R37/2

Library

CHESTER COLLEGE

This book is to be returned on or above the last date stamped below.

BRITISH RIVERS

List of contributors

R. I. Ferguson, Department of Earth and Environmental Science, University of Stirling, Stirling FK9 4LA

J. Lewin, Department of Geography, University College of Wales, Llandinam Building, Penglais, Aberystwyth, Dyfed SY23 3DB

M. D. Newson, Institute of Hydrology (Plynlimon), Staylittle, Llanbrynmair, Powys

D. E. Walling, Department of Geography, University of Exeter, Amory Building, Rennes Drive, Exeter EX4 4RJ

R. C. Ward, Department of Geography, University of Hull, Hull, Humberside HU6 7RX

B. W. Webb, Department of Geography, University of Exeter, Amory Building, Rennes Drive, Exeter EX4 4RJ

T. R. Wood, Principal Hydrologist, Severn–Trent Water Authority, Abelson House, Coventry Road, Birmingham

BRITISH RIVERS

Edited by **JOHN LEWIN**

University College of Wales, Aberystwyth

London
GEORGE ALLEN & UNWIN
Boston   Sydney

1981

First published in 1981

GEORGE ALLEN & UNWIN LTD
40 Museum Street, London WC1A 1LU

British Library Cataloguing in Publication Data

British rivers.
  1. Rivers – Great Britain
  I. Lewin, John
  551.48′30941   GV1283

  ISBN 0–04–551047–4

Set in 10 on 12 point Times by Bedford Typesetters Ltd
and printed and bound in Great Britain by
William Clowes (Beccles) Limited, Beccles and London

Preface

This book is intended for a wide readership, but it started for a particular reason. I have recently been serving on the organising committee for the Second International Conference on Fluvial Sedimentology, to be held at Keele University in September 1981. The conference theme of 'Modern and ancient fluvial systems: sedimentology and processes' brings together many scientists from different disciplines with a practical working interest in the physical nature of rivers. I realised that there was no easy way in which either foreign visitors or those with a working or leisure interest in British rivers could in fact brief themselves about the distinctive nature of rivers in this country. This seemed all the more unfortunate because of the tremendous amount of research recently accomplished and the volume of new information now available on British rivers. This comes especially from work by Water Authorities in England and Wales, River Purification Boards in Scotland, the Department of the Environment and the Water Data Unit, the Institute of Hydrology and the Hydraulics Research Station (both Natural Environment Research Council), the Water Research Centre, and numerous individuals in Universities and Polytechnics.

If such august organisations and individuals were jointly to admit a fault, it might be that they do tend to accumulate data on tape and in cupboards, and when they do publish their findings, this can be in obscure reports and esoteric journal articles. The significance of particular findings may be only apparent to a few people with a working knowledge of a vast literature of previous investigations.

This book, then, is a joint effort to describe and explain the physical nature of contemporary British rivers. Benefiting from the work previously mentioned, and adding our own particular experience, we have looked at six aspects of British rivers which we expect to be of interest to a wide range of engineers, scientists and all those concerned with rivers. Where possible we try to deal with the whole of Britain, though this objective is at times frustrated because of the uneven availability of information. Our several viewpoints also cannot include *all* aspects of rivers, and those requiring biological information, navigation guidance, or analysis of the long-term geological development of river systems may be disappointed. But we hope that this book will be appreciated for what it does contain, and that those concerned with river study, management or sheer enjoyment will feel that some interesting and valuable perspectives have been opened up by the end of it.

John Lewin
Aberystwyth
January 1981

Acknowledgements

R. C. Ward wishes to acknowledge the helpful co-operation received during the preparation of Chapter 1 from members of staff at the Water Data Unit, the Institute of Hydrology and the Welsh Water Authority. M. D. Newson wishes to thank Graham Leeks for reading the text of Chapter 3, and the staff of the Institute of Hydrology, on whose work at Plynlimon much of this chapter is based. D. E. Walling and B. W. Webb are indebted to a large number of officers in the Regional Water Authorities of England and Wales, in the River Purification Authorities of Scotland and in the Department of the Environment for Northern Ireland who generously supplied data concerning water quality in British rivers: their thanks are also due to the Water Data Unit, DOE, for provision of information, and to Miss S. Burn and Miss H. Blackman of the University of Exeter, whose assistance with data compilation and processing is gratefully acknowledged. T. R. Wood is grateful to the Director of Operations, Severn–Trent Water Authority, for permission to publish Chapter 6 and the opinions expressed within it are not necessarily those of the Severn–Trent Water Authority: he would also like to thank David Brewin and John Martin for reading the section on water quality and for their several helpful comments and suggestions. J. Lewin is very grateful to his wife for her help in the preparation of the text and the index.

The following individuals and organisations are thanked for permission to reproduce illustrative material:

The Director, Institute of Hydrology (1.10c, 1.18a,d, 2.14, 3.2, 3.3, 3.8, 3.9c, 3.10a,c, 3.11, 3.14a, 3.16a); Blackwell Scientific Publications (1.11a); Institute of British Geographers (1.19c, 3.7, 4.3); J. A. Catt and Oxford University Press (2.3); Oxford University Press (2.4); A. S. Potts and the Editor, *Geografiska Annaler* (2.5a); Geological Society of London (2.5b); B. J. Bluck (2.10e); Edward Arnold Ltd (2.15); J. L. Ternan (3.13); Geobooks Ltd (4.1, 4.6a); Geological Society of America (4.6b, 4.15); the Editor, *Progress in Physical Geography* (4.8, 4.23); Figure 4.11b reproduced by permission of the Controller, HMSO, courtesy of Hydraulics Research Station, Wallingford, England; Elsevier Publishing Co. (4.12); John Wiley & Sons Ltd (4.6b, 4.15, 4.17); State University of New York (4.24); the Controller, HMSO (5.1, 5.2, 6.1, 6.2, Tables 5.1, 5.3, 5.4, 5.5, 5.6); Director of Operations, Severn–Trent Water Authority (6.4, 6.5, 6.7, 6.10); Binnie and Partners (6.8).

Contents

X

List of tables

NOTE ON UNITS USED

Lengths are given in millimetres (mm), metres (m), and kilometres (km). 1 m is 3.28 feet or 1.09 yards, 1 km is 0.621 miles, 1 mm is 0.039 inches.

Volumes are given in cubic metres (m³), litres (l) or megalitres (Ml). 1 m³ is 35.31 cubic feet or 1000 l. 1 Ml = 1000 m³ = 10^6 l. 1 l is 0.22 gallons, 1 Ml is 0.220 million gallons or 0.81 acre-feet.

Weight (mass) is given in grams (g), kilograms (kg) and tonnes (t). 1 kg is 2.20 lb, 1 t (metric) is 0.98 tons. 1 t is 1000 kg, 1 kg is 1000 g, 1 g is 1000 mg.

Flow rates are given in cubic metres per second (cumecs or $m^3 s^{-1}$) or megalitres per day (Ml d^{-1}). 1 $m^3 s^{-1}$ is equivalent to 35.315 cubic feet per second (cusecs) or 19.01 million gallons per day. 1 Ml d^{-1} is 0.220 million gallons per day.

Concentrations are given in milligrams per litre (mg l^{-1}) and sediment yields in tonnes per square kilometre per year (t $km^{-2} yr^{-1}$).

Other units are explained where necessary in the text.

1 River systems and river regimes

R. C. Ward

The hydrological data base

The first systematic river gauging in Britain was carried out by Captain W. N. McClean in 1912 in Scotland but by the time of publication of the first *Surface water year book of Great Britain,* which referred to the water year 1935–6, there were still only 27 gauging stations, seven of which had been set up by McClean (Boulton 1966). During the 1950s and 1960s, however, there was a rapid expansion of the gauging network so that by the end of 1973 the re-named *Surface water: United Kingdom* (DOE 1978c) listed 1205 gauging stations. The rapidity of recent growth is illustrated in Figure 1.1 by the bar graphs of starting dates of gauging station records and by the fact that the average length of record to 1973 of gauging stations in the United Kingdom was only 11.6 years.

River discharge is calculated by converting records of water level (or stage). The relationship between stage and discharge, i.e. the rating or calibration of the gauging station, may be obtained by installing a gauging structure, e.g. a weir or flume, or by determining the water velocity and cross-sectional area over a range of flows at the gauging site, i.e. the *velocity–area method.* The accuracy of gauged discharges therefore depends on the following factors: (a) the accuracy and reliability of water level measurement which should normally be satisfactory; (b) the accuracy and reliability of the assumed stage–discharge relationship, which will normally be better for structures than for velocity–area sections, but which

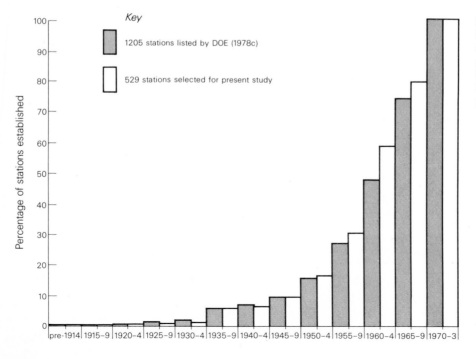

Figure 1.1 Bar graphs illustrating the date of commencement of river gauging records at 1205 stations listed by DOE (1978c) and at 529 stations selected for the present study.

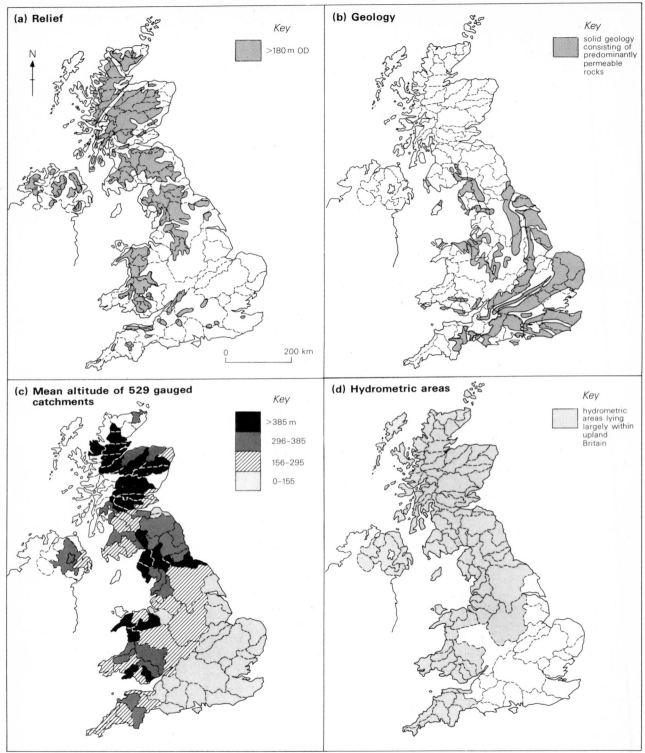

Figure 1.2 The geographical setting of river catchments in the United Kingdom. (a) Generalised relief; (b) outline of solid geology; (c) mean altitude by hydrometric area of 529 gauged catchments; (d) hydrometric areas – shaded areas are those lying predominantly within 'upland' Britain.

will deteriorate in both cases as a result, for example, of seasonal weed growth, channel profile changes, and backwater effects; and (c) the concurrency of rating and stage records with respect to changes in the control. Of the 1205 gauging stations listed by DOE (1978c) 56% used control structures, 39% used velocity–area sections, and 5% used some other method, including in some cases a combination of structures and velocity–area sections.

Hydrological data are collated and published for a variety of areal units. At a fairly coarse scale they are available for each of the 10 Water Authorities in Britain and separately for Northern Ireland. At an intermediate level, data are available for each hydrometric area of which there are 105 in the United Kingdom. Finally, at the most detailed level, data are available for individual gauged catchments most of which are represented in publications such as DOE (1978c). In this chapter data for hydrometric areas and for selected gauged catchments have been used as the basis for much of the discussion.

The hydrometric areas (HAs) are mapped in Figure 1.2d. Those which lie predominantly within 'upland' Britain, i.e. those northern and western parts of the country having substantial areas above 180 m (see Fig. 1.2a) and whose solid geology consists largely of old, hard, impermeable rocks (see Fig. 1.2b), have been shaded. Although convenient in many respects, hydrometric areas are far from being ideal units. For example, they are of disparate size, the largest (HA 54) being 30 times larger than the smallest (HA 101). Also some represent the drainage area of a single river system (e.g. HA 32) and others (e.g. HA 105) are drained by well over 100 individual river systems (Smith & Lyle 1979). Nevertheless they have been used extensively in this chapter as the basis for comparative chloropleth mapping of both hydrological and geomorphological characteristics (see also Table 1.3).

The average gauging density for the United Kingdom which is represented by the 1205 gauges listed by DOE (1978c) is approximately 200 km^2 per gauge but as might be expected, the spatial distribution of these gauges is far from uniform although the situation is better now than with the much smaller number of gauges which have existed in the past. Two aspects of the distribution of river gauging stations are illustrated in Figures 1.3 and 1.4. The number of currently operational gauges for each hydrometric area for the years 1953, 1963 and 1973 is shown in Figure 1.3a, b and c respectively. The four categories of shading in these and many of the other maps are based on the quartile and quartile–median ranges. In the case of Figures 1.3 and 1.4 the 1973 ranges were determined and these ranges were also used for the 1953 and 1963 maps in order to emphasise the growth and development of the gauging network. It is clear that the major inadequacies of the earlier periods have been largely rectified except in peripheral areas and especially in northern and western Scotland. The density of the gauging network, expressed as the number of square kilometres per gauge for each hydrometric area, is shown in Figure 1.4a, b and c for the same three years. This diagram includes a few now abandoned gauges for which data are still readily accessible. Again there has been a substantial improvement with time although this is less apparent in the case of the larger hydrometric areas which, despite their large number of gauging stations nevertheless have a comparatively sparse areal coverage.

However, both Figures 1.3 and 1.4 must be interpreted with caution for a number of reasons. First, many rivers, especially the larger ones, are gauged in several places, e.g. DOE (1978c) listed 11 gauges for the Trent (HA 28), eight for the Spey (HA 8), seven for the Severn (HA 54) and five for the Thames (HA 39). The gauging network thus has a 'nested' structure which is further exaggerated by

3

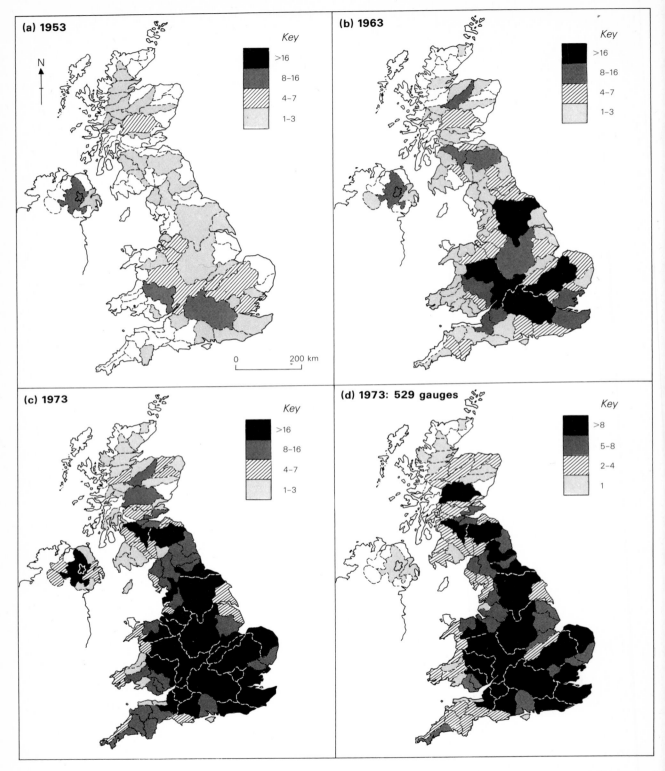

Figure 1.3 Distribution of 1205 river gauging stations by hydrometric area. (a) 1953; (b) 1963; (c) 1973. (d) Distribution of 529 selected river gauging stations in 1973.

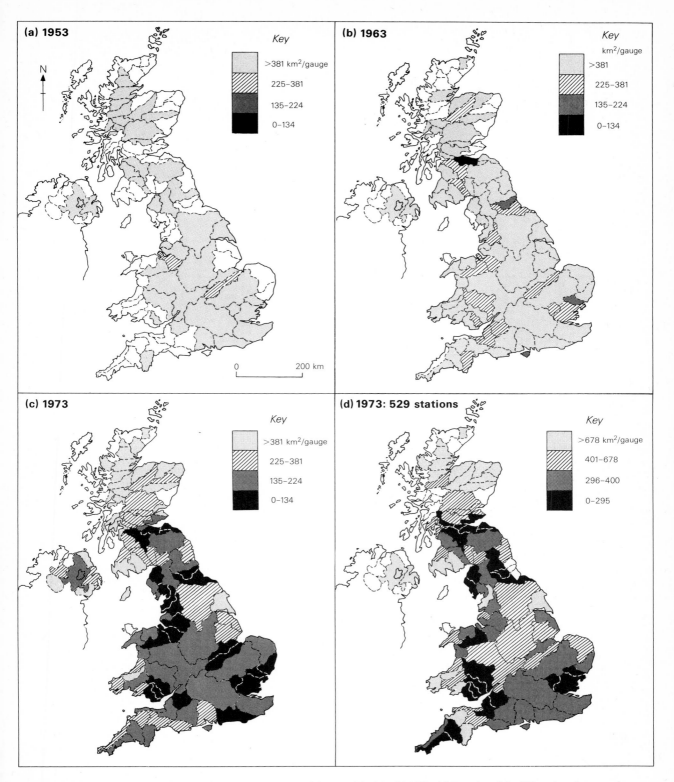

Figure 1.4 Density of the 1205 station river gauging network. (a) 1953; (b) 1963; (c) 1973. (d) Density of the 529 station river gauging network in 1973.

the fact that tributary flows gauged at upstream locations are themselves measured again at downstream stations on the main river. In other words, multiple gauging of catchments does not provide an equivalent set of independent discharge values since downstream stations incorporate upstream flows.

Secondly, a substantial proportion of many hydrometric areas remains ungauged, even at the present time. This may result in some areas, e.g. HA 29, from the fact that gauging stations exist on only some of a number of rivers which flow independently to the sea. In other areas, especially where rivers have shallow gradients, it results from the fact that the lowest gauging station is located some considerable distance upstream from the tidal reach. The ungauged lengths of rivers having the largest catchment in each hydrometric area are shown in Figure 1.5d. It will be seen that in lowland Britain the final 17 km at least of most major river courses remains ungauged.

River data interpretation is complicated not only by the type and distribution of the gauging stations but also by the extent to which recorded discharges have been affected by human interference. In the sense that afforestation and deforestation, urbanisation and land drainage works, for example, influence the volume and timing of river flows, it could be argued that the discharge of *all* British rivers is affected by man. Unfortunately many of these and similar effects are subtle and may be difficult to quantify although an indication of the rivers most affected by urbanisation is given in Figure 1.9c. More tangible, and therefore potentially more quantifiable, influences result from the regulating effects of reservoirs and the abstraction from and return of water to rivers.

Some indication of the spatial distribution and magnitude of such influences is given in Figure 1.5 which illustrates the proportion of gauging stations in each hydrometric area which is influenced by (a) regulation of river flows by impounding, regulating and HEP reservoirs, (b) reduction of river flows by the abstraction of surface water or groundwater for domestic, industrial and agricultural needs and (c) the augmentation of river flows by effluent returns from sewage works and industry. Again, these maps should be interpreted with caution since within a given catchment area abstraction and effluent return may be largely complementary; only when water is transferred from one river catchment to another is there a predictable *significant* effect on discharges.

Despite their importance, quantitative adjustments of river data to take into account the effects of human modifications are not necessarily made as a matter of course. Indeed, of the approximately 12 000 station-years of British river flow data archived by the Water Data Unit, less than 25% have been so adjusted. However, this compares favourably with many other countries, e.g. the USA, in which *no* adjustment is made to gauged river flows before their publication.

Because of the nested structure of the gauging network not all gauging stations listed by DOE (1978c) have been incorporated into the hydrological data base for this chapter. Instead the downstream station for each river has been used where this is currently operational and no severe calibration problems are known to exist. Where the downstream station has been abandoned recently in favour of a new or pre-existing station, both sets of data have been used. Finally, in order to improve spatial coverage, the data from unreplaced abandoned stations have been used in three cases, i.e. the Shin at Lairg (HA 3), the Beauly at Erchless (HA 5), and the Allt Bhlaraidh at Invermoriston (HA 6). Following these procedures, a total of only 529 gauging stations were selected for use in this work. It is desirable, therefore, to estimate the representativeness of this limited selection of gauging stations by comparing them with the 1205 gauging stations listed by DOE (1978c).

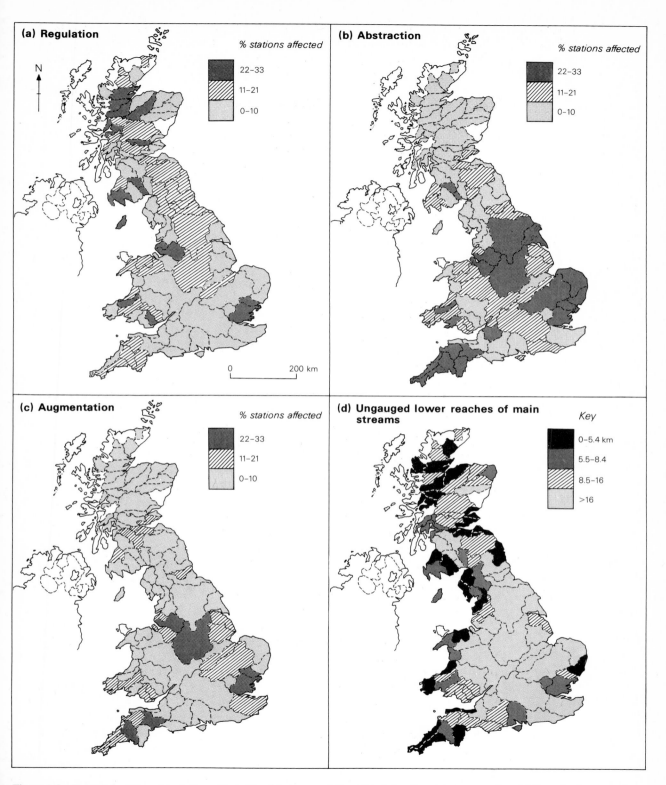

Figure 1.5 Percentage of gauging stations affected by: (a) river regulation; (b) abstraction; (c) augmentation. (d) Length of ungauged lower reaches of main streams.

The bar graphs in Figure 1.1 show that the pattern of growth in numbers of the selected stations closely resembles that of the entire population, particularly during the period through to the mid-1950s. Thereafter the next 15 years saw a proportionately greater establishment of selected gauging stations with a correspondingly smaller growth in the 1970s. The average length of record for the 529 stations is slightly shorter (11.5 years) than for the entire population. Comparison of Figures 1.3c and d and of 1.4c and d confirms that the geographical distribution of the selected stations resembles very closely that of the full 1205 stations, when the reduced numbers and network density are taken into account. It is suggested, therefore, that data from the 529 selected stations are likely to be representative of gauged river data in general and may reasonably be used as one basis for discussions of catchment characteristics and hydrological characteristics of British rivers. Certainly the altitudinal distribution of the gauged catchments (see Fig. 1.2c) compares very closely with the broad relief divisions suggested in Figure 1.2d.

Catchment characteristics

Not surprisingly, in view of the limited areal extent of the British Isles as a whole, British rivers and river catchments are very small. Table 1.1 lists the top 20 of the 529 gauged rivers used in this chapter. These have been ranked on the sum of the ranks of gauged length, gauged catchment area and mean annual discharge. Outside the top 20 only two rivers have gauged lengths of 100 km or more, no river has a gauged catchment area of 10 000 km² or more, although the Thames comes very close, and only the Tay has a mean annual discharge of more than 100 m³ s⁻¹.

Table 1.1 Major British rivers ranked in terms of length, area and mean annual discharge.

River and station number		Length		Area		Qbar		Rank on
		km	rank	km²	rank	m³ s⁻¹	rank	Σ ranks
Thames	039001	239	1	9950	1	67.40	6	1
Trent	028009	149	5	7490	2	82.21	2	2
Wye	055901	225	2	4040	6	71.41	5	3
Tweed	021009	140	6	4390	4	73.85	4	4
Severn	054001	206	3	4330	5	62.70	7	5
Tay	015006	110	12	4590	3	152.21	1	6
Spey	008001	137	7	2650	9	55.86	8	7
Ness	006007	107	13	1840	13	76.60	3	8
Ouse	027009	117	9	3320	7	40.45	13	9
Aire	027003	114	11	1930	12	36.89	17	10
Tummel	015012	90	22	1720	14	54.89	9	11
Clyde	084005	105	14	1700	15	37.40	16	12
Tyne	023001	89	23	2180	11	43.45	11	13
Dee	012001	116	10	1370	21	35.70	18	14
Eden	076002	102	16	1370	22	31.02	22	15
Ribble	071001	94	20	1140	28	31.72	20	16
Gt Ouse	033001	184	4	3030	8	14.16	62	17
Avon	054002	125	8	2210	10	14.43	59	18
Tywi	060001	82	31	1090	32	38.34	15	19
Tees	025009	103	15	1260	25	19.46	39	20

Comparison with some of the world's major rivers in Table 1.2 provides a useful perspective and emphasizes the fact that the scale of operation of geomorphological and hydrological processes and of related drainage-basin management techniques in Britain is miniscule in a global context.

Table 1.2 Comparative data for world and British rivers.

River	Length km	Area 000s km^2	Qbar 000s m^3 s^{-1}
Amazon	6437	7050	180
Congo	4700	3457	41
Ob–Irtysh	5410	2975	15
Mackenzie	4241	1841	11
Ganges–Brahmaputra	2897	1621	38
Zambezi	3540	1330	7
Tigris–Euphrates	2740	1114	1
Danube	2850	816	7
Columbia	1950	668	7
Rhine	1320	160	2
Thames	239	10	0.06

Smith and Lyle (1979) estimated, from an analysis of topographic maps at the scale of 1:625 000, that there exist in Britain 1445 river systems. If a total land area of 229 900 km^2 is assumed, each river system would drain an average area of about 159 km^2. As Smith and Lyle acknowledged, counting errors associated with map scale mean that the total number of river systems is in fact substantially greater than their estimate, although they demonstrated that most of the underestimate resulting from the count at the 1:625 000 scale compared with a count at the 1:63 360 scale concerned small, low order, especially first and second order, systems. Figure 1.6a shows the distribution of estimated catchment size derived by dividing the total area of each hydrometric area by the total number of river systems as estimated by Smith and Lyle and then, as in most of the other choropleth maps in this chapter, basing the system of shading on the quartile and quartile–median ranges of the resulting values. The pattern which emerges, as one would expect, shows that the larger catchments are associated with the 'inland' hydrometric areas, many of which have a rather small number of river systems (see also Fig. 1.8c), with the smaller catchments being concentrated almost exclusively in the peripheral coastal areas.

The comparative choropleth map showing the distribution of catchment size for the 529 gauged catchments presents an essentially similar pattern although the distribution curve is rather different. Thus mean catchment area is much larger at 366 km^2, the median value of 269 is slightly higher while the upper and lower quartile values are respectively substantially lower and higher. The values ranged from 1370 km^2 (HA 12) to 30 km^2 (HA 101).

A similar comparison between general and selected gauged catchment conditions is presented for river length in Figure 1.6c and d. The mean values mapped in Figure 1.6c were derived by dividing the total length of rivers having a summer flow of at least 0.052 m^{3}s^{-1} by the total number of streams as counted by Smith and Lyle. The appropriate river length data for hydrometric areas in England and Wales were supplied by the Water Data Unit from information originally

9

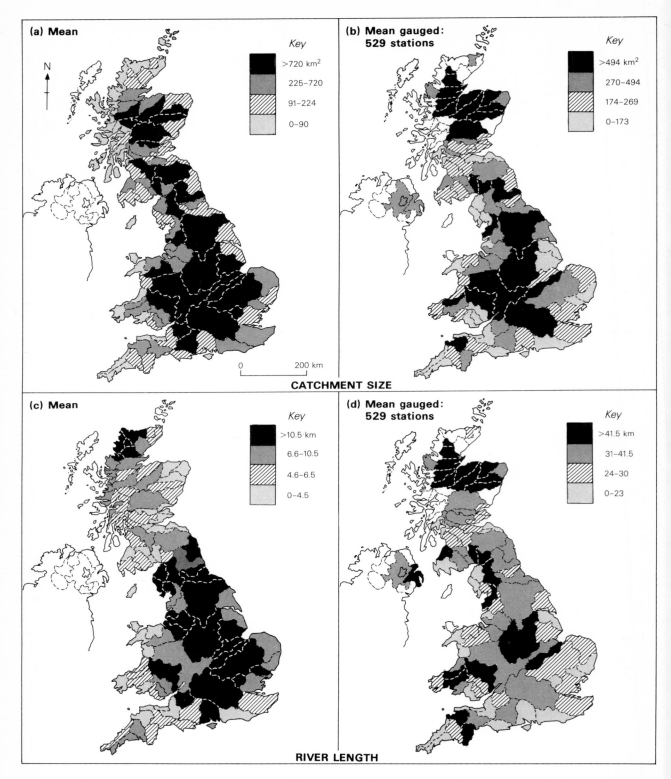

Figure 1.6 Mean catchment size: (a) river systems counted by Smith and Lyle (1979); (b) 529 selected catchments. Mean river length: (c) rivers counted by Smith and Lyle (1979); (d) 529 gauged rivers.

compiled for the *River pollution survey of England and Wales 1975* (DOE 1978b). Corresponding river lengths for Scottish hydrometric areas were not available from this source but have been estimated from the regression of total river length on total number of streams for hydrometric areas in the 'upland' parts of England and Wales (see Fig. 1.7).

Clearly this is not an entirely satisfactory derivation since the lower order segments of larger rivers are counted as separate streams. On the other hand dividing total river length by the total number of river *systems* would have been no more satisfactory since a single river system may comprise a number of major tributary streams. Having regard to the under-counting inherent in the scale of map analysis employed by Smith and Lyle, the values shown in Figure 1.6c may in fact be reasonably representative. Again the longest rivers tend to be associated with the larger, inland hydrometric areas and the shorter ones are found in the coastal periphery, particularly of Scotland, Wales and southern England. For Britain as a whole, a total estimated river length of 58 380 km divided by the 7835 streams counted by Smith and Lyle yields an average length of 7.45 km. Within the hydrometric areas mapped in Figure 1.6c the values range from 30 km (HA 70) to 2 km (HAs 14, 20, 61 and 102) with a median value of 6.5 km.

Figure 1.6d shows that the mean lengths of the selected gauged rivers are substantially greater. The average length for all hydrometric areas is 32.6 km, with a median value of 30 km and a range from 116 km (HA 12) to 10 km (HA 101). This upward shift would be expected both because of the tendency for gauging stations to be established on the larger rivers and also because the lowest gauging station on each river has normally been selected for the present study.

Drainage density has long been recognised as a significant and sensitive catchment characteristic which, as Gregory and Walling (1973) observed, not only provides a link between the form attributes of a catchment and the processes operating along the stream courses but also reflects a variety of topographic, lithological, pedological and vegetational controls. As with virtually all drainage network measurements, the numerical values derived depend largely on the scale of the maps or air photographs used or on the assiduity of the field observer.

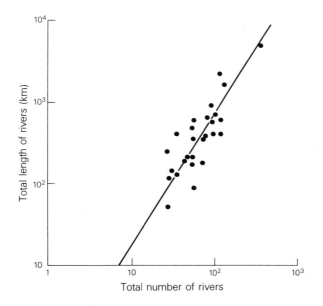

Figure 1.7 Relationship between total river length (Water Data Unit data) and total number of streams (Smith & Lyle 1979) for hydrometric areas in 'upland' Britain.

Provided the method of derivation is applied consistently however the values obtained should provide the basis for valid comparisons between different areas. Values of average drainage density, as defined by Horton (1932), i.e. length of streams per unit of drainage area, are mapped by hydrometric area in Figure 1.8a and have been calculated by dividing the total length of rivers, as defined for Figure 1.6c, by the area of each hydrometric area. Horton suggested that drainage density values would vary within the range 0.93–1.24 km km^{-2} for steep, impervious areas having a high precipitation to nearly zero in permeable basins with high infiltration rates (Gregory & Walling 1973). The values mapped in Figure 1.6c range from 1.46 (HA 95) to 0.02 (HA 20). Because the definition of stream length used in the calculation of drainage density is directly related to a specified summer flow, comparisons between the drainage densities derived here and those for areas outside Britain should be made with caution.

Values of stream frequency, expressed as the number of streams counted by Smith and Lyle (1979) divided by the area of each hydrometric area, provide an alternative measure of network density with emphasis on the *number* of channels rather than their length, and are mapped in Figure 1.8b. Regional distinctions are even more coherent than in Figure 1.8a and emphasise the comparative sparsity of the network over lowland Britain, the minimum value being 0.007 streams km^{-2} (HA 30), and the high values of western uplands in Scotland, North Wales and South-West England, the maximum mainland value of 0.107 occurring in HA 95.

Two further measures of network density are shown in Figure 1.8c and d. The number of river systems gives some indication of the complexity of the drainage network and tends to reflect both the interaction of a number of geomorphological variables (lithology, structure, drainage history, etc.) and also the length of 'drainable' coastline in each hydrometric area. In 14 HAs only one river system is represented: in nine others there are 30 or more river systems, including three HAs in the Scottish Islands which each have more than 100 river systems. Inevitably, there is a large measure of inverse relationship between the number of systems and the order number of the highest system as determined by Smith and Lyle. Interestingly, despite the large size of several of the hydrometric areas in lowland Britain no system within this part of the country has an order number greater than four, a value which is in fact exceeded in only four hydrometric areas.

Figure 1.9 illustrates the distribution of a number of variables which may operate within catchments having a given size and elevation and a given length and complexity of drainage network to affect the timing, distribution and speed of passage of runoff. Clearly there are a large number of such variables, some of which may be excluded from consideration because their effect on river discharge is insignificantly small or impossible to measure, others because their *detailed* distribution within a catchment or hydrometric area is what matters and not their average values, although in fact it could be claimed that this is true of *all* variables which affect river discharge.

The storage capacity of lakes and reservoirs will tend to attenuate flood peaks and to sustain dry weather flows. This ameliorating effect will depend partly on the number of lakes and reservoirs and partly on the proportion of the catchment draining through them. Neither measure is sufficient in itself since a large number of lakes on the headwaters of a major river system will have little effect on flows some distance downstream, whereas although most of a river system may drain through one large lake in its lower reaches, the greater part of the system, upstream of the lake, will not benefit from its presence.

The number of lakes and reservoirs were counted for each hydrometric area by

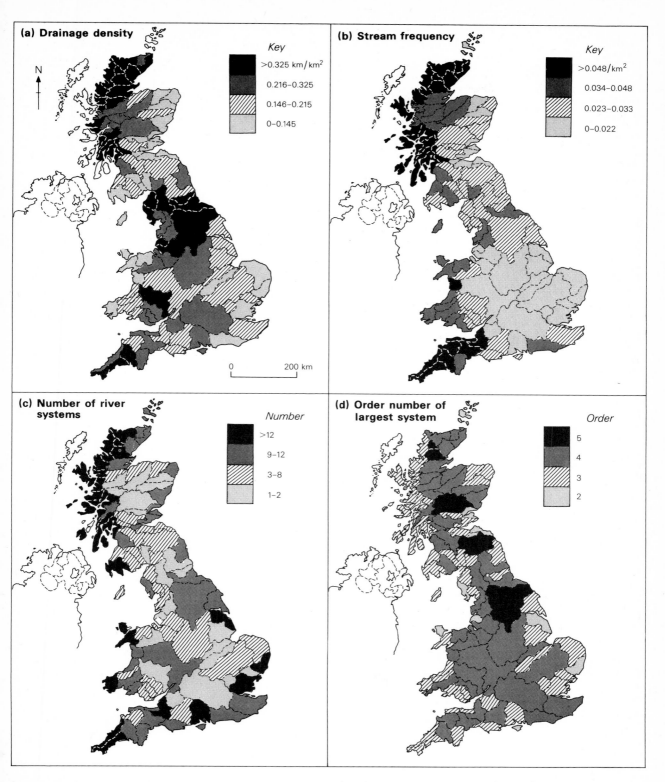

Figure 1.8 Drainage network characteristics by hydrometric area. (a) Drainage density (km km^{-2}); (b) stream frequency (km^{-2}); (c) number of river systems; (d) order number of largest river system (based on data presented by Smith & Lyle 1979).

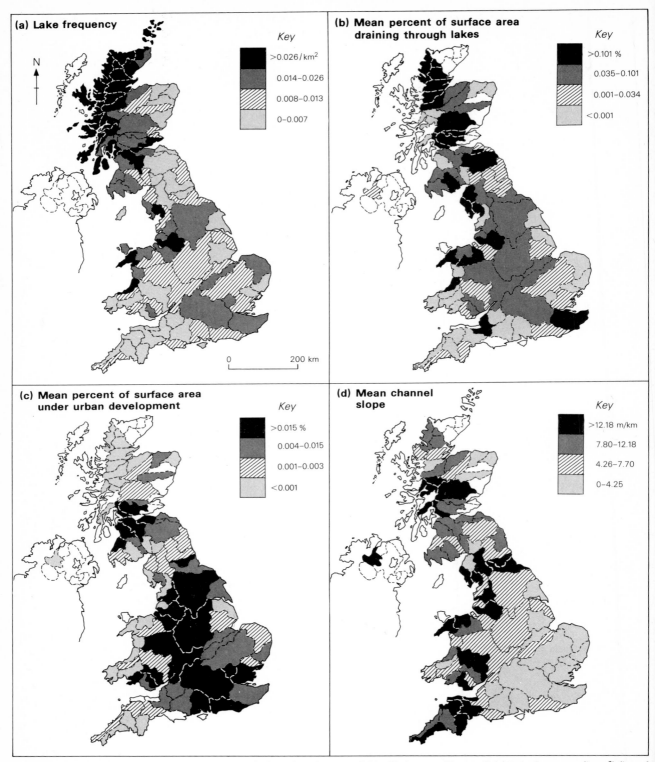

Figure 1.9 Distribution by hydrometric area of selected catchment variables likely to modify runoff. (a) Lake frequency (km^{-2}) (based on data presented by Smith & Lyle 1979); (b) mean percentage of surface area draining through lakes; (c) mean percentage of surface area under urban development; (d) mean channel slope (m km^{-1}). (b, c and d are based on data presented in NERC 1975a).

Smith and Lyle (1979), their total of 5505 for Great Britain representing an average frequency of 0.024 km^{-2}. Average frequencies for each hydrometric area are mapped in Figure 1.9a, the values ranging from 0.400 for the Hebrides (HA 106) to zero in HAs 9 and 11. The distributional pattern of proportion of catchment area draining through lakes in Figure 1.9b largely reinforces the lake frequency distribution, with high values in parts of Scotland, the Lake District, Lancashire and North-West Wales. However, marked disparities between the maps occur in several hydrometric areas in western Scotland and the border country and also in HAs 34, 38 and 52.

Urbanisation of previously rural catchments completely changes their hydrological behaviour through the reduction in vegetation cover, evapotranspiration and infiltration capacity. Runoff is affected both through a substantial increase in the quickflow component and also through the reduction of water quality. A general indication of those British rivers most likely to be affected by urbanisation is given in Figure 1.9c which shows the distribution by hydrometric areas of the mean percentage of catchment surface under urban development. Low values are confined almost exclusively to peripheral hydrometric areas and most of the high values occur in England, with outliers in South Wales and lowland Scotland.

Slope is an important hydrological and geomorphological variable but difficult and laborious to quantify in a meaningful way. Surrogate values are often employed, one of them being channel slope which may be measured relatively easily and precisely and which, as Strahler (1950) demonstrated, may be closely related to valley-side slope. Furthermore, mainstream slope is closely related to tributary slopes and may be used therefore as an index of catchment slope characteristics. Following US Geological Survey procedure, the NERC flood studies team (NERC 1975a) defined mainstream slope between the 10 and 85 percentiles of mainstream length, measuring upstream from the gauging station. These percentiles, by omitting the extreme slope values, appear to give a better prediction of mean annual flood. The values mapped in Figure 1.9d are the mean values for the catchments listed in NERC (1975a) for each hydrometric area. With comparatively few exceptions the spatial distribution of channel slope closely reflects the relief characteristics mapped in Figure 1.2.

Hydrological characteristics

River discharge varies both temporally and spatially in response to the changing balance between the various components of the hydrological equation. This can be stated simply for streamflow as

$$Q = P - (E + \Delta G + \Delta S)$$

where Q is streamflow, P is precipitation, E is evaporation from land and water surfaces and ΔG and ΔS are changes in storage of groundwater and soil moisture respectively. Thus in the British Isles, where rainfall is comparatively consistent from month to month, streamflow values tend to be highest in winter when evaporation is low and groundwater and soil moisture storage are high, and lowest in the summer months when evaporation is high and groundwater and soil moisture storage are low. Similarly, spatial variations of streamflow reflect the relationships between the underlying distributions of precipitation and evaporation and in particular the fact that over most of England more than 50% of

15

precipitation is lost as evaporation, although elsewhere in the British Isles the proportion is smaller, falling to less than 25% in parts of Wales and in the Western Highlands of Scotland.

In this section of the chapter, river discharge is discussed first in the general context of the water balance and then in terms of its regime characteristics and their spatial expression.

River discharge and the water balance

Precipitation is the raw material for streamflow and its distribution for the British Isles is shown in Figure 1.10a. Average annual totals range from about 500 mm in parts of the South-East to nearly 5000 mm on some high ground in North Wales, the Lake District and western Scotland and it is clear that, broadly speaking, rainfall amounts are strongly correlated with relief. Amounts are fairly evenly distributed throughout the year although most places receive marginally more in the winter (October–March) than in the summer half of the year.

Some indication of the frequency with which streamflow is replenished by precipitation is given by the average number of rain days (having at least 0.25 mm of rain) per year shown in Figure 1.10b. Although values as low as 0.25 mm are unlikely to have any apparent effect on streamflow, even such small inputs of precipitation, if maintained over prolonged periods, may reduce the rate of recession of streamflow below what would have occurred otherwise. It will be noted that even in the driest areas rain falls on almost half the days of the year and that on average the wettest areas have less than 100 dry days annually.

Streamflow response to rainfall is rapid, especially in the small river basins so typical of the British Isles, but precipitation falling as snow will have no obvious effect on river discharges until melting takes place. In normal circumstances snow accumulation and melt do not play a major part in modifying regimes of river discharge in Britain. Only in the Scottish Highlands and in limited areas of the northern Pennines does the average annual number of mornings with snow lying exceed 50. Furthermore, as Figure 1.10c illustrates, annual maximum depths of snow accumulation are modest, exceeding 300 mm only in the northern half of the country, and contributing to river discharge in the form of the water equivalent of the snow pack only about one-tenth of the accumulated depth.

The amount of water available for streamflow is determined primarily by the balance between precipitation and evaporation from land and water surfaces (i.e. evapotranspiration). Values of *potential* evapotranspiration, which indicate the maximum possible evaporative losses for a given climatological location in conditions of unlimited moisture supply, are mapped in Figure 1.10d. The derivation of this map, which is based on a variety of sources, was detailed by Ward (1976). The pattern of isopleths shows both a broad latitudinal decrease from south to north and also a marked decrease away from the coast. Both characteristics reflect the availability of net radiation although the higher coastal values are probably also a reflection of the additional drying power associated with higher windspeeds in coastal areas. Conversely, reduced values in the main upland areas are largely associated with low radiation availability.

Except in the wetter areas values of *actual* evapotranspiration are normally lower than the potential values because of the reduced opportunity for evaporation from drying soil and vegetation surfaces. The reduction of soil moisture content below the optimum 'field capacity' is referred to as the soil moisture

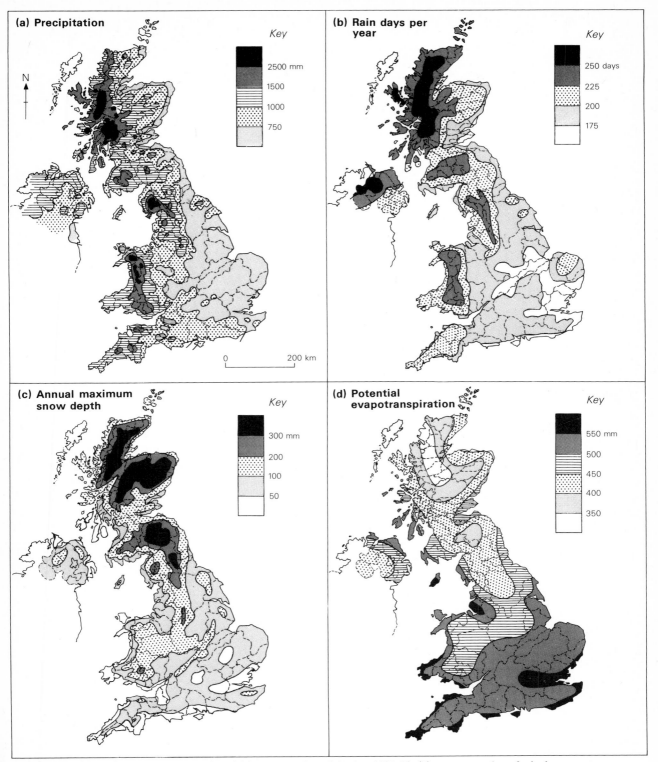

Figure 1.10 Selected hydrological variables I. (a) Mean annual precipitation, 1901–30; (b) average number of rain days per year, 1901–30 (a and b are based on cartographic data in *Climatological atlas of the British Isles*, HMSO 1952); (c) median annual maximum snow depths, 1946–64 (based on an original map in NERC 1975a); (d) mean annual potential evapotranspiration (based on data published in *British rainfall* and in MAFF 1967).

deficit and Figure 1.11a shows mean annual potential soil moisture deficit, calculated on the (unrealistic) assumption that there is no limit to soil moisture
depletion. The map indicates that the greatest constraints upon potential evapotranspiration will occur in the south and east, whereas in the north and west mean
soil moisture deficit is so low that evapotranspiration is likely to take place at the
potential rate. This is largely confirmed by the pattern of actual evapotranspiration illustrated in Figure 1.11b. Again the derivation of this map was discussed
by Ward (1976). Based on measured data from a large number of river basins, the
map shows that over most of England and Wales actual evapotranspiration values
lie between 400 mm and 499 mm.

On an annual basis, which allows ΔG and ΔS to be ignored, streamflow
represents the residual of precipitation minus actual evapotranspiration. Mean
annual runoff is mapped in Figure 1.11c with low values (below 500 mm precipitation equivalent) in the South-East, in the lee of the Welsh mountains and along
eastern coastal areas of northern England and southern Scotland, and high values
(exceeding 1500 mm) confined to Dartmoor, the Welsh and Cumbrian mountains
and the western Highlands of Scotland.

The proportion of precipitation which appears as river discharge, i.e. the
discharge ratio, provides a useful integration in dimensionless form of the various
factors controlling river discharge which have been discussed already. Discharge
ratios mapped in Figure 1.11d range from values of less than 25% in East Anglia to
values in excess of 75% in some western areas.

Regime characteristics and their spatial expression

In this section an attempt is made to characterise variations of discharge with time,
over a wide range of time scales, to illustrate both general trends and detailed
contrasts in regime characteristics. In addition, consideration is given to the
spatial expression of some of these regime characteristics.

The comparative brevity of gauged streamflow records in many countries has
tended to inhibit discussion of runoff trends over any but short periods of time.
However, attempts have been made to reconstruct streamflow data for long
periods by using either simple water-balance accounting models based on readily
available data sets such as precipitation and air temperature (cf. Thornthwaite &
Mather 1955) or correlation and regression analysis in which runoff is predicted or
postdicted from rainfall data alone. An interesting example of the latter approach
was provided by Marsh and Littlewood (1978) who used precipitation data from
1728 to 1976 to estimate annual runoff from England and Wales. Eleven-year
simple moving averages of these values are shown in Figure 1.12 together with
11-year simple moving averages of mean annual rainfall over England and Wales,
as presented by Rodda, Sheckley and Tan (1978).

The suggestion of a slight upward trend in rainfall totals which was observed by
Rodda *et al.* inevitably reappears in the estimated runoff totals. Thus although the
249-year mean runoff value is 435 mm, the five successive 50-year means (49 years
for the final period) are 413 mm, 417 mm, 453 mm, 447 mm, and 443 mm.
Alternatively one could recognise the possibility that 150 years in which there was
a clear upward trend was followed by a period of 100 years, since the late 1870s, in
which there has been a scarcely discernible downward trend.

Average annual flows are a useful starting point for analysis and discussion but
it is the way in which river discharge varies with time during the year that is such an
important additional factor in influencing the operation of many hydrological and

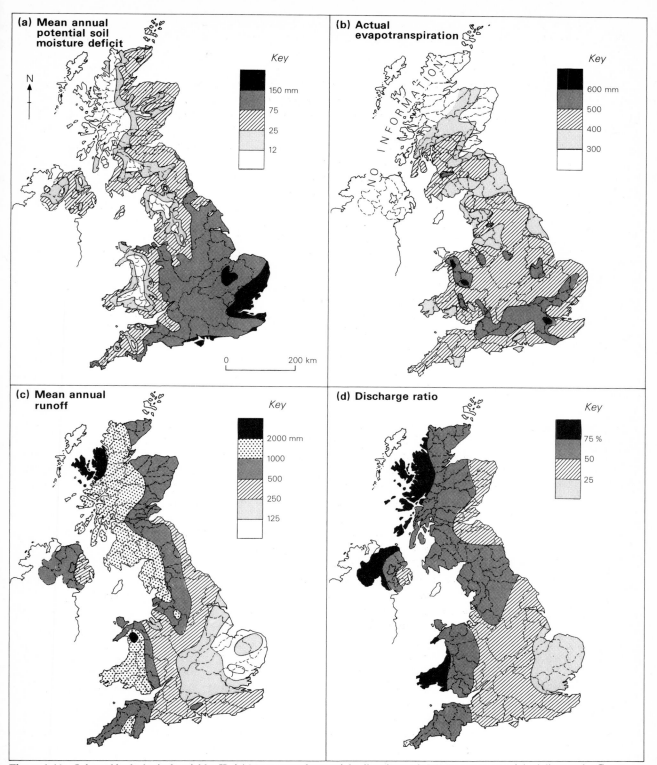

Figure 1.11 Selected hydrological variables II. (a) Mean annual potential soil moisture deficit (based on an original diagram by Green 1964); (b) mean annual actual evapotranspiration; (c) mean annual runoff (based largely on data presented in Water Resources Board 1971, and DOE 1978c); (d) mean discharge ratio, calculated as the median value for each hydrometric area.

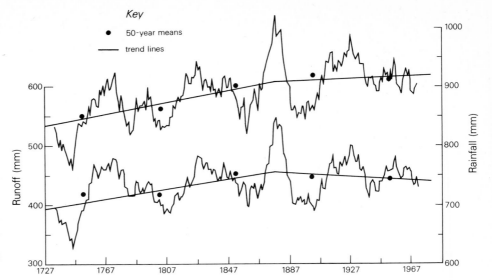

Key

● 50-year means

— trend lines

Figure 1.12 Eleven-year
moving averages of rainfall
(top) and runoff (bottom),
1728–1976, 50-year means and
estimated trend-lines (based on
data presented by Rodda,
Downing & Law 1976, and
Marsh & Littlewood 1978).

geomorphological processes. Particularly in terms of analysing either the effects
of water movement on the transport of dissolved and suspended solids through
and within a drainage basin or the range and availability of river flows from a
resource-management viewpoint it is necessary to determine the frequency with
which a certain discharge value occurs, the times of occurrence during the year of
periods of high and low discharge and the magnitude of the seasonal variations
between high and low discharges.

River flow values for daily (or occasionally weekly or monthly) periods may be
arranged according to their frequency of occurrence and plotted as a flow-
duration curve, i.e. a curve showing the percentage of time that specified flows are
equalled or exceeded during a given year or period of years. For ease of comparison and presentation the examples shown in Figure 1.13 have been made
dimensionless by dividing the daily discharge values by the average daily discharge
values for the period concerned. This technique thereby combines in one curve
the entire range of river discharges, although not of course in chronological order,
and the shape of the curve will reflect the complex combination of hydrological
and catchment factors which determine the range and variability of river discharge.

Flow-duration curves which slope steeply throughout, cf. Tees (HA 25) and
Tamar (HA 47) in Figure 1.13, denote highly variable flows with a large quickflow
component (i.e. water reaching the stream channels rapidly via surface or shallow
sub-surface routes), whereas gently sloping curves, cf. Ver (HA 39) indicate a
large baseflow component (i.e. water reaching the stream channels only comparatively slowly, having been held in temporary storage on or below the ground
surface). Furthermore, as Searcy (1959) observed, the slope of the lower end of
the flow-duration curve characterises the perennial storage of the drainage basin,
so that a flat lower end indicates a large amount of storage.

Since the slope of a flow-duration curve provides a quantitative measure of
streamflow variability considerable attention has been paid to the derivation of
suitable indices of that slope. For example, the US Geological Survey have long
related the flow available 50% of the time to the flow available 90% of the time
(Searcy 1959). In Britain, Hall (1968) found that for a wide variety of rivers the
mean daily flow was exceeded 30% of the time and the modal flow was exceeded

20

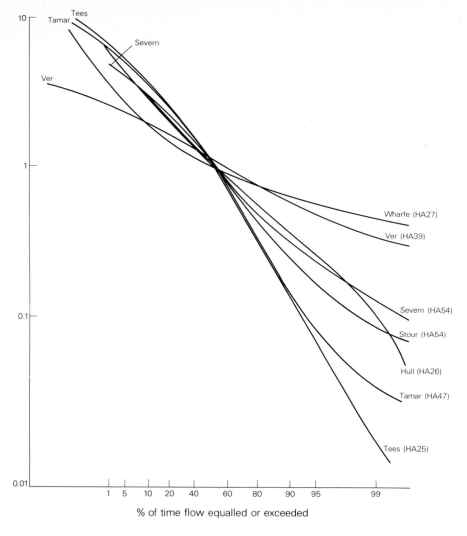

Figure 1.13 Mean flow duration curves for seven rivers.

70% of the time, and suggested that the ratio of mean and modal flows could be related to geological and catchment characteristics.

That there is a certain similarity of behaviour amongst British rivers is indicated by the fact that of 58 flow-duration curves for rivers widely distributed throughout Britain, which were examined by the present author, 32 had 30%:70% ratios of 2–2.99, 12 fell into each of the adjacent classes, i.e. 1–1.99 and 3–3.99, while the remaining two had 30%:70% ratios greater than 4.0. Flow duration curves representative of the largest (2–2.99) group are those for the Hull, Wharfe and Severn in Figure 1.13 (HAs 26, 27 and 54) which can, therefore, be considered to behave as 'typical' British rivers. Low values are exemplified by the Ver (1.79) and the Stour (1.40) and high values by the Tamar (4.32) and the Tees (4.42) (HAs 39 and 54, and 47 and 25 respectively).

Additional information about river basin hydrology may be obtained from a consideration of river flows arranged in chronological order, i.e. the hydrograph, for periods of varying length. Thus, at one scale, the variation of mean monthly flows through the year reflects the relationships between the basic components of the catchment water balance and in particular the interactions between

21

climatological and hydrological factors. At another scale, from the annual succession of daily or shorter period flows, it is possible to learn much about catchment response to inputs of precipitation, i.e. the runoff-producing process, and about the relative importance of the quickflow and baseflow components of catchment runoff.

The pattern of seasonal runoff variations described by a graph of mean monthly river flows is often referred to as the 'regime' of a river or stream, although in fact this term was adopted early in the century by British irrigation engineers working in India to describe that state of equilibrium when there is neither accretion nor deposition of the transported solids load. Earlier consideration of some runoff characteristics of British rivers (Ward 1968) showed that regimes could be represented adequately by ten-year hydrographs of mean monthly discharges and that of the 37 regimes examined, 29 had one period of high and one period of low flow each year. The remaining eight regimes, all of which occurred on rivers in the north and west, seemed to show certain features of Pardé's 'régimes complexes originels' (Pardé 1955) associated either with the increased effectiveness of summer precipitation or with the effects of snowmelt during the spring.

Six selected river regimes are plotted in dimensionless form, i.e. mean monthly flow/mean annual flow, in Figure 1.14. The examples cover a wide range of geographical location and also show quite marked geological contrasts. The Scottish Dee drains a catchment consisting largely of granite and Precambrian grits and schists; the Lune drains an area of Carboniferous limestone in its headwaters region followed by Silurian flags and shales and millstone grit in its middle and lower courses respectively; the Severn an area of massive rocks of Palaeozoic age in the west and south and Triassic sandstones and marls overlain by

Figure 1.14 Regime graphs for six rivers.

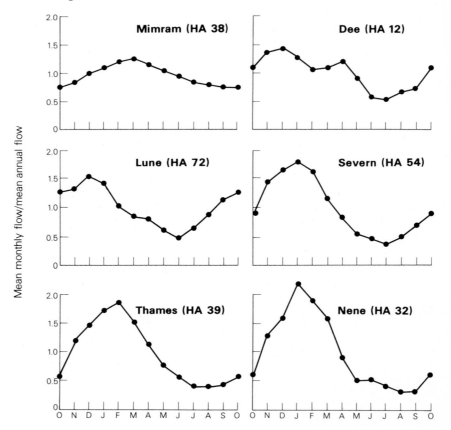

glacial deposits in the north and east; the Nene a catchment of Jurassic clays, limestones and sandstones, with spreads of glacial sands, gravels and boulder clay; the Thames an area of Jurassic limestones and clays, Cretaceous sands, sandstones and chalk, Tertiary sands and clays and large areas of glacial drift; and finally, the Mimram drains an area which is predominantly chalk extensively covered by clay-with-flints.

Despite this geographical and geological variety, however, the regime graphs show certain similarities. Apart from the Dee, all have a relatively uncomplicated pattern of a single period of high water followed by a single period of low water. The main points of contrast lie in the seasonal range of the discharge values and in the timing of the periods of high and low water. The least seasonal variation is exhibited by the Mimram whose average maximum monthly flow is only 1.3 times the annual mean and whose mean minimum monthly flow does not fall below 75% of the mean annual flow. This situation appears to reflect the dominance of baseflow from the chalk of this catchment. Surprisingly, at first sight, the Dee also shows a muted seasonal contrast in flow, with maximum and minimum values representing respectively less than 1.5 and 0.5 times the mean annual flow. In this catchment groundwater storage is unlikely to be a major factor; instead maximum flows appear to be reduced by the fact that a significant proportion of winter precipitation occurs as snowfall, its appearance as runoff being delayed until melting takes place, while low flows during the summer are maintained at a comparatively high level because of the reduced depletion of precipitation by evapotranspiration compared with the other rivers illustrated. The Lune, Severn and Thames form an intermediate group, having maximum flows of between 1.5 and 2.0 times the annual mean and low flows of slightly less than one-half the annual mean. Finally, the Nene shows a markedly greater seasonal contrast in flow than the other rivers illustrated, with a monthly maximum value of more than twice the annual mean and a monthly minimum value considerably smaller than one-half the annual mean. This particular seasonal pattern seems to reflect one or more of a variety of factors which may affect the catchment water balance including generally low precipitation values, a limited amount of groundwater storage and a high magnitude of evapotranspiration during the summer months, as well as the less easily discernible effects of factors such as variations of land use.

There are also variations in the timing of periods of maximum and minimum flow for the rivers illustrated in Figure 1.14. Monthly maximum flow occurs in December for the Dee and Lune, January for the Severn and Nene and in February and March for the Thames and Mimram respectively. The month of minimum flow ranges from June–July, through August and September and finally to October for the same rivers. Again Ward (1968) noted such differences and detected the elements of a consistent regional variation in regime characteristics as illustrated in Figure 1.15.

For the 59 rivers whose regimes were examined in the present study the months during which maximum and minimum flows occurred are plotted in Figure 1.15a and b respectively. Despite differences of detail the two distributions are broadly similar in the sense that the time of occurrence of both maximum and minimum flow becomes gradually later towards the south and east. Thus mean monthly maximum flow in Scotland, North-West England and the western fringes of Wales occurs in December but is as late as February or even March in some eastern areas. Similarly, the mean minimum monthly flow occurs in June over central and western Scotland, northern England and parts of northern and western Wales, and even in May for some of the Cheshire rivers, but is as late as September in

23

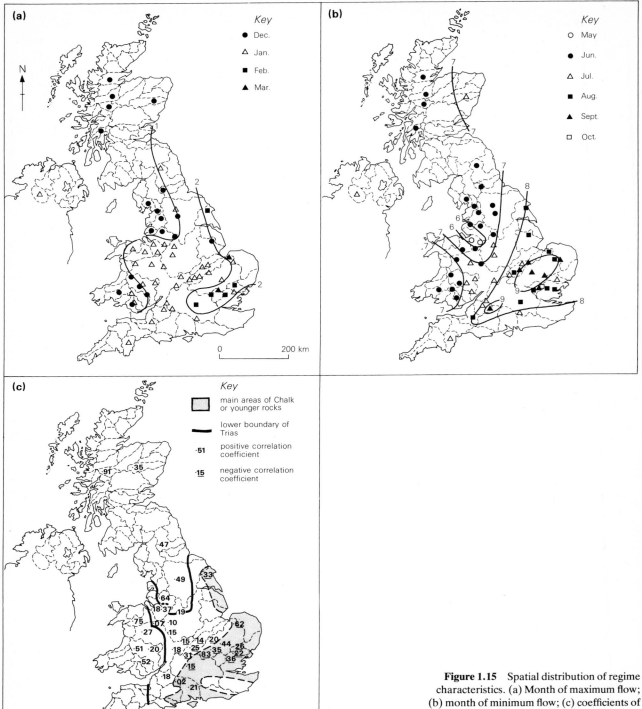

Figure 1.15 Spatial distribution of regime characteristics. (a) Month of maximum flow; (b) month of minimum flow; (c) coefficients of correlation between mean monthly values of precipitation and runoff and their relationship to geological conditions.

parts of eastern or central southern England. These patterns appear to reflect the effects of hydrogeology and other catchment characteristics, together with the increasing effectiveness of evapotranspiration towards the south and east, rather than any direct effect of precipitation regime. For example, in the case of three rivers having runoff minima in September, i.e. the Mimram, Cam and Semington Brook, the mean monthly rainfall minimum occurs in April, whereas for the Lochy, Irwell and Irfon, all of which have runoff minima in June, the mean monthly rainfall minima occur in April, March and May–June respectively. However, Rodda, Downing and Law (1976) suggested that the earlier occurrence of periods of low flow in the west and north may be due to the fact that average monthly rainfalls decline early in the year in the mountainous west, especially in northern Britain, so that the six months with the lowest amount of precipitation in western Scotland are normally February to July.

If, as has been suggested, the main factors influencing the relationship between rainfall and runoff are geology and the increasing effectiveness of evapotranspiration towards the south and east, it might be expected that coefficients of correlation between mean monthly values of precipitation and runoff would show a definite spatial pattern. Figure 1.15c indicates that, in fact, the highest positive correlation coefficients occur in the north and west where hard, old, crystalline rocks, having little groundwater storage capacity, encourage the rapid transmission of precipitated water into the stream channels. Conversely, the highest negative values, indicating a tendency towards an inverse relationship between the two variables, occur almost at the heart of the large areas of sedimentary water-bearing rocks (particularly within the areas of chalk and younger rocks) which together constitute such a large part of the English Plain and which encourage infiltration and percolation and the sub-surface storage of precipitated water with its subsequent gradual release into stream channels. Although little attempt has been made in Figure 1.15c to show details of geology, the lower boundary of the Bunter–Keuper series which marks the approximate lower limits of the porous sedimentaries is throughout much of its length located in the transitional zone of low positive and negative correlation coefficients which separates the areas to the north and west, where runoff is clearly positively related to precipitation, and the areas to the south and east where this relationship is considerably more complex.

Although the sort of broad similarities discussed above between river regimes presented on the basis of monthly mean flows may be expected, river flow variations based on daily or shorter-period data are likely to vary considerably and indeed at this level of detail each river must be considered unique. The six hydrographs of daily mean discharge shown in Figure 1.16 and Figure 1.17 must be regarded, therefore, simply as examples selected to illustrate broad contrasts in catchment hydrology rather than as formal representatives of identifiable categories of flow variation. Daily mean discharges in 1972 for three comparatively large rivers are shown in Figure 1.16, where the obvious contrast is between the flashy behaviour of the Lune, the subdued behaviour of the Thames with its much larger baseflow component and the intermediate character of the Dee. Three smaller rivers are illustrated in Figure 1.17 which also refers to 1972. Again the comparison may be made between the large and moderate baseflow component of the Avon and Nene respectively. The regime of the Elan, like that of many reservoired rivers, is entirely controlled except in times of high flow.

Two aspects of the flood behaviour of British rivers are illustrated in Figure 1.18, i.e. an index of flood potential in the form of an estimate of mean annual flood (Fig. 1.18a) and an indication of flood experience during the period of river flow gauging in the form of the highest instantaneous gauged discharges (Fig. 1.18b). The best estimate of mean annual flood (BESMAF) was derived by the NERC Flood Studies Team by extending the recorded flood experience by correlation with nearby flood records. Where such extension was not possible the arithmetic mean of annual maximum floods was used (NERC 1975a).

The pattern of isopleths drawn through the BESMAF values is a fairly predictable one. Apart from small, isolated areas of higher ground or relatively impermeable surfaces, lowland Britain has BESMAF values substantially below $0.25 \, \text{m}^3 \, \text{s}^{-1} \, \text{km}^{-2}$. The average values for HAs 29 and 30 combined and for HAs 34 and 35 combined is 0.06 and for HAs 42 and 43 combined it is 0.05. High values, above $0.75 \, \text{m}^3 \, \text{s}^{-1} \, \text{km}^{-2}$, are restricted to Dartmoor, the Welsh mountains, areas of the Pennines and Cumbria, the Southern Uplands and parts of western and northern Scotland.

Although the data are presented cartographically in different ways, a comparison of BESMAF with the distribution of highest instantaneous gauged dis-

Figure 1.16 Hydrographs of daily discharge during 1972 for the Lune, Dee and Thames.

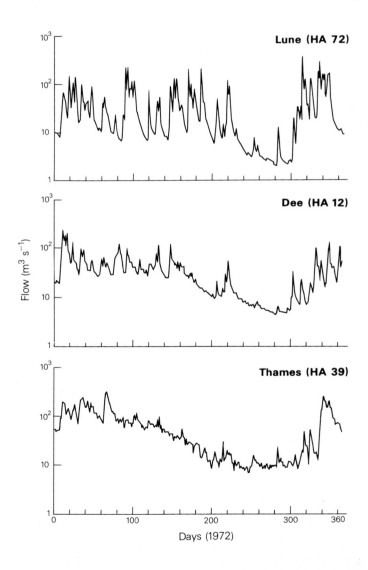

26

charges, averaged for each hydrometric area (Fig. 1.18b), reveals a striking similarity. In both cases it should be noted that the comparatively low values of flood-flow per unit area over south-eastern England may be misleading in the sense that they are to some extent compensated by the large area of the catchments concerned. The highest instantaneous gauged discharge for the Thames at Teddington (HA 39), for example, is approximately 790 $m^3 s^{-1}$, which exceeds that for the Tees at Broken Scar (HA 25) of 679 $m^3 s^{-1}$ or for the Clyde at Blairston (HA 84) of 577 $m^3 s^{-1}$. The usefulness of maximum gauged discharges as an index of flood potential obviously depends upon the length of record since long records are more likely than short ones to incorporate rare, high magnitude events. Extension of the comparatively brief gauging records of most British rivers will, therefore, gradually increase the values currently mapped in Figure 1.18b until they approach useful 'design flood' dimensions in terms of their magnitude–frequency relationships.

NERC (1975a) found that the relationship between mean annual flood and the flood of a given return period varied between a number of identifiable regions

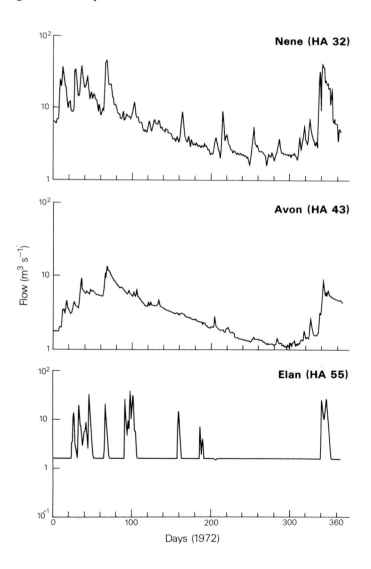

Figure 1.17 Hydrographs of daily discharge during 1972 for the Nene, Avon and Elan.

27

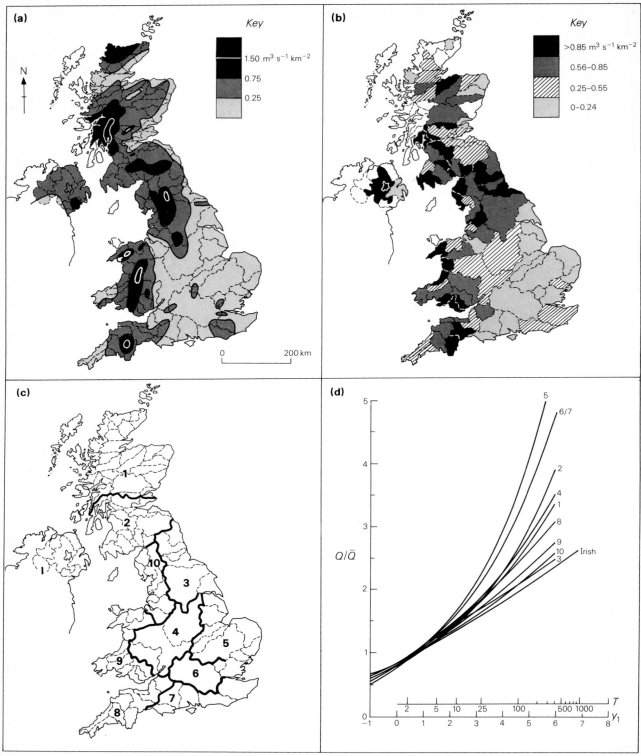

Figure 1.18 Selected flood discharge characteristics. (a) BESMAF (estimated mean annual flood) values; (b) mean maximum instantaneous gauged discharges for each hydrometric area (based on data presented in DOE 1978c); (c) regions defined by the NERC Flood Studies team; (d) curves showing the relationship between floods of a given return period (Q) and the estimated mean annual flood ($\bar{Q}$) for the 11 regions shown in c (a and d are based on original diagrams in NERC 1975a).

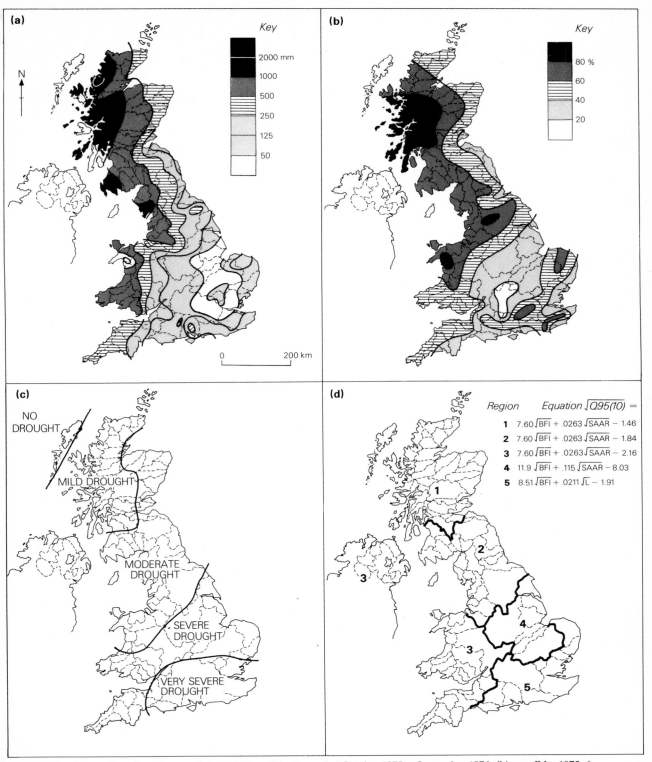

Figure 1.19 Selected low-flow characteristics. (a) Runoff for the period October 1975 to September 1976; (b) runoff for 1975–6 expressed as a percentage of mean annual runoff; (c) categories of drought during 1975–6 (based on an original map by Atkinson 1980); (d) regions defined by the NERC Low Flow Studies team (based on data presented in Institute of Hydrology 1980).

within Britain. These regions which were subsequently combined in various ways for predictive purposes, are shown in Figure 1.18c and the curves indicating the average distribution of $Q/\bar{Q}$ in each region are shown in Figure 1.18d.

At the other hydrological extreme, the low-flow characteristics of rivers also have particular significance. Low-flow studies of British rivers received a tremendous stimulus as a result of the 'great British drought' of 1975–6 which generated a substantial literature of its own culminating in the publication of a comprehensive *Atlas of drought in Britain 1975–6* (Doornkamp, Gregory & Burn 1980).

The severity of the 1975–6 drought was by no means uniform throughout the British Isles. England and Wales were undoubtedly worse affected than Scotland or Northern Ireland. Over much of the country, however, the period of 16 months from May 1975 to August 1976 was the driest for 250 years and many authorities therefore concluded that, particularly during the last 12 months of this period, baseline dry weather conditions were established for many hydrometeorological and associated variables. Certainly, in terms of river discharge, the effects of the drought were quite dramatic. Figures 1.19a and b show that except in limited areas of western Scotland, the western Pennines and Snowdonia runoff was reduced by substantial amounts. Indeed over much of southern England runoff values were less than 40% of the long-term mean although even within this area there were 'islands' of comparatively higher runoff seemingly associated partly with areas having a smaller reduction of precipitation below the long-term mean and partly with catchment conditions favouring the storage and slow release of base flow to the stream channels.

Atkinson (1980) categorised the severity of the 1975–6 drought largely in terms of the precipitation characteristics during the period, as 'mild', 'moderate', 'severe' and 'very severe'. The spatial distribution of these categories is shown in Figure 1.19c and it is interesting to observe the remarkable coincidences with the pattern of regions demarcated by the Institute of Hydrology's Low Flow Study team (Institute of Hydrology 1980a) and illustrated in Figure 1.19d. The underlying philosophy of the Low Flow Study was that low flow indices extracted from river flow records could be related statistically to catchment characteristics in a way which would permit the prediction of low flows at ungauged sites. It was found that the 95 percentile ten-day flow Q95(10) can be determined from a knowledge of (a) the base flow index (BFI), which is a measure of the proportion of base flow under the flow hydrograph, and either (b) the annual average rainfall in the current standard period (SAAR) or (c) main stream length (L). Figure 1.19d illustrates that for three of the five regions depicted, i.e. regions 1, 2 and 3, the low flow equations differ only in the constant term, although regions 4 and 5 require two totally different equations. There is little doubt that the *Low flow studies report* fills a substantial void in our understanding of the dry-weather flow characteristics of British rivers.

Table 1.3 Hydrometric area data.

Hydrometric area	Area	Mean catchment area		Mean river length		Drainage density[c]	Stream frequency[d]	Lake frequency[e]	Urban area[f]	Draining to lakes[f]	Channel slope 10–85 percentile[f]
		All[a]	Gauged	All[b]	Gauged						
	km^2	km^2	km^2	km	km	$km\,km^{-2}$	km^{-2}	km^{-2}	$\%$	$\%$	$m\,km^{-1}$
1	877	80		6		0.43	0.075	0.022			
2	1372	137		9		0.73	0.085	0.039			
3	1909	147	147	12	43	1.18	0.101	0.040	0	0.472	12.17
4	2173	241	962	8	53	0.37	0.048	0.040	0	0.449	6.70
5	1075	358	850	5	62	0.23	0.047	0.044	0	0.518	3.8
6	1993	1993	1219	7	59	0.27	0.039	0.043	0	0.430	11.6
7	1821	364	499	6	63	0.21	0.035	0.016	0	0.084	8.6
8	2788	2788	899	7	65	0.25	0.034	0.013	0.003	0.080	4.7
9	1545	193	566	4	43	0.07	0.020	0	0.012	0	4.2
10	1415	142	387	4	37	0.09	0.023	0.006	0	0	3.5
11	1336	1336	1270	3	100	0.07	0.020	0			
12	2117	2117	1370	6	116	0.15	0.026	0.009	0.005	0.052	3.9
13	2027	203		5		0.12	0.025	0.007			
14	1070	119	217	2	27	0.03	0.014	0.009			
15	5080	5080	801	10	40	0.32	0.031	0.019	0.003	0.130	19.5
16	976	976	345	3	35	0.08	0.025	0.015	0.008	0.334	10.7
17	1444	160	191	3	25	0.04	0.014	0.034			
18	1626	407	263	5	36	0.16	0.031	0.025	0.018	0.182	9.9
19	915	305	135	3	24	0.05	0.020	0.023	0.157	0.101	8.6
20	676	169	115	2	18	0.02	0.013	0.007	0.015	0.004	11.6
21	5355	1071	494	9	37	0.21	0.024	0.007	0.007	0.143	7.0
22	2052	187	219	11	33	0.29	0.027	0.009	0.003	0.005	8.7
23	2916	2916	589	7	39	0.21	0.031	0.007	0.002	0.031	5.4
24	1197	599	209	13	30	0.35	0.028	0.006	0.016	0.027	15.8
25	2238	224	304	11	31	0.41	0.038	0.008	0.007	0.056	26.7
26	2125	177	316	7	29	0.18	0.025	0.004	0.005	0	1.5
27	11366	1033	586	16	41	0.46	0.029	0.014	0.054	0.081	7.6
28	10436	3479	799	21	42	0.22	0.011	0.013	0.091	0.043	4.8
29	1905	136	72	10	13	0.17	0.016	0.009	0	0	4.6
30	3366	1683	161	20	26	0.15	0.007	0.007	0.003	0.011	3.2
31	1601	1601	268	11	35	0.15	0.014	0.011	0.004	0.051	2.6
32	2369	2369	497	11	51	0.11	0.011	0.018	0.013	0.073	4.3
33	8582	2861	388	19	30	0.18	0.009	0.008	0.007	0.015	1.6
34	3694	528	202	9	26	0.12	0.013	0.014	0.003	0	1.4
35	1600	123	135	8	21	0.10	0.013	0.003	0.014	0	2.2
36	1043	522	164	15	20	0.15	0.011	0.002	0.002	0	2.5
37	3149	185	174	7	29	0.14	0.020	0.010	0.034	0.018	2.6
38	1419	1419	190	11	18	0.19	0.017	0.023	0.063	0	3.7
39	10943	5472	525	14	32	0.22	0.016	0.018	0.207	0.035	4.2
40	4784	478	240	5	24	0.18	0.033	0.015	0.012	0.147	4.0
41	3086	257	135	3	17	0.14	0.047	0.013	0.061	0.025	6.6
42	2735	130	256	14	19	0.22	0.015	0.008	0.129	0	4.1
43	2974	991	454	6	36	0.16	0.025	0.004	0.006	0	0.5
44	1324	132	165	5	23	0.15	0.032	0.008			5.2

31

Table 1.3 – *continued*

Hydrometric area	Area	Mean catchment area		Mean river length		Drainage density[c]	Stream frequency[d]	Lake frequency[e]	Urban area[f]	Draining to lakes[f]	Channel slope 10–85 percentile[f]
		All[a]	Gauged	All[b]	Gauged						
	km^2	km^2	km^2	km	km	$km\,km^{-2}$	km^{-2}	km^{-2}	%	%	$m\,km^{-1}$
45	2253	250	223	6	37	0.28	0.051	0.002	0.003	0	14.5
46	1512	137	314	5	42	0.25	0.047	0.007	0	0.019	29.9
47	1820	152	190	8	24	0.40	0.053	0.003	0	0	9.6
48	1559	37	49	8	13	0.42	0.050	0.010	0	0.004	12.2
49	1249	48	80	5	15	0.31	0.059	0.003	0.002	0	8.5
50	2146	268	745	4	68	0.19	0.053	0.003	0.002	0	14.9
51	528	53	76	4	11	0.23	0.053	0.006			17.8
52	2761	197	91	4	17	0.21	0.049	0.006	0.015	0.133	6.6
53	2220	1110	365	18	29	0.27	0.015	0.005	0.010	0	2.8
54	11421	952	510	9	40	0.16	0.017	0.010	0.019	0.043	7.4
55	4184	2092	736	14	43	0.40	0.029	0.005	0.001	0.021	15.7
56	1741	348	172	7	28	0.22	0.031	0.009	0.028	0.040	8.0
57	926	309	158	9	27	0.27	0.029	0.016	0.065	0.089	7.7
58	1028	129	76	5	16	0.22	0.045	0.007	0.010	0.010	12.6
59	861	86	228	4	38	0.15	0.039	0.012	0.025	0	10.4
60	2048	228	418	5	45	0.21	0.045	0.003	0	0	5.7
61	1481	55	191	2	25	0.06	0.037	0.005	0	0	6.6
62	1027	342	894	5	98	0.19	0.041	0.008	0.001	0	1.8
63	846	77	176	5	39	0.17	0.035	0.028	0	0.125	10.3
64	1343	122	184	3	20	0.14	0.053	0.014	0	0	5.2
65	1317	88	44	3	12	0.13	0.039	0.033	0	0.523	51.5
66	1503	301	220	4	27	0.14	0.035	0.018	0	0.052	14.2
67	2117	1059	290	9	26	0.23	0.025	0.012	0.002	0.250	11.1
68	1886	377	285	12	37	0.26	0.022	0.021	0.016	0.011	4.5
69	2687	672	270	16	31	0.36	0.022	0.035	0.185	0.141	22.8
70	618	309	40	30	14	0.39	0.013	0.021	0	0.052	4.7
71	1488	1488	303	9	28	0.30	0.034	0.024	0.019	0.046	14.4
72	1648	330	635	8	55	0.31	0.040	0.008	0	0	6.2
73	1202	200	165	13	25	0.29	0.023	0.027	0.013	0.463	12.2
74	914	91	54	12	15	0.36	0.030	0.014	0	0.454	13.8
75	1219	244	156	15	20	0.43	0.029	0.011	0.001	0.534	1.7
76	2397	2397	371	13	46	0.41	0.031	0.007	0.001	0.086	12.2
77	998	333	581	5	49	0.22	0.046	0.002	0	0.016	3.8
78	960	960	501	3	42	0.09	0.028	0.009	0	0	10.6
79	1480	493	297	4	35	0.10	0.025	0.009	0.012	0.040	6.7
80	1526	191	199	5	33	0.20	0.037	0.026	0	0.301	12.1
81	2047	120	186	5	22	0.14	0.026	0.021	0.003	0.084	8.1
82	1078	270	296	4	45	0.15	0.036	0.026	0.028	0.095	7.4
83	1515	168	204	6	27	0.26	0.043	0.017	0.077	0	11.6
84	3040	760	242	7	26	0.21	0.029	0.029	0.111	0.035	11.3
85	814	271	361	5	36	0.34	0.066	0.025	0.056	0.562	15.5
86	861	32	86	5	16	0.33	0.063	0.033			
87	720	34		6		0.67	0.103	0.026	0	0	94.6
88	808	48		7		0.62	0.094	0.093			

Hydrometric area	Area	Mean catchment area		Mean river length		Drainage density[c]	Stream frequency[d]	Lake frequency[e]	Urban area[f]	Draining to lakes[f]	Channel slope 10–85 percentile[f]
		All[a]	Gauged	All[b]	Gauged						
	km^2	km^2	km^2	km	km	$km\,km^{-2}$	km^{-2}	km^{-2}	%	%	$m\,km^{-1}$
89	1391	126		6		0.33	0.052	0.041			
90	1177	45		6		0.30	0.052	0.033	0	0	30.6
91	1327	1327		5		0.23	0.041	0.025	0	0	117.7
92	1153	36		8		0.59	0.078	0.049			
93	1679	48		7		0.32	0.047	0.052			
94	1061	39	441	7	40	0.57	0.081	0.104			6.4
95	2196	41		14		1.46	0.107	0.181	0	0.381	8.7
96	1958	65		11		1.00	0.090	0.100			
97	912	91	413	5	25	0.32	0.059	0.059			
101	381	42	30	10	10	0.30	0.031	0.003			
102	714	55		2		0.07	0.038	0.025			
103	572	72		3		0.13	0.042	0.007			
104	2163	27					0.092	0.059			
105	2508	22					0.078	0.058			
106	2733	21					0.105	0.400			
107	697	63					0.019	0.069			
108	1279	8					0.233	0.152			
203	5000[g]		336		38						
205	1800[g]		445		43						

Notes

[a] Area of HA divided by total number of systems counted by Smith and Lyle (1979).

[b] Total stream length (Water Data Unit data) divided by total number of streams counted by Smith and Lyle (1979). N.B. Total stream length values for Scottish HAs have been estimated (see text).

[c] Total stream length (Water Data Unit data) divided by area of HA. N.B. Total stream length values for Scottish HAs have been estimated (see text).

[d] Total number of streams counted by Smith and Lyle (1979) divided by area of HA.

[e] Total number of lakes and reservoirs counted by Smith and Lyle (1979) divided by area of HA.

[f] Means are calculated for each hydrometric area from the individual catchment data presented by NERC (1975a).

[g] Estimated area.

33

2 Contemporary erosion and sedimentation

J. Lewin

This chapter looks at the evidence for 'contemporary' erosion and sedimentation by rivers in Britain, broadly that which is apparent over a matter of decades or perhaps a century or two. A simple framework for looking at such activity is provided by Figure 2.1. This emphasises that erosion, transport and sedimentation are components of the same fluvial system, and that the overall transfer of material from hillslope to ocean is accomplished through a number of steps, some of them effectively repeated time and again. For example, soil material may be weathered on site for millennia, and then rapidly eroded from a hillside – only to be stored as slope-foot colluvium for further centuries before being picked up again at an eroding river bank. From then on material may be moved short distances (and be mechanically broken down on the way) from cut bank to sedimenting channel margin where again it may be stored as part of the floodplain for centuries before being picked up once more by the migrating river channel. These processes are also not all physical and inorganic: soil leaching may lead to preferential removal of mobile elements, while organic processes may lead to selective solute uptake.

It follows from what has been said so far that fluvial systems in Britain necessarily have *temporal* components and dependencies. What is being transported past one particular point along a stream may have arrived there via different pathways and over different timespans: some (fine) sediment may have been washed long distances from hillside to stream mouth in a single storm, but some (coarse) material may have been initially weathered from slopes under cold Pleistocene conditions, then stored in a gravel terrace, and finally moved intermittently again from gravel bar to bar during the 10 000 years of the Holocene. 'Contemporary' activity is conditioned by the past in a complex way and it takes much longer for sediment to pass along the various pathways in the system than it does water. At the same time, precisely where and when and how water is flowing

Figure 2.1 Erosion and sedimentation in a fluvial system. The arrows show the movement of material between domains.

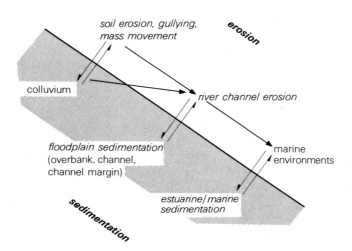

soil erosion, gullying, mass movement

erosion

colluvium

river channel erosion

floodplain sedimentation (overbank, channel, channel margin)

marine environments

sedimentation

estuarine/marine sedimentation

within a drainage basin provides the essential means for material transport. Thus the flow hydrographs and river regimes discussed in Chapter 1 are commonly linked to transport rates, as discussed in terms of water quality in Chapter 5. Other environmental factors, such as frost action or biogenic activity, can also be important, but a more important consideration to appreciate at this point is that water movement also has *spatial* dimensions and dependencies. Thus diffuse sub-surface soil water flow on slopes may allow the transfer of colloids and solutes; ground saturation in hollows may lead to overland water flow and surface erosion, spring heads may produce steep head-cuts, and channelled flow may lead to both vertical incision and lateral cut-bank development. All these may operate differentially over time from winter to summer and from storm runoff event through intervening dry spell.

The final general point to appreciate is that catchments provide very varied opportunities for sediment production by virtue of the materials present. In Britain, much of the landscape is mantled by superficial deposits (glacial and prior fluvial sediments in particular) and it is these especially which are now being redistributed by river action. At the same time, much of the Holocene has been characterised by sufficient slope stability to allow the development of mature soils both on these superficial deposits and on weathered bedrock. Contemporary fluvial erosion thus commonly involves pre-prepared material (including that now made especially available by tillage, urban development or other human activities), so that every catchment may have a unique mosaic of sediment sources: soils, deep superficial deposits, some ploughed land and some forest, undercut river cliffs, seepage saps and so on. As far as the evidence available allows it, the next few sections summarise the nature of these erosional and depositional contexts and processes. A distinction is made between long-term tendencies towards, or sites for, erosion and sedimentation (here termed 'progressive'), and those which may prove transient within a matter of years or decades ('cyclic'). For example, areas of erosion (cut banks, pools, scour holes) or sedimentation (shoals or bars) may be found essentially within river channels and these may be replaced or reformed from storm to storm. These may be important for the transfer of sediment but they do not necessarily persist as intact features, and from a practical point of view it is helpful to distinguish the transient from the progressive even though the distinction may be a little arbitrary at times.

Progressive erosion

Sediment sources

In some places, streams may derive sediment directly from bedrock, but spectacular though features like waterfalls, rapids and potholes may be locally (Fig. 2.2), these seem to provide only a small part of the sediment British rivers transport at present. These relate in particular to materials that have been subjected to prior breakdown, which now form valley-bottom or valley-side superficial deposits and soils. In seeking to provide generalisations on a national scale, examination of a map is helpful here. Table 2.1 lists the types of deposit mapped by the Institute of Geological Sciences on the Quaternary Map of Britain (1977). Some of these are very localised in their extent (1,4,7), but others may be of general significance despite an apparently limited distribution on what is necessarily a generalised small-scale map.

35

Figure 2.2 The bed of the
River Findhorn near
Randolph's Leap, showing
pools, rapids in the low-flow
inner channel, and potholes in
the exposed bedrock ribs.

Blown sand (2) has been mapped extensively around the Moray Firth, in
Strathclyde around Ayr, in Lancashire, and in Lincolnshire and Humberside.
Wind action remains an important agent of erosion in eastern England (Radley &
Simms 1967, Robinson 1968), and the former extent of loess (periglacial wind-
deposited sediment) is also significant for present fluvial processes. Catt (1978)
has suggested that such silty material (also designated loam or brickearth (12),

Table 2.1 British superficial deposits.

Category (after IGS 1977)	*Study examples*
1 landslip	Skempton and Hutchinson (1976)
2 blown sand	Catt (1978), Radley and Simms (1967), Robinson (1968)
3 peat	Tallis (1973)
4 lacustrine clays, silts and sands	Gaunt *et al.* (1971), Oldfield (1977)
5 alluvium	Bluck (1971, 1976), Horton (1970), Rose *et al.* (1980)
6 river terrace deposits	Clayton (1977), Cross and Hodgson (1975), Wills (1938)
7 raised beach and marine sediments	Sissons (1976), Tooley (1974)
8 glacial sands and gravels	Shaw (1972)
9 boulder clay	Boulton *et al.* (1977)
10 plateau gravels	—
11 clay-with-flints	Hodgson *et al.* (1967), Loveday (1962)
12 brickearth	Catt (1978)

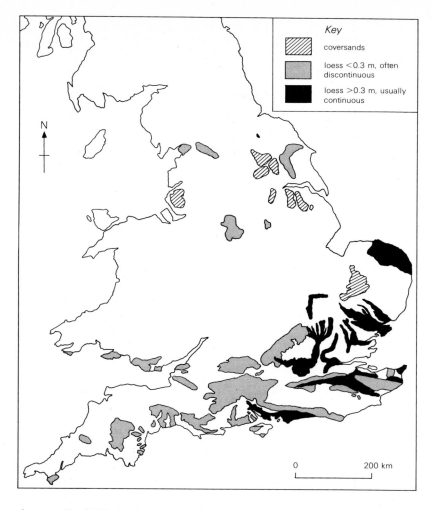

Figure 2.3 The distribution of loess and coversands in southern Britain, based on Catt (1977).

though not all of this is simple loess) once formed a ubiquitous cover probably 1–4 m thick south of the Late Devensian ice limit. Although many areas still retain more than 30 cm of loess, especially on chalk and limestone permeable bedrock (Fig. 2.3), much has been weathered, eroded and fluvially redistributed so that it is now incorporated into alluvial and colluvial sediments. It seems possible that South-East England in the Late-glacial shared some of the features of accelerated erosion now to be seen in the loess terrains of the southeastern United States, although the present extent, and texture, of alluvial valley floor sediments in Britain owes something to prior glaciation nearby.

By contrast, peat deposits (3) are extensive in upland Britain. It has been estimated, for example, that peat covers 7.5% of Wales (Taylor & Tucker 1970) mostly on plateau surfaces above 350 m and where precipitation is over 125 cm a year. Such peats have formed over about the last 5000 years; they are often shallow but can exceed 3 m in depth, and at present they may be actively eroding (Crisp 1966, Tallis 1973). Many lowland rivers also have organic fens alongside, as in the Fenlands, East Anglia and Somerset Levels. Here peat losses may follow drainage and cultivation. In 130 years, peat levels have been lowered by 3.9 m at the Holme Post near Peterborough (Hutchinson 1980).

Boulder clay (9), both from Devensian and earlier glaciations, is mapped very   37

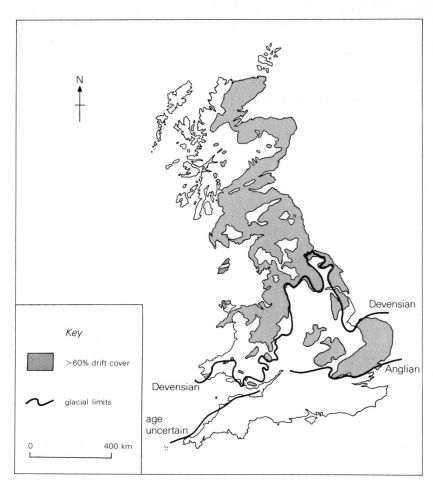

N

Key

>60% drift cover

glacial limits

Devensian

Anglian

Devensian

age
uncertain

0   400 km

Figure 2.4 Glacial limits in Britain (after Bowen 1978) and the distribution of extensive glacial drift (after Boulton *et al.* 1977).

widely north of the Thames. Figure 2.4 shows the limits of Devensian glaciation, which probably reached its maximum extent around 18 000 years ago, together with the probable maximum extent of earlier glaciation. It also shows the large area of glacial sediments, though for details of these it is advisable to consult much larger-scale geological maps. Even outside the areas of extensive glacigenic sediments, there are often patchy deposits which can form important sediment sources for contemporary rivers. Figure 2.5a shows an area in mid-Wales where till, till solifluced downslope under cold periglacial conditions, and thick stratified scree may all contribute sediment to the present channel where they are undercut and gullied. By contrast, some parts of Scotland subjected to intensive scour by glaciers and largely devoid of superficial deposits may actually yield very little sediment to judge from the sedimentation in lakes, or lack of it (Pennington *et al.* 1972). Both within and beyond glacial limits, however, periglacial cold conditions generally led to structural disturbance, mass movement, and accelerated fluvial transport and the deposits that resulted are widely distributed (Higginbottom & Fookes 1971).

In all, the Quaternary has provided contemporary streams with a complex inheritance of variable sediment sources which may include both true tills, glacial sands and gravels (8), solifluced slope and other sediments (head and coombe deposits among them), and prior fluvial terrace or terrace-like sediments (6,10).

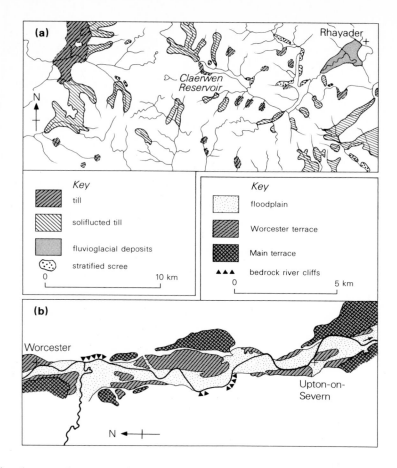

Figure 2.5 (a) The distribution of glacial and periglacial sediments in a part of mid-Wales, based on Potts (1971); (b) terraces and modern alluvium along the River Severn near Worcester, after Wills (1938).

In upland areas these may function as in the small stream valley in South Wales shown in Figure 2.6: there the present stream is incised into superficial deposits, with a now inactive system of gullies being present in addition. Active input of sediment is confined to a few shallow slips and undercut banks, but the heterogeneous size mix of superficial deposits provides both cobble-sized (over 6 cm) material transported as bed-load and a range of finer sediments transported in suspension. Elsewhere in Britain, rivers may derive sediment from both bedrock and their own previous fluvial deposits. Figure 2.5b shows a section of the River Severn below Worcester. Before the river was effectively stone-lined to limit navigation damage, it cut laterally into fragments of the Worcester and Main terraces (the last an outwash train from Devensian ice; see Fig. 2.4), into high Trias bedrock cliffs, and into its own recent, fine alluvium.

A general conclusion to draw is that British rivers can provide themselves with coarse sediment by their own incision, headward extension or lateral channel migration; these may be in the form of materials which are largely coarse, like many terrace sediments and glacial gravels, or mixtures (diamicton) of various origins which have both coarse and fine components. Fine sediment may be derived from these, but they can also come from sorted wind-derived silts and from surface soils. Organic sediments, from both upland and fen, may also border stream channels. What is less common in present-day Britain are sand-bed rivers and ones where there are high rates of slope material input unless, that is, cultivation practice facilitates it.

Figure 2.6 The Nant Garw, near Brynamman on the Black Mountain, Dyfed, showing gullied superficial deposits to the left of the stream.

Finally to complete the complexity of contemporary British fluvial sediment sources, we should note the complexity of solid geology in Britain, and therefore of soils developed on various present materials. The latter include calcareous brown earths and rendzinas on chalk and limestone, high base status brown earths over much of the rest of lowland England, and acid brown earths and podsols in upland Britain. Superficial deposits vary even this picture, however, and examination of Soil Survey maps and reports is advisable for local information. In particular, soil type may vary with valley form, depth of superficial sediment and hillslope hydrology, and there are inter-relationships in both directions between soil type and erosion activity (e.g. Huggett 1976).

Erosion domains

A much improved understanding of the ways in which fluvial systems are capable of picking up sediment and developing their channels has recently begun to emerge, in particular through advances in the study of hillslope hydrology (Kirkby 1978), soil erosion (Morgan 1979) and river channel morphology (Gregory 1977). For example, water may move on hillslopes as overland flow (either because of ground saturation, or exceedance of soil infiltration capacity), shallow subsurface flow, or groundwater flow, and these may be associated with the wash, rill, piping and springhead erosion of sediment. Which process dominates may depend on both the nature of surface materials and the nature of precipitation (such as its timing and intensity) and other environmental factors.

Many of these recent developments are theoretical in nature or based on a limited number of type sites, only a few of which are in Britain. But the emerging theoretical importance of localised erosion, as at streamheads, is not incompatible with much earlier empirical research in Britain (reviewed in Douglas 1970), and it

40

Table 2.2 Active fluvial erosion sites. *Progressive erosion*

1	Hillslope	(a) creep, wash, rill and solution processes	Huggett (1976)
			Kirkby (1967)
			Morgan (1980)
			Young (1960, 1978)
		(b) localised mass movement	Crisp *et al.* (1964)
			Newson (1975b)
			Skempton and Hutchinson (1976)
2	Streamhead	(a) seepage, overland flow generation	Bunting (1961),
			Burt (1979)
			Finlayson (1978)
			Tuckfield (1973)
		(b) piping	Gilman and Newson (1980)
			Jones (1971)
		(c) network extension	Ovenden and Gregory (1980)
		(d) gullying	Fairbairn (1967)
			Gregory and Park (1976b)
			Harvey (1974, 1977)
			Thomas (1956)
			Tuckfield (1964)
3	Channel, involving	(a) bedrock	Finlayson (1978)
		(b) superficial deposit	Hill (1973)
			Knighton (1973)
			Lewin and Brindle (1977)
		(c) alluvium	Hooke (1979)
			Thorne and Lewin (1979)

is possible to marry theoretical advance with older observation to identify the likely erosion domains of the present landscape. Table 2.2 presents domains and a listing of studies that have been undertaken.

Research published in the 1960s, notably by A. Young and M. J. Kirkby, showed low rates of downhill creep and even slower rates of surface wash (Table 2.3); though observations were over rather brief periods and precision is difficult, rates of the same order of magnitude have been confirmed both by longer-term observations (Young 1978) and by ingenious inference from the form of earlier Quaternary structures (Chandler & Pook 1971). Much higher rates of soil erosion have been observed on agricultural land (Evans & Morgan 1974, Al-Ansari *et al.* 1977, Morgan 1980) amounting to between 2 and 200 tonnes per hectare for small areas during storms. Such material may be fed into streams or it may remain as a colluvial footslope deposit. 'Hillwash' or 'ploughwash' deposits following wood-

Table 2.3 Rates of slope material movement (volumetric movement measured in $cm^3 \, cm^{-1} \, yr^{-1}$).

	Surface wash	Soil creep
Young (1960)	0.08	0.5
Kirkby (1967)	0.09	2.1
Young (1978)		0.61
Chandler and Pook (1971)		0.3

41

Figure 2.7 Slope failure on a tributary of the River Wye, Powys, following extreme precipitation in August 1973.

land clearance and cultivation in the Holocene may reach 5 m in thickness in chalk dry valleys (Evans 1966) where streamflow removal is inactive.

Localised mass movement may also actively occur on some slopes: this may involve slides (Skempton & Hutchinson 1976) and flows (Grove 1953) on clay and in peat (Crisp *et al.* 1964, Newson 1975b). Many of the clay slides represent the latest of several reactivations of earlier Pleistocene movement. Again, such movement may involve the redistribution of material on slopes rather than the direct input of sediment into streams, but stream undercutting and concentrated water flow may create instability such that rivers become the direct recipients of mass movement debris. Figure 2.7 shows a shallow slide of superficial deposits over shale bedrock along the line of a small stream following heavy rainfall in 1973. Streamwater inflow, water movement along the bedrock interface, and mass increase by saturation are likely to have been responsible for localised instability, with direct transfer of the released sediment into the lower stream.

Moving to the second streamhead domain (Table 2.2), several different types of sediment source are possible. These include seepages (Bunting 1961, Tuckfield 1973), soil pipes (Jones 1971, Gilman & Newson 1980) and spring heads, though in terms of sediment production volume the gullying of superficial deposits seems to be the most important. Thus Harvey (1974) showed that small gullies cut into glacial till in the Howgill Fells were producing sediment at a rate of around $400\,t\,ha^{-1}\,yr^{-1}$. Gullying can be a complex process (involving piping, frost action, flowslides and other processes); it may also be enhanced by artificial drain outlets (Fairbairn 1967, Gregory & Park 1976b) and deforestation (Tuckfield 1964). But gullying, some currently active and some not, is in any case widespread in suitable superficial deposits (Thomas 1956).

Figure 2.8 The actively undercut bank of the Afon Tywi, Dyfed.

Streamhead hollows may also receive fine slope sediments eluviated from soils and be the sites for enhanced solute concentrations in soil waters (Huggett 1976, Burt 1979). It is possible that delivery to and especially loss from such areas may lead to streamhead extension in which chemical processes are importantly localised in these areas of persistent saturation.

Within channels (domain 3 in Table 2.2), sediment may be derived from bed scour or bank erosion; this may involve bedrock, various superficial deposits or recent alluvium. Information is almost lacking on bedrock erosion (though see Finlayson 1978), but till (Hill 1973) and soliflucted till (Lewin *et al.* 1974, Lewin & Brindle 1977) can provide sediment which is especially significant in many upland environments where other sources are inoperative.

Lateral migration and cut bank recession is characteristic of some but not all British meandering rivers (Fig. 2.8): change rates and patterns are discussed in Chapter 4, and we need to note only two points here. First, the bank erosion process involves slope failure the form of which depends on bank composition and condition, and the mechanical forces applied. These include river scour, the action of frost heave and ice segregation, and bank moisture effects. Banks may retreat through granular removal, slip failure, or in the common case of composite banks with cohesive fine sediment overlying incohesive coarse ones, by cantilever collapse (Thorne & Lewin 1979). Embayments may be enlarged by large scale eddies, so that banks are not always smoothly curving in plan (Knighton 1972).

The second point is that cut-bank erosion is part of a dynamic channel geometry and may to a variable extent be balanced by point bar sedimentation (e.g. Knighton 1972). This is illustrated hypothetically in Figure 2.9 in which various combinations of upstream sediment input, downstream sediment output, and rates and patterns of lateral movement are illustrated. It is perfectly possible to have high rates of lateral mobility without very high rates of sediment throughput, 43

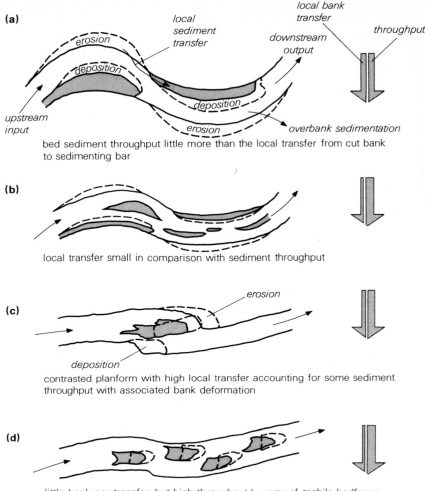

(a)

local bank
transfer

local
sediment
transfer

downstream
output

throughput

erosion

deposition

local bank transfer

downstream output

deposition

upstream
input

erosion

overbank sedimentation

bed sediment throughput little more than the local transfer from cut bank
to sedimenting bar

(b)

local transfer small in comparison with sediment throughput

(c)

erosion

deposition

contrasted planform with high local transfer accounting for some sediment
throughput with associated bank deformation

(d)

little bank-bar transfer, but high throughput by way of mobile bedforms
(bars, shoals)

Figure 2.9 Possible
relationships between lateral
channel movement and
downstream sediment flux.

or low rates of lateral movement which nonetheless have high sediment throughput rates. Bank erosion may not necessarily be associated with long-distance
sediment transport and high sediment yield.

Finally we should consider channel bed scour. The large number of medieval
bridges and other water level-related structures such as fish weirs, locks and mill
races, does not suggest that progressive bed scour or stream incision is a very
marked British phenomenon, at least in comparison with the arroyo trenching of
the American southwest. However, localised bed lowering can certainly occur,
especially in relation to the movement of channel bar forms, and scour may be
found in association with confining structures which lead to overdeepening.

Dominating sources and domains

Although individual studies have identified both sediment sources and the process
domains which exploit them, it remains difficult to specify which are dominant in
terms of gross down-channel sediment yields. In fact enough is now known to
suggest that generalisations applicable to Britain as a whole could be misleading,

and that the pattern is both scale and event dependent. Further complication is provided by the significance of non-denudation material, both in the form of atmospheric fallout and precipitation (Crisp 1966, Cryer 1976) and human activity (Hall 1967), and by the dominating export of material in solute rather than particulate form (see Table 5.13). This is one explanation for the high rate of ground lowering as well as physical downslope movement recorded on a slope by Young (1978), but generally speaking solute loss is recorded in terms of stream-flow yield rather than being measured 'on site', this being much more difficult. However, loss of material in ways that it is difficult to trace by physical measurement do seem to be very important (e.g. Huggett 1976, Burt 1979, Waylen 1979).

Table 2.4 Identified sources for suspended sediment.

		Material	Area (km²)	Specified source
Drewton Beck, Yorks Wolds	(Imeson 1970b)	chalk	7	river banks and spring head
Hodge Beck, N. Yorks Moors	(Imeson 1970b, 1974)	Jurassic clays, shales and limestones	18.9	burnt moorland, river banks
Catchwater Drain, Humberside	(Imeson & Ward 1972)	glacial sediments	15.4	river bed and banks
Maesnant, Dyfed	(Lewin *et al.* 1974)	mudstones and grit, with periglacial sediments	0.54	streambank bluffs, sheep hollows and pipes
six east Devon catchments	(Walling 1971)	Cf. overlying greensand and marl	0.111 to 6.397	mainly channels and adjacent slopes
East Twin, Somerset	(Finlayson 1978)	sandstone	0.18	overland flow areas
Jackmoor Brook, Devon	(Walling *et al.* 1979)	brown earth soils	9.3	surface runoff from cultivated areas, variable during storms
Ystwyth, Dyfed	(Grimshaw & Lewin 1980a)	Lower Silurian sediments	170.0	channel and non-channel sources approx. equal, depends on events

Some attempts to identify within-catchment sources for suspended sediments are listed in Table 2.4. Some of these rely on a relative evaluation of erosion source areas, but recent attention in Britain has focused on the possibility of examining diagnostic characteristics of yielded sediments in an attempt to identify their sources directly. Sediment properties examined include mineralogy (Wood 1978), contained pollutants (Lewin & Wolfenden 1978), magnetic properties (Walling *et al.* 1979), and colour (Grimshaw & Lewin 1980a). When extended more widely, these approaches could prove very useful.

One problem arises through the storage of eroded materials for short or long periods at various points within the river system (see Fig. 2.1), and this has been observed in a number of studies. Finlayson (1978) has suggested that for a small Mendip catchment, the source areas for sediment are those consistently producing overland flow, these being the peat surfaces in the upper part of the catchment and the channel itself lower down, but that extreme floods are crucial for the export of sediment which may remain as channel fill between extreme events. Again in the North Yorkshire Moors high rates of sediment production from unvegetated moorland have been demonstrated by Imeson (1974), but he suggests that perhaps only a third of this contributes to stream sediment load. A contrasting case is presented by Walling (1978), based on an analysis of data from two stations 13 km apart on the River Culm in Devon. Here downstream loads were observed to be less than upstream during a flood event, despite active channel erosion and a tributary entering along the reach. These three examples show that temporary sediment storage as colluvium and alluvium takes place in Britain as in the United States (see, for example, Costa 1975, Trimble 1977), so that the identification of immediate as well as ultimate sediment sources and sinks is necessary. An understanding of the whole sediment system is required.

As far as sediment is concerned, it seems likely that for coarser particles bank erosion, bed scour and the gullying of alluvial sediments and superficial deposits are dominant sources; additional finer sediment may derive in particular from agricultural land and as a result of other human activities that will be discussed later. Solutes are also apparently affected by agricultural practice and in particular by catchment lithology: this is discussed in Chapter 5.

Cyclical erosion and sedimentation

Bed material sediments in particular may move relatively slowly through a river system, and in so doing may assume forms and a segregation by sediment size that may be of some practical significance. Thus in coarse sediments, bars of various types may form both stable and mobile shoals of around the same dimensions as channel width: these may perform particular ecological functions, as for spawning fish, or they may be dredged by water authorities in the belief that this may improve floodwater movement or modify bank erosion. Sediment moving along the channel in bar forms, or moving as individual particles or diffuse sheets, may become incorporated into floodplains for prolonged storage, the time period being dependent on the rates of lateral mobility or vertical change in migrating channels. Such sediment may be topped by finer overbank flood deposits, the latter being dominant in certain environments.

Figure 2.10 shows some of the varieties of bar form that coarse sediment may assume on British cobble and gravel rivers: in mountain streams sediment size may approximate channel depth and a range of boulder jams and bedrock forms are found as described in Chapter 3. Gravel bar forms include mid-channel or medial forms which are sometimes classified as longitudinal or transverse (often lobate) according to the relative magnitudes of cross and downstream dimensions (Fig. 2.10, a and b), diagonal bars which cross from one side of the river to another (Fig. 2.10c), and a variety of point or lateral bars attached to one of the river banks (Fig. 2.10d,e,f). Such forms have been studied on both Scottish (Bluck 1971, 1976, 1979) and Welsh (Lewin 1976, 1978a) rivers, and their development may be associated with a wide variety of channel planform change (Lewin *et al.* 1977).

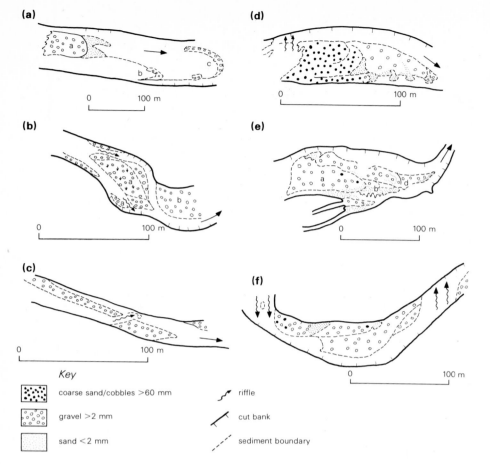

Key

- coarse sand/cobbles >60 mm
- gravel >2 mm
- sand <2 mm
- riffle
- cut bank
- sediment boundary

Figure 2.10 Channel bar forms on gravel rivers. (a) Lobate transverse bars on the River Spey; (b) longitudinal, a, and point, b, bars on Afon Dyfi, Powys; (c) diagonal bar on Afon Rheidol, Dyfed; (d) attached complex of lobate bars with downstream tail on Afon Ystwyth, Dyfed (see Lewin 1976); (e) complex of lateral bars, River Tulla, Scotland (based on Bluck 1976); (f) point bar complex, River Rheidol, Dyfed.

Point or lateral bars in particular have been shown to vary widely: some may be platform-like, others are compound consisting of several amalgamated elements or lobes, and others modified by marginal erosion or chute dissection. Inner depressions may also represent unsedimented portions of former channel now blocked off from the main flow (dead sloughs) (Fig. 2.11). Over time, bars may grow in a downstream direction or across the channel, while forms may be transformed one to another, as when medial bars migrate downstream distorting to diagonal or attached forms (Bluck 1979). Bar processes are also river-stage dependent, so that high-flow bars become dissected at intermediate flows, or added to by marginal accretion. Pools between bars may equally be scoured at high flows and infilled by prograding delta forms at low ones.

The role of bar forms in sediment transport is variable. Point bars may be the recipients of cut-bank erosion material from nearby upstream, and they may be found in locations that are stable with respect to evolving meander planforms. Bed sediment transport rate here is little more than a local flux between erosional and depositional sites. On the other hand, there is evidence that bars can move through meandering channel forms (Lewin 1978a) at least under extreme flows, and here local channel erosion may not be the immediate sediment source. Such bars may not be stably located with respect to planforms, and in fact the passage of a mobile bar or set of bars may locally deform the channel as it passes (Fig. 2.9). Whether bank erosion is forcing or following bar development may vary over time

47

Figure 2.11 Point bar on the Afon Ystwyth, looking diagonally upstream. The coarse bar head sediments extend across the centre of the picture, with fine bar tail sediments downstream. These include a delta where a lateral channel debouches into a dead slough in the foreground. A chute bar may be seen at the head of this slough on the extreme left.

(Lewin 1976), but the distinction is an important one for understanding both form developments and bed sediment transport rates.

Sediment size relations within channels and bars may be complex, and related in part to the sediment size range available to the river. Thus gravel, sand, silt and clay are all found within the meandering River Endrick near Glasgow (Bluck 1971), but the finer sediments are noticeably rarer on many rivers draining the Palaeozoic shales of mid-Wales (Lewin 1978a). In the first instance sediment sizes reflect source material, which is then resorted according to the mode of river transport. Upper river reaches commonly retain coarser sediments with a

Figure 2.12 A tail of rippled sand in the lee of bar-top vegetation on the River Spey at Garmouth.

Figure 2.13 Bar top shale-derived sediment, River Ystwyth, Dyfed. The card is 10×15 cm, with river flow during emplacement being from right to left. Orientation and imbrication of the coarser sediment can be seen, together with the packing of finer sands and gravel between and beneath the coarse 'paved' surface.

secondary sand population, whereas finer sediments are winnowed away downstream (McManus 1979). Downstream fining of sediment may also arise through mechanical abrasion and fracturing of the larger particles. Size segregation also occurs within channel reaches, with coarse or fine material on pool bottoms (depending in part on the timing of prior flow events), coarse sediment on bar heads and riffles, and a bar tail of finer sediments downstream which are deposited by lower flows around the emergent bar head and which may be reworked during successive high flows (Fig. 2.11). Size segregation may also occur in other ways, for example in the form of shadow deposits in the lee of bed obstacles (Fig. 2.12).

Within unit bars, a sediment size mix may be characteristic, with voids between larger particles infilled by finer ones (Fig. 2.13). At the surface, finer fragments may be absent so that the bed appears armoured with coarser fragments protecting the erosion of finer materials beneath: packing or imbrication may also increase bed resistance.

Erosion regimes

Channel dimensions and change rates, gullying, and sediment and solute yields have all been related to river discharges and other environmental factors in a number of individual studies (e.g. Harvey 1969, 1977, Hooke 1979, Knighton 1972, Walling 1971). British rivers do not have extreme regimes by world standards. Figure 2.14 shows flow return periods (annual series) plotted against discharge as a ratio of mean annual flood for Britain and for other rivers or regimes. From this it may be appreciated that the 50-year flood may be only just over twice the size of the mean annual, but that in other areas such floods may be relatively much larger. Such extreme floods are capable of scouring out whole valley floors, but this does not appear to be generally characteristic of British environments, although floods may have singular effects (Newson 1980a) which may persist for many years on smaller streams (Anderson & Calver 1980).

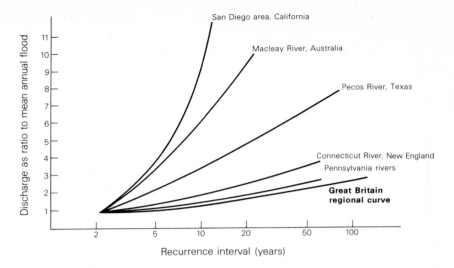

Figure 2.14 Flood return
period (annual series) for
selected regions and rivers
(after Abrahams & Cull 1979)
and for Britain (after Natural
Environment Research
Council 1975a).

River flow is also not the only physical factor of importance in determining rates of erosion. Even when direct bank scour is concerned, banks prepared by prior wetting may erode more than ones that are dry at equivalent discharges (Knighton 1973). Such wetting is more common in winter. Frost incidence appears to be of minor importance (Knighton 1973, Hooke 1979) on large-scale river banks though not in gully development (Harvey 1974). Bank erosion may occur at quite low discharge on parts of a river bend (Thorne & Lewin 1979), with more general cut arc development or a shift in erosion loci at higher ones.

The relative importance of higher flows varies with the nature of the process involved. Thus Knighton (1972) reported that 79% of bank erosion on the Bollin-Dean took place during flows that occurred for less than 5% of the time; in a study of five east Devon catchments, Walling (1971) found the corresponding figures for suspended and dissolved loads were 88.4–94.9% and 28.5–56.8% respectively. Though more data are unfortunately hard to come by, and comparisons can in any case be difficult because of the different basis for calculations (e.g. using instantaneous or daily mean flow data), it is clear that rarer flows are more important for sediment movement, and particularly for coarse sediment which may only be fed into streams following rare floods, thence to move infrequently once competence thresholds are crossed. For channel development, special significance has been placed on flows at bankfull stage (sometimes assumed to be the 1.5-year flood on the annual series) (Nixon 1959, Hey 1975a), though many empirical studies have suggested that both lower and higher flows are responsible for particular channel features or channel development in particular environments. More information is needed, both on the effects of extreme events and on process rates which are difficult to relate to causative events such as the loss of solutes or fine material from slopes.

Progressive sedimentation

River-derived sediments are accumulating especially in floodplain and estuarine environments in contemporary Britain. Many such environments may in fact have considerable depths of alluvial and other superficial deposits, with a bedrock floor related to low Quaternary sea levels that may be 100 m below the present land surface. Contemporary sedimentation thus forms a surface skin over what may be a considerable volume of prior sedimentation (Dury 1964b) that may have involved a number of episodes of cut and fill.

In upland valleys, river mobility is such that coarse channel sediments occupy much of the valley floor, the surface of which represents an amalgam of relict bar forms and migratory channel patterns topped off with a small amount of fine overbank flood sediment. Figure 2.15 shows four cross-profiles of the Rheidol valley, all within 2 km of each other, with dates showing former channel locations and arrows giving the direction in which the migrating river shifted across the valley. The floodplain here has been built up largely of coarse gravel in lateral and medial bars, with fine sediment accumulating especially in cut-offs, sloughs, inner bar margin and bar tail areas. Some signs of incision during lateral migration and of floodplain convexity in cross profile, possibly indicating aggradation along the channel, are both present. However vertical changes in the short term (around 100 yr) are not nearly so marked as lateral movements.

A strongly-contrasted picture is presented by many lowland rivers in Britain which have remained rather fixed in position without pronounced sediment input or transfer during the Holocene. The valleys of east Norfolk have deep alluvial fills, estuarine or lagoon clays and silts towards the sea, but peats and organic

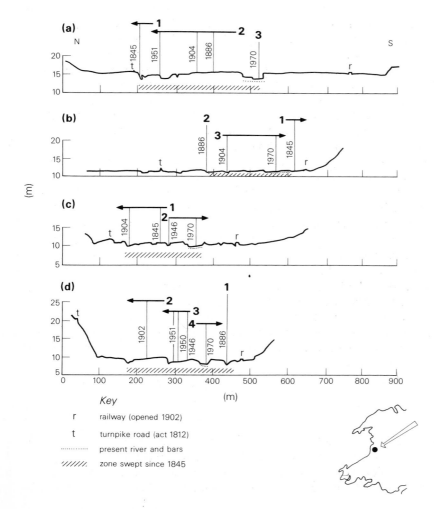

Figure 2.15 Cross-profiles of the Afon Rheidol floodplain, showing also the location of the channel at different dates and the inferred sequences of channel movement.

Key

r railway (opened 1902)

t turnpike road (act 1812)

.... present river and bars

/////// zone swept since 1845

51

muds inland. Deep excavation of peats led to the artificial creation of the Broads (Lambert *et al.* 1960) where organic fills rather than mineral ones had developed. The River Gipping provides a not dissimilar case from Suffolk (Rose *et al.* 1980). Here the floodplain has been characterised by backswamp fen development behind levées along the channel during the Holocene, with some recent overbank deposition of clay that may be associated with agricultural activity. A slightly different situation is found along the River Nene (Horton 1970): here a ribbon of coarser recent sediments is found isolated within the surface sediments adjacent to the channel, with clays underlying the floodplain beyond. Other examples are given by Dury (1964b) who regards valley infilling as the result of stream shrinkage rather than aggradation in the usual sense.

A third type is provided by the lower Severn (Beckinsale & Richardson 1964). This has rather prominent natural levées adjacent to the channel which may be 3 m higher than the nearby alluvial valley floor. A reasonable supply of fine sediment and a relatively stable channel appear to have led to the predominance of over-bank sedimentation in the creation of the valley floor. Interestingly the upper part of the floodplain sediments consists of silty clay in which there is a pronounced colour contrast. Shotton (1978) concluded from examination of sections on both the Severn and Warwickshire Avon that the upper generally buff-red member resulted from deforestation and accelerated soil erosion starting around 2500 years ago. Elsewhere Dury (1964b) has ascribed colour contrasts to the effects of gleying, and the average sedimentation rate of the upper horizons is not in fact greater than the 4.6 mm yr^{-1} Shotton suggests for 'normal' overbank sedimentation on the Avon.

Floodplain deposition in post-Roman (Limbrey 1978) or perhaps in post-Mesolithic times (Jacobi 1978) following deforestation and cultivation, has also been suggested from archaeological evidence, but perhaps the strongest indications of fluctuations in long-term progressive sedimentation come from lake sediments (Mackereth 1966, Pennington & Lishman 1971, Oldfield 1977). From these it appears that much of the Holocene has been represented by relatively reduced erosion conditions, and thus lake sedimentation, by comparison both with the Late Devensian and with what has happened since forest clearance. Again there are comparisons to be made with North America (Costa 1975, Trimble 1977), except that in Britain 'post-settlement alluvium' covers a much longer time period. It is also interesting to note that a wide variety in the proportion of coarse to fine alluvium and of organic content is possible, depending in particular on the nature of sediment supply and lateral river mobility.

For finer sediments, estuaries form major depositional sites; with the notable exception of the River Spey which carries coarse sediment right to its mouth where it is dispersed by wave action, the 20 largest British rivers (Table 1.1) all have estuarine mouths and here deposition of both fluvial and marine sediments takes place in mixed and saline waters. The same applies to many smaller rivers, notably in western Scotland, Essex and Cornwall. Tidally-influenced rivers are shown in Figure 2.16 together with the major estuaries.

In such environments although net water flow is seawards, tidal inflow and outflow may be much stronger and the inward movement of littoral and offshore sediments can be most important, though variable around the British coast. Thus tidal ranges can vary from up to 16 m in the Bristol Channel to less than 1 m in some Scottish sea lochs, and although some estuaries like the Firth of Tay may have a large input of fresh water and fluvial sediment, this may be less significant in others like the Wash. For the Clyde, Fleming (1970) has estimated that very little

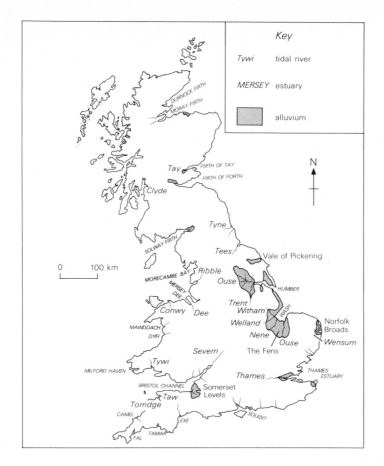

Figure 2.16 Major British estuaries, tidal rivers and areas of alluvium.

sediment is derived from the sea and that dredging virtually balances the river input. By contrast, Hall (1967) has suggested that for the Tyne estuary around 350 000 t derive from rivers and 250 000 t come from offshore. This is calculated from estimates of dredging volumes and river inputs (including sewage and spillage), and taking marine contributions as the difference. The dominance of marine influence may further be illustrated by the Humber where it has been estimated that over 3×10^6 t of silt may be in suspension in the estuary during a winter spring tide, by comparison with the 0.4×10^6 t carried in by rivers. During spring tides, water flow into the estuary past Spurn Head can be $1700 \times 10^6 \, \mathrm{m^3 \, s^{-1}}$, whereas the supply of river water during floods is only around $1550 \, \mathrm{m^3 \, s^{-1}}$ (NERC 1979b).

As in rivers, estuarine sediments may be physically mobile involving the migration of bedforms, ebb and flood channels, and the repeated uptake and redeposition of sediment. But the conservative nature of estuaries with regard to sediment does mean that river sediments are likely to remain there somewhere, with sediment movement being dependent on estuarine stratification and circulation, but with movement in a landward direction along the bottom possible, including the landward return of rubbish (Board 1973). Secondly, it is the finer river sediments that generally reach estuarine environments, and here rather different chemical processes may affect them, involving for example flocculation of clays in saline waters, the desorption of some heavy metals from suspended sediment, and the replacement of oxidising by reducing conditions (see, for example, Biddle &

53

Miles 1972, Burton & Liss 1976). Estuaries may thus have serious environmental problems associated with the accumulation and the release of river and other pollutants, a fact which has long been recognised (Royal Commission on Environmental Pollution 1972, Natural Environment Research Council 1975b) and which is in evidence in the considerable volume of physical, chemical and biological research currently being undertaken in estuaries.

The largest area of alluvium in Britain lies around the Wash (Fig. 2.17). From what has been said above, it may be appreciated that sedimentation in such areas (others include the Vale of York, Thames estuary and Somerset Levels) is derived partly from offshore sources and also involves marine sedimentation, peat and salt marsh development as well as fluvial processes (Godwin & Clifford 1939). The

Figure 2.17 The Wash and the Fens, showing the former coastline, natural and artificial channels and alluvial sediments.

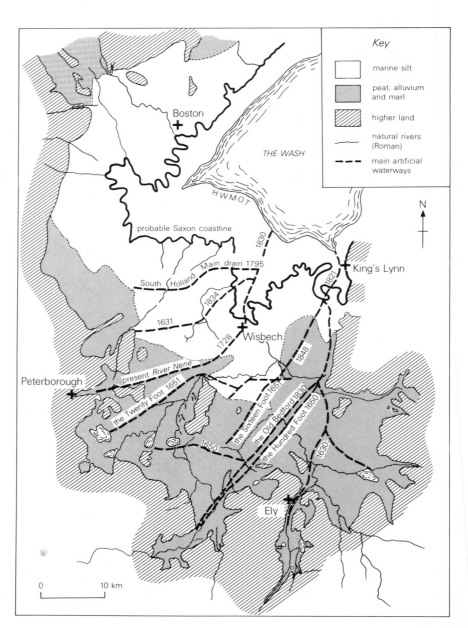

54

latter may have been much affected by human activities as around the Wash where the natural drainage system has notably been replaced by an artificial one over the centuries (Fig. 2.17). The levée and channel sediments of old river courses ('roddons') have remained as sinuous silty ribbons (now often ridges) between extensive organic fen deposits (Godwin 1938), but the progressive reclamation shown in Figure 2.17 has been of generally marine sediments.

Man's activity

It has been said (admittedly in the United States) that sediment is our greatest pollutant (Robinson 1973); in quantity and now in quality both the rates and processes involved in eroding and depositing sediments have been grossly affected by human activity. This arises through the acceleration or modification of processes delivering sediment to river channels, through modification of river channels and river regimes so as to affect sediment flux, and through the addition of substances in quantities otherwise unknown.

In Britain, localised but significant soil erosion has been readily identified on agricultural land (Evans & Morgan 1974, Morgan 1980). An interesting example is provided by enhanced sediment yields on the River Almond, a tributary of the River Tay in Scotland, which have been attributed to the turnip harvest (Al-Ansari *et al.* 1977). Here it was suggested that for one four-day harvest period during dry weather in December, just over 1 km² yielded an extra 35 t of sediment to the river. It is, of course, particular cropping, tillage, burning, or drainage practices which are likely to affect sediment yields. In the case of coniferous afforestation, Painter and others (1974) have pointed to the increased sediment yields that may result from deep ditching. Ovenden and Gregory (1980) have also shown how stream networks have been modified and extended in Britain, in particular replacing diffuse seepage areas with ditches or field drains. It is thus most unlikely that sediment delivery to streams in Britain is in any real sense 'natural', and as was earlier suggested in discussing hillwash sediments, this has not really been the case at least in some degree for millennia. But erosion has been enhanced in the last century or so because of activities ranging from industrial processes in South Wales (Bridges 1969) to recreational activity in the Cairngorms (Bayfield 1974) (see Fig. 2.18).

Channel erosion on larger rivers has also been at least partly managed for centuries. Writing of South Wales in about 1820, G. A. Cooke put it as follows: 'Some proprietors, when the waters come down, curse the streams, and leave them to take their course; others erect jetties, and turn the torrent like a battering ram against their neighbour's land on the other side, who in his turn erects other jetties to turn back the stream: so that, in time of flood, the torrent is buffetted alternately from one side to the other; but in general it takes ample revenge on both parties' (Cooke, n.d.). In southern and eastern England before the railway age, many river courses were more systematically stabilised or improved for navigation with bank protection, and the provision of cuts, locks and towpaths. On the River Severn in the 19th century, this involved extensive dredging and the blasting of shoals with gunpowder to maintain a 6 ft deep channel (see Hadfield 1966, 115–27 and 282–90), while the Hampshire Itchen was apparently made navigable as early as the 12th century (Hadfield 1969). Other channel modifications include fish and mill weirs (some with flash locks alongside which at the time were recognised as producing bed scour problems), and the clearing and

Figure 2.18 The Cardingmill valley on the Long Mynd, Shropshire, showing some effects of recreational use.

enlarging of channels to improve drainage, activities which continue to this day. Thus the dimensions, plan layout and patterns of sediment transfer on many lowland rivers represent a modification of what would naturally be the case, the most visible sign of which are localised or extensive river training works. These range from car bodies and sunk barges through to revetments or spurs made of sheet piling, concrete, stone (either as large, loose blocks or in wire gabions), or reinforced fill.

Urbanisation, now affecting around 10% of the land area of England and Wales, may produce its effects both in terms of enhanced sediment yields during building operations (Walling & Gregory 1970) and because of the modified characteristics of urban runoff thereafter (Hollis & Luckett 1976, Knight 1979, Park 1977). This may lead to an increase in channel capacity. A contrasting decrease in capacity has also been widely identified below reservoirs in Britain (Gregory & Park 1974, Petts 1979). By 1970, 297 large dams had been constructed in England and Wales and 143 in Scotland, and these may have at least long-term effects on erosion and sedimentation (Grimshaw & Lewin 1980b). Admittedly, neither downstream scour nor reservoir infilling by sediment such as to diminish their capacity are usually regarded as serious problems in Britain. For example, Ledger and others (1974) show that in 120 yr two small Scottish reservoirs appear to have lost only around 3–10% of their capacity. This compares with a country-wide *annual* average of approaching 2% in the United States (Dendy 1968). However, reservoirs do deplete downstream suspended sediment loads (by trapping the sediment from what can be high-yield upstream areas) and they do decrease the frequency with which coarse sediments in downstream channels are transported. This may alter rates of channel change and the nature of beneficial overbank sedimentation. The observed decrease in channel capacity below reservoirs, though no doubt due in part to a failure to occupy the whole pre-reservoir channel, may also involve channel-side infilling and aggradation especially using material fed in by unregulated tributaries. In practice, adjustments may be complex in the long term, with individual reservoirs and river systems behaving differently (Petts 1979).

Addition of substances to river sediments may be of various kinds: these include glass, brick, aggregates, rubber, bitumen, and organic and humic compounds from urban areas (Ellis 1979); heavy metals from mining and industrial processes and atmospheric fallout (Davies 1980); and sewage discharges, particularly into estuarine environments (Porter 1973). Under low-flow conditions many rivers may be dominated by urban effluent, with the accumulation of stream-bed sludge (Richards & Wood 1977). All may be transported fluvially and variously incorporated into floodplain and estuarine sediments where further recycling and pedogenic or diagenic alterations may occur. These include translocation within the sediment or release to waters following changes in acidity or redox conditions, microbial activity, plant uptake, or the presence of saline water.

In river systems, high levels of pollutant concentration may be related to river erosional and depositional activity. For example, in the case of heavy metals from mining activity in mid-Wales (Davies & Lewin 1974, Lewin *et al.* 1977, Wolfenden & Lewin 1977) it is possible to relate metal concentration in floodplain sediments to depositional domains and to both the timing and the location of sedimentation with respect to former mining activity. There is a fall-off in metal concentration downstream of input points for mining debris, a progressive decrease in concentration in sediments emplaced since mining activity ceased, and an association between high concentrations and the loci of fine sediment deposition.

It should be appreciated that with metals as with other pollutants, transfer processes are not purely physical involving chemically inert substances; most may be chemically interactive with waters and fine sediment so that during transport or deposition there may be changes of state between solute and solid forms involving adsorption and complexing with organic matter and with hydrous iron and manganese oxides.

Conclusions

Erosion and sedimentation can be major destabilising activities in river systems, causing serious problems for river management. River systems were formed by such processes in the first place so that their continuation should be expected. There is much scattered evidence for this in British rivers, and this has been presented in terms of the sediment sources available, and the erosion system operating. To understand both it is necessary to appreciate the Quaternary context and the induced effects of human activity. The earlier Holocene was a period of sluggish erosional activity, though one fortunately of pedogenic development; enhanced soil loss, the erosion of Quaternary sediment fills, and numerous effects of human activity are characteristic of the present-day British environment.

Certain parts of fluvial systems are also more active than others: exploitation of available sediment sources is known to be effective at streamheads and on agricultural land in particular, whilst some floodplains (notably the middle courses of rivers) are the scene for sediment recycling by actively migrating rivers. All such activities vary seasonally and in response to individual forcing events, as in the case of extreme floods which may produce slope failures and channel effects that may subsequently work through the system.

We do not yet have nearly enough information about these activity patterns and rates, but the rates do not seem to be large by world standards. However, they are not negligible and over centuries and decades may make a difference to soil quality, channel dimension or depositional environment. This chapter has stressed in particular the importance of sediment storage on slope, floodplain and estuary. Here although the 'natural' flux rates involved may not be large, accelerated erosion and the incorporation of pollutants may lead to long drawn-out quality problems. What Britain lacks in terms of overall bulk sediment flux may be more than offset by quality deterioration as natural and man-created material transfer proceed side by side. Commendable efforts towards water quality improvement, channel management and soil conservation have to be made on the understanding that each may have antecedents and consequences which are worked through a dynamic system over a very long time span. Fluvial processes will remain active in Britain, and our actions have left us with more complications to cope with.

3 Mountain streams

M. D. Newson

Mountains or uplands?

The altitude, relief and scenery of the west and north of Britain are only locally mountainous, but the area covered by 'uplands' (20–30%) means a predominance of short, relatively steep rivers throughout Britain. Although the typical river of the upland type has its source at 500 m in a peat bog rather than at 5000 m in a glacier, there are climatological and geomorphological reasons for describing the fluvial *processes* in the upper parts of this river as mountainous in character.

The network of climatological recording stations in Britain is very sparse in the uplands, but the available data suggest that climatological lapse rates in north and west Britain are amongst the steepest in the world (Taylor 1976), leading to very high annual rainfall totals (6530 mm at Sprinkling Tarn in the Lake District in 1954), a dispiriting combination of strong winds (more than 250 gales per annum on Ben Nevis) and low temperatures (more than 100 airfrosts per annum on Plynlimon) and, in severe years a deep and long-lasting snow cover (average snow cover varies from 20 days on southern hills to 50 days in Scotland). A decrease of mean temperature of just 1.3°C over 40 years would promote glacial conditions once more in the Scottish Highlands (Manley 1975); at present these most truly mountainous river basins in Britain show a spring flow peak from snow melt.

It is, however, the dominance of glaciers in the recent geological past in upland Britain which gives perhaps the best justification of the adjective 'mountain' for our fluvial processes; the materials involved in present-day fluvial action are not dissimilar to those in a continental river with its source at 5000 m. Church and Ryder (1972) have used the terms *paraglacial* and *post-paraglacial* for eras in which the sedimentary legacy of glaciation interacts with other processes. In the case of Britain the paraglacial state of upland streams is most obvious from the very coarse material which lines their channels; where incision has not yet occurred to bedrock the major roughness elements of the channel may be of cobble or boulder size (Fig. 3.1). Lower reaches, as rivers leave the upland zone, show fine examples of gravel-bed rivers, especially in England and Wales; in Scotland the cobble zone may extend well downstream and there have been comparisons between the alpine glacial outwash environment and the lower reaches of the Spey (Lewin & Weir 1977). Nevertheless, Scotland also has sand bed rivers within the upland zone – the nature of Pleistocene deposits and the timing of the most recent glaciation is the determining factor in sediment size.

A more detailed definition

For defining mountain or upland streams, numerical *geomorphological* classification has advantages beyond a consideration of glacial and periglacial deposits,

Figure 3.1 A mountain stream in the strict sense: River Derwent in the English Lake District.

and maps of morphometric indices were recently prepared for Britain as part of the Flood Study (NERC 1975a, Newson 1978). Since morphometric variables are inevitably well correlated together, a principal components analysis was undertaken to investigate the use of a single classificatory index for the British fluvial system. Figure 3.2a shows mapped eigenvalues for the principal component WET/DRY, integrating the effects of rainfall, soil moisture and morphometry. The Exe/Tees line, often quoted as the boundary between the uplands and lowlands of Britain (Stamp 1950) appears as the WET/DRY boundary too. The steepness of Britain's rivers on a world scale is particularly notable (Fig. 3.2b). Only the Severn, Thames and Great Ouse in Britain approach the low gradients of larger continental rivers, and major rivers like the Spey, Tay, Tees and Wye are much steeper. The seminal study by Bathurst, Li and Simons (1979), further stresses large-scale roughness elements as diagnostic of 'mountain' streams. It proposes an approximate sub-division of channel slopes based on the scale of roughness elements: above 100 m km^{-1} channels become dominated by falls and pools; below 4 m km^{-1} small-scale roughness elements comprise most of the channel. Although the slope index portrayed in Figure 3.2b is specifically designed for flood studies and represents an average gradient, it may be taken that the areas shaded as being steeper than 10 m km^{-1} are those in which extensive river reaches are dominated by large scale roughness elements or falls and pools: mountain streams. In addition, there is a zone at the upland margin of South-West England, Wales, the Pennines and Scottish Uplands and Highlands which has the river characteristics of small-scale piedmonts (Kopaliani & Romashin 1970). In many cases alluvial sediments have come to dominate bank materials in this zone, but although sediments are highly reworked, the Pleistocene influence is still strong.

It is possible to summarise the several characteristics of mountain and piedmont streams in Britain briefly discussed above as follows. *Mountain streams* have steep channels and side slopes without an intervening floodplain of significance in terms of water or sediment storage; a dominance of bed-load sediment transport except

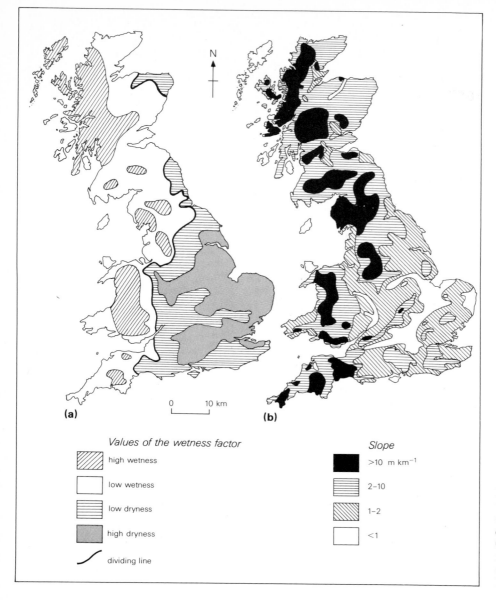

Figure 3.2 Morphometric identification of mountain streams. (a) The principal component WET/DRY; (b) re-mapped values of the morphometric variable stream slope (after NERC 1975a, Newson 1978).

Legend for map (a): **Values of the wetness factor** — high wetness, low wetness, low dryness, high dryness, dividing line.

Legend for map (b): **Slope** — >10 m km^{-1}, 2–10, 1–2, <1.

Scale: 0 — 10 km

in those areas where the Pleistocene legacy includes finer materials which have formed erodable river banks; and a flashy regime in which flood spates apparently dominate in terms of geomorphological effectiveness. Flow resistance is complex and generally controlled by large-scale roughness elements.

In *piedmont streams* the most noticeable change is the lessening of channel gradient; although side slopes may be steep they are separated from the active channel over most of its length by a floodplain which is the central feature in a geomorphological regime dominated by storage and reworking of mountain-derived sediments. Mountain-derived flooding is still important in terms of geomorphological effectiveness although suspended sediment movement tends to dominate over bed-load. Flow resistance is generally controlled by channel elements of intermediate scale.

61

The study of mountain streams in Britain

Only a small part of the expansion of catchment-area field research in Britain since 1960 has focused on mountain streams (Newson 1979a); much of the early effort in support of the International Hydrological Decade was of short duration or has not produced published results. Of 49 experimental catchments listed in 1970 (NERC 1970), 24 fell within the larger, mountain and upland area defined above; however, only five of these were established with a fluvial geomorphology bias. At the time of writing, less than ten have produced results and only the Plynlimon experimental catchments (Newson 1979b) have been fully operational for more than a decade. Much of this chapter has to be based on work at Plynlimon; it may well not be relevant in parts of the area defined above, especially in Scotland. George Borrow, author of *Wild Wales,* wrote of Plynlimon as 'more like what the Welsh call a *rhiw* or a slope than a *mynydd* or mountain'.

The reason for the bias towards research on hydrology as distinct from fluvial geomorphology in the uplands may be that hydrological processes can be studied over periods as short as one flood event. But long-term catchment studies which require much greater resources are also essential to studying the effects of dynamically changing variables (e.g. land-use change at Plynlimon). It is crucial that such investigations obtain data during extremes of flood and drought; lengthy records are therefore essential and government funding has been available to date at Plynlimon to secure them. The calibration of extremes is even more essential to fluvial geomorphology, where magnitude:frequency concepts are once more attracting research interest. The 'rare' event in upland areas has profound effects on both sediment supply by slope failure and the transport of coarse material downstream (Newson 1980a), yet it is notoriously difficult to study.

If the fluvial geomorphology of mountain streams has been under-researched there is an even bigger gap in the study of the slopes which contribute sediment to them. Since the pioneering field work of Young (1958a) and Kirkby (1963, 1967) there have been few instrumented studies of hillslopes (largely because of the inherent difficulties of obtaining reliable results) and a morphological approach has been more common (Young 1972).

Apparently, students of hydrology have largely ignored channels for slopes, whilst those of fluvial geomorphology have done the reverse. This situation leads to serious gaps in our literature on mountain channel flow processes, which are only just beginning to be a popular topic for study (Beven, Gilman & Newson 1979, Bathurst 1978), and on slope development. Although the situation is a fair reflection of the relative control exercised by slope and channel runoff in hydrology and the relative impact of sediment transport and sediment supply in fluvial geomorphology, there can be little fundamental progress in our understanding of mountain or piedmont streams until our approach becomes more comprehensive and is long-term enough to include the effects of extremes.

The hydrology of British 'mountain' streams

Since the urbanisation of Britain during the Industrial Revolution, the lowland centres of population have relied on the high rainfall inputs to upland catchments (with relatively low outputs through evapotranspiration) to provide them with water resources. Upland supplies have had two further advantages: they have been considered pure and cheap to connect to the consumer – by gravity in pipelines or, latterly, in river channels by regulating flows from reservoirs. The major disadvantage of upland supplies is their irregular timing and extremes: reservoir storage is essential and the damming of upland valleys is seldom easy politically, especially in the case of dams in Wales built to supply water to England. Scottish water resources are, by comparison, abundant (Scottish Development Department 1973).

Rainfall

The westerly location of the major upland areas of Britain puts them in the path of the prevailing moist airstreams and cyclonic disturbances from the Atlantic. Although the whole country is subject to these airstreams, there is a marked intensification of rainfall over the uplands, particularly in advance of surface cold fronts (Browning, Pardoe & Hill 1975). Variation in the tracks taken by depressions moving across the British Isles therefore exerts a control on both seasonal patterns in upland rainfall and on extremes of rainfall. The uplands have a winter maximum of rainfall; in spring and early summer there is a greater tendency for anti-cyclones to 'block' the path of depressions. The three months November–January produce as much rainfall in the uplands as the five succeeding months. British upland rainfall is generally of low intensity (on a world scale). As Figure 1.10 shows, it is possibly the number of rain days rather than the total rainfall which seems excessive in contrast with the lowlands. Although the proportion of total time occupied by rainfall in the uplands reaches a maximum around 18%, it must be remembered that over large areas of lowland Britain the proportion is nearer 5%; this has been found to be a key parameter in assessing the hydrological impacts of land-use change.

Figure 3.3 Two major types of rainfall intensification which promoted upland flooding in Britain. (a) The winter, frontal rainfall of 2 and 3 November 1931; (b) the local convective storm over the headwaters of the Severn, 15 August 1977.

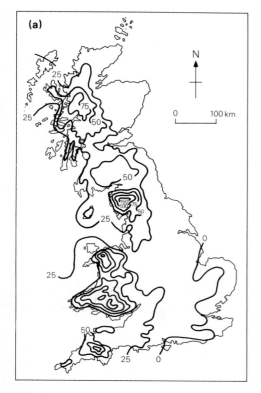

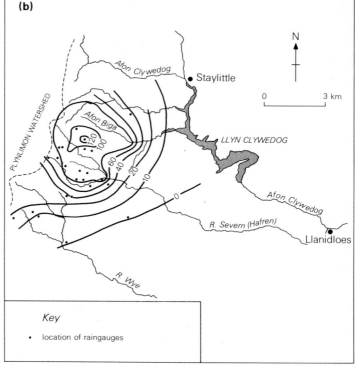

Key

• location of raingauges

Despite the generally low intensities of rainfall, a characteristic of mountain streams is a flashy regime, the result of episodic heavy falls. During winter these are mainly associated with cold fronts (Holgate 1973) and intensities of 6 mm hr^{-1} appear to be critical in causing spates in upland channels, although for geomorphological effectiveness much more intense falls are required (Newson 1980a). Although the network of daily-read storage raingauges in the uplands is relatively sparse, work by Bleasdale (1963) and Rodda (1967) points to the frequent occurrence of large daily falls, mainly from frontal activity. The other major source of intense rainfall is the isolated convectional rain storm, typical of severe flooding in summer. The poor recording-raingauge network, especially in Scotland, spoils our appreciation of their importance. Thus, although only five of Jackson's (1974) 'top 50' two-hour rainfalls were recorded in the uplands a probabilistic approach to these shorter durations (Jackson 1971) indicate prominent areas of upland, especially in Scotland, liable to very heavy storms. Figure 3.3 illustrates the spatial characteristics of the two major types of rainfall intensification.

Except at high altitudes in the Scottish Highlands, snowfall in the British uplands is unreliable from year to year in both depth and duration. The problem of measuring mixed precipitation is seldom tackled adequately by official hydrological networks even though snowmelt exacerbates flooding (Johnson 1975) and the spring snowmelt runoff in Scottish Highland rivers coincides conveniently with a rainfall minimum. The snow measurement problem is perhaps best solved by a combination of several simple techniques: melting snow caught by carefully-sited standard raingauges, measuring depths and densities manually and measuring natural rates of snow-melt in specially-adapted recording raingauges (e.g. Hudson 1977).

Runoff and extremes of runoff

Generally more than 70% of rainfall runs off in British upland catchments, although there are few gauged streams within the mountain zone to investigate the highest runoff coefficients; it is likely that these are in excess of 90% (Reynolds 1969). The major problems of gauging are the steep gradient and bedload movements (Harrison 1965). Attempts to overcome these have been by the design of the 'Plynlimon' flume and by the more recent but untried techniques of electromagnetic and ultrasonic gauging. Some success has been achieved with Crump and flat-Y weirs, although flood afflux and sedimentation are always a problem. The operation of those full-range structures which do exist is costly, including excavating bedload, repairing abrasion of surfaces and even completely replacing stations destroyed in floods (Fig. 3.4).

In view of the sparsity of flow gauging it is fortunate that, for the short pasture vegetation which dominates the uplands, it has been found that the Penman estimate of annual rates of evapotranspiration (E_t) is accurate. This allows estimates of runoff for ungauged areas from the more plentiful records of rainfall and from estimates of Penman E_t obtained from climate measurements. Following Penman's 1950 paper, therefore, there has been a tendency for approximations of annual runoff to be based on an annual catchment loss in the uplands of 460 to 535 mm. Pioneering catchment studies as a check on runoff from rainfall came as early as the 1920s from W. N. McClean (e.g. 1927) and from Wales in the 1950s (Risbridger & Godfrey 1954, Lewis 1957). However, even Penman estimates require instruments and observers. Neither are conveniently

(a)

(b)

Figure 3.4 The problems of full-range flow gauging in upland streams. (a) The River Dunsop weir at Footholme (West Pennines) wrecked by the flood of August 1967; (b) a new full-range structure on the Dunsop, shown at low flow.

available in the remoter uplands and to this end the Institute of Hydrology has developed automatic weather stations for its Plynlimon experiment and, more recently for mountain-top locations (Strangeways 1972, Curran *et al.* 1977). However, although the station can fill in detail of *potential* evapotranspiration over small areas of upland, a crucial aspect of evapotranspiration measurement in the uplands is the effect of tall vegetation on *actual* evapotranspiration. A 'natural'

65

Mountain streams dominance of short 'moorland' vegetation in the British uplands is the result of deforestation from the Neolithic period onwards. The attempts by public and private organisations to re-establish upland forests in Britain has been of great interest to water resource specialists since Law (1956) first alerted them to the likely increases in evaporation from a forested catchment by the interception of rainfall. This topic is returned to below. In fact, 'moorland' vegetation in the British uplands also includes such intermediate crops as Bracken (*Pteridium*) and Heather (*Caluna*). The water relations of these species are little researched so far. Losses from upland catchments are, nevertheless, small compared with rainfall and even if completely afforested, the upland catchment would still be the main-stay of lowland water resources. Figure 3.5 shows a typical rainfall map of the important Severn catchment during a week in winter stressing the very high proportion of the total water resource that comes from the uplands. The corollary of the rainfall distribution is that a substantial source of hazard by flooding also exists in the upland area. Regulation of the flows of the Severn using major upland reservoirs is clearly a powerful tool in basin management.

Although there is currently keen interest amongst water suppliers in annual runoff, especially in relation to land use, it is perhaps the extremes of runoff in the uplands which present the engineer with most problems when developing water resources; although a dam must be built to guard against drought, it must also itself be protected against the threat of catastrophic flooding. Flow ranges of more than three orders of magnitude are common in upland streams and flood peaks may be reached in less than an hour. In droughts the absence of aquifer rocks in the British uplands leads to very low flows indeed; during the 1975–6 drought, dry river beds were not an uncommon sight in the upland areas affected.

The most spectacular and damaging mountain floods in Britain have not been

Figure 3.5 A typical weekly rainfall contribution in winter to the upland part of the complex River Severn water resource system. Major points of regulation and of abstraction are shown.

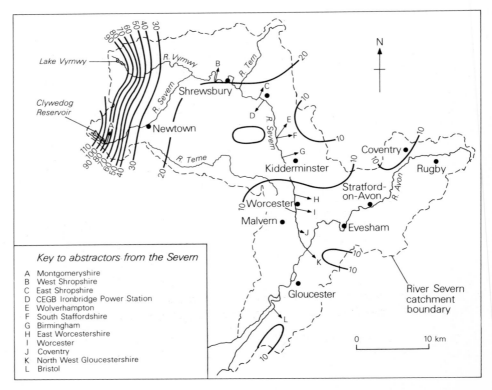

Key to abstractors from the Severn

A Montgomeryshire
B West Shropshire
C East Shropshire
D CEGB Ironbridge Power Station
E Wolverhampton
F South Staffordshire
G Birmingham
H East Worcestershire
I Worcester
J Coventry
K North West Gloucestershire
L Bristol

(a)

(c)

(b)

Figure 3.6 Filling the data gaps: fieldwork and flow extremes in upland Britain. (a) Volumetric gauging of the trickle of flow in the upper Wye, Plynlimon, during the 1976 drought; (b) flow by-passing the same flume as (a) during the January 1975 flood; (c) the use of surveyed 'trash marks' in estimating peak flood discharges on ungauged streams or where structures have been overtopped or even destroyed.

those brought about by a winter day's rainfall of 100 mm, not even when exacerbated by melting snow, both of which conditions tend to lead more commonly to hazardous flooding in the piedmont and lowland zone. Instead, it is that caused by a short, often convective, rain storm in summer in which 'physiographic aggravation' by steep slopes and channels leads to a very high peak discharge (Newson 1975a, 1980a). The Lynmouth flood of 1952 illustrates the fatally rapid rise of water which drowned 34 people and the massive damage to property brought about by large volumes of coarse sediment and huge individual boulders. A recurring theme in reports of headwater flooding, such as that at Lynmouth, is that the neglect of such small channels by official maintenance procedures (dredging, tree-clearance etc.) exacerbates the flood problem; temporary dams form and break during the flood, causing very damaging surges of flow. Fortunately, not many centres of population occur so close to the banks of such a steep channel as that at Lynmouth; most other reports of such flooding have been more of interest to geomorphologists than to students of the flood hazard. More frequently, the output from an upland catchment affected by intense heavy rainfall causes only agricultural damage within the upland area and little effect downstream (e.g. Newson 1979a). Routing the typical winter flood from an upland source area to downstream sites is achieved quite successfully by simple methods of correlation in Britain; the rivers are short enough to predict downstream flood levels and timing based on the passage of the flood wave past observed sites within the upland zone. Flood warning also tends to be simply but

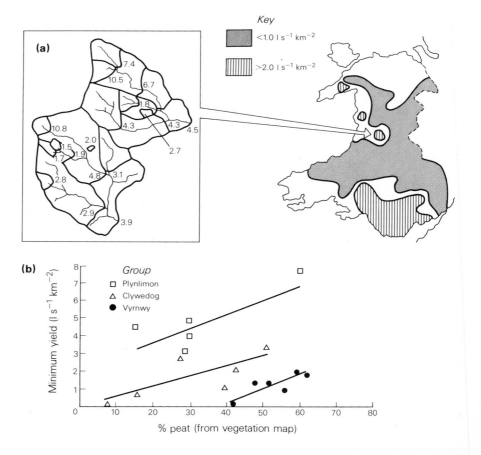

Figure 3.7 Drought in the uplands. (a) Flow yields (minimum) during the 1976 drought in Wales, inset of Plynlimon catchments shows importance of inputs from the peaty drifts of the headwater. (b) A graphical relationship between peat cover and minimum streamflow yields (1976) in mid-Wales.

effectively organized (Harding & Parker 1972) through police and wardens. As Smith and Tobin (1979) show, upland towns and villages are seldom accorded structural protection against flooding, though Newtown on the Severn was given such a scheme as a pre-requisite to government-sponsored urban expansion. The introduction of a flood-retaining capacity into the operating rules for regulating reservoirs has produced protection for upland towns, at least in terms of public perception and this, often unfounded, confidence in the degree of protection afforded by river regulation can extend much further downstream.

The sparsity of flow-gauging stations on upland streams makes it often necessary to estimate flood peaks; even where flow structures do exist they may be overtopped or by-passed simply because structures to cope with the very great flow ranges are extremely expensive (e.g. Fig. 3.4). Raingauges may be scarce in the area of interest or even damaged by landslides. Inevitably, upland flood data collection involves detective work (see Newson 1975b). *Bucket catches* are often used to estimate point rainfalls and *trash marks* (Fig. 3.6c) for peak river levels. Past estimates of peak flows from peak levels must be viewed with some suspicion.

The shortage of gauging stations in the uplands is not so serious at the low-flow extreme where, in serious droughts, there is normally sufficient time to perform numerous 'spot' river gaugings to compute minimum stream-flows or catchment yield per unit area. For very small flows, the most direct measurement is volumetric and during the 1976 drought such gaugings were used in both Wales and Scotland to establish minimum yields; the Institute of Hydrology used the technique to check low-flow calibrations in the 'Plynlimon' flumes (Fig. 3.6a). Figure 3.7a shows the results of 'spot' gauging rivers in Wales during the 1976 drought. It illustrates the very low yields which prevailed in the central uplands with the exception of two headwater areas characterised by gritty periglacial deposits and deep peat; the detail of the Plynlimon catchments shows the very localised occurrence of the highest drought yields. Later it proved possible to relate the yields within catchment areas to the map area of peat (Newson 1980c and Fig. 3.7b).

The dominant rocks of the British uplands are impermeable Precambrian, Lower Palaeozoic and Carboniferous rocks of which only the latter, which includes massive limestones, can be called an aquifer of any importance (Newson 1973). There is consequently little to report on groundwater studies in upland areas apart from a rather imbalanced concentration on karst limestones. Of the water supplies from karst aquifers, that to Bristol has been most researched by water tracing (Atkinson, Smith, Lavis & Whitaker 1973, Atkinson & Drew 1974), and by catchment budgeting (Atkinson 1977). The latter study established quantitatively the role of fissure flows in the Carboniferous limestone, as opposed to 'normal' Darcian aquifer flows; pollution threats were therefore in the minds of the water authority who helped sponsor the Mendip work (see Atkinson 1971). Because of the importance of fissure or 'conduit' flows, the regime of karst-fed rivers in the uplands is also 'flashy', in marked contrast to that expected from groundwater supplies. The influence of this regime is especially noticeable in the rivers of the Yorkshire Dales but, in contrast to the Mendip Hills near Bristol, the much more extensive Yorkshire karst is little studied hydrologically outside of the extensive cave systems.

Filling the data gap in upland hydrology – predictions by engineers, models by geographers

The relative shortage of empirical data for upland catchments so far described has had two major effects: necessity has forced the engineer to make good use of what does exist to predict ungauged values needed for design, and opportunity has found the researcher attempting to create a firm theoretical base for modelling. Geographers have been especially active in the latter field because the spatial aspects of the runoff process are clearly evident in 'wildscapes' such as the uplands.

Until the Dolgarrog disaster in 1925 (Fearnsides & Wilcockson 1928) the design of spillway capacity for the ever-increasing number of British upland reservoirs had never been based on an integrated body of hydrological data. There had been few disasters; that at Dale Dyke, Sheffield (Amey 1974, Harrison, republished 1974) being the most completely documented. Dolgarrog, however, prompted the Reservoir (Safety Provisions) Act, 1930 and to facilitate the safe design of spillways the Institution of Civil Engineers produced a guide to catastrophic and 'normal maximum' flood peaks, using a plot of recorded and estimated peaks against catchment area – the so-called envelope curve. No further dam disasters occurred, although the estimated flood peaks during the Lynmouth flood in 1952 shocked the profession into a revision of the envelope curve (Dobbie & Wolf 1953). However, the centre of interest in engineering flood design began to shift to the gathering body of lowland flow records and the improving statistical appreciation of extremes, largely through the work of E. J. Gumbel. Cole (1966) derived mean annual floods for England and Wales; prediction by relationship with catchment area showed the influence of the higher rainfall and steeper slopes of the uplands clearly. Later the Flood Study of the early 1970s (NERC 1975a) used these regional factors of morphometry and climate explicitly in estimating the size of the mean annual flood (AMAF) in regression equations of the form:

$$\text{AMAF} = \text{AREA}^a \text{STREAM FREQUENCY}^b \text{SLOPE}^c \text{RUNOFF}^d \text{SOIL}^e \text{LAKE}^f \text{URBAN}^g$$

Although the Flood Study provided regional versions of this basic equation to reduce the standard error of estimate, the residuals from the single nationwide equation which led to the regionalisation did not show mountain streams to be worthy of separate treatment. Whether they do in fact require separate flood prediction methods will require the collection of much more data from small upland catchments.

One may consider the statistical treatment of flood peaks described briefly above as most useful to the engineer designing land drainage or flood protection in the lowlands. To the designers of upland reservoir spillways the very extreme flood is still the centre of interest. The profession has, however, moved in another direction from the 1933 envelope curve and its revisions to aid this basic upland design problem. The unit hydrograph, used in conjunction with the more abundant rainfall information (including meteorological estimates of the 'probable maximum precipitation') has become the basic tool in such designs. Here, too, the Flood Study introduced quantification of regional factors of morphometry and climate. The basic dimension of the unit hydrograph is its time to peak (TP) and this was predicted using a basic equation of the form:

$$\text{TP} = \text{MAINSTREAM LENGTH}^a \text{SLOPE}^b \text{URBAN}^c \text{RUNOFF}^d$$

Despite including in the data base for this equation a number of steep, small upland catchments, the times to peak predicted (and those recorded over much of upland Britain) are generally much longer than those suggested by, for example, equations derived in the United States for catchments of similar area and slope. Possibly the depth and character of the soil cover in the British uplands is crucial here; comparisons between truly mountainous catchments, where bedrock dominates the surface and undrained peat-covered moorland catchments illustrate the much more rapid and voluminous flood response of the former. Dunne (1978) links the slower response of soil-covered catchments in the humid-temperate zone to the absence of Hortonian overland flow which arises where surface soils are unable to infiltrate water at the rate being supplied in precipitation. The Flood Study recommends catchment lag-time, identified by temporary gauging as a basis for predicting time-to-peak. Dunne's observation is also relevant to the fact that the Flood Study prediction does not succeed in the case of retrospective comparison with 'catastrophic' floods, such as that at Lynmouth. Research into the slope and channel runoff processes leading to this non-linearity at very high flood is clearly needed; for processes in the slope phase are likely to be behind the quick response in extreme floods, and they may even show up in reducing times to peak of smaller floods in some catchments (see Fig. 3.8). Although the impact of urbanisation in the lowlands is included in the Flood Study time-to-peak equation, that of the major upland land-use effect – drainage for agriculture and forestry – could not be detected as significant even though it has been determined as such from individual studies of small catchments (e.g. Robinson 1980) and has been suggested as a possible cause for increased flooding in mid-Wales (Howe, Slaymaker & Harding 1967).

In designing for drought, the engineer concerned with reservoirs has until recently had even less data upon which to work than in the case of floods. Reservoir storage has frequently to be assessed on the basis of estimated yields: direct gauging records are rarely available. The most popular of the traditional techniques was that of basing yield upon the rainfall in the 'three driest years' (Glasspoole 1924) and using a conversion such as the Lapworth Chart (Skeat &

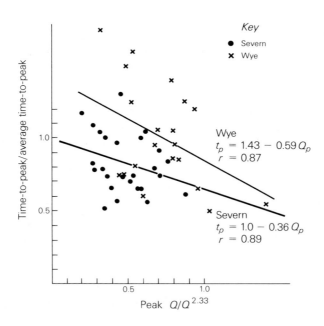

Figure 3.8 Linearities and non-linearities of upland flood response.

Wye
$t_p = 1.43 - 0.59 Q_p$
$r = 0.87$

Severn
$t_p = 1.0 - 0.36 Q_p$
$r = 0.89$

71

Dangerfield 1969) to match design yield for supply with natural yield and the requisite storage volume which the dam must create. The Lapworth Chart was based on gauged records from 17 catchments. Retrospectively, we may conclude that it builds in a probability of supply failures of between one in 50 years and one in a 100 years. The increase in hydrometry during the 1960s and 1970s has as yet provided little help with the problem in that very long records are necessary; as an interim the most frequent strategy has been to calibrate a mathematical model of natural yield from the proposed reservoir catchment by using a long record of flows lower down the same or an adjacent catchment. Naturally, the data collected during the drought of 1975–6 has had the effect of improving our knowledge of low flows, as have the recent Low Flow Studies using regression equations based on catchment characteristics (Institute of Hydrology 1980), of which the base-flow index (BFI) proved the most successful. Using the BFI, catchment area and annual average rainfall it is possible to predict the ten-day flow total exceeded 95% of the time and the mean annual minimum ten-day flow, i.e. an approach through flow duration curves is taken and suites of curves allow the two basic predictions to be extended to other durations and other probabilities.

The 1975–6 drought also refined the philosophy of the probability of failure for which reservoirs are designed and the flexibility of supplies which are essential to operational viability during a prolonged drought. The traditional 'three driest years in 100' criterion has, therefore, been replaced by a spectrum of designs tailored to our improved knowledge of low flows, demand and operations. One of the operational constraints – that of releasing compensation water from a reservoir to maintain the ecological viability of the stream – was found during 1976 to have been conservative; much lower compensation flows are now known to be adequate and statutory Drought Orders are the means of implementing them. On the other hand, the use of river channels and regulating reservoirs to supply lowland centres of demand was shown to have some problems in 1976, resulting from bank storage of the released water and losses by evapotranspiration through riparian plants.

Identifying and measuring the processes of runoff as a basis for modelling

The revolution in our spatial concept of flood runoff, from that in which surface flows from the whole catchment produce flood peaks, to that where subsurface flows hold the key to the generation of surface flows from quite small parts of the catchment (partial contributing area) has attracted geographers to upland hydrology in numbers over the last 15 years. However, much of the early work on throughflow (e.g. Weyman 1970, 1973, 1974) was performed on brown earth soils, typical of the periphery of the uplands and in these soils the 'classic' throughflow–partial area model works well. In the peats and peaty podsols of the upland core, as Weyman identified at the head of the East Twin (Mendip Hills) catchment, there are likely to be complications. Jones (1971) was the first in Britain to describe the phenomenon of soil piping which has turned out to be widespread in peaty upland soils (Newson 1976a, Jones 1978, Gilman & Newson 1980) and Knapp (1974) has identified general inhomogeneity of soil moisture movements (all these studies in upland mid-Wales). The piping study of the Wye catchment on Plynlimon pointed out that although pipes exhibited high flow velocities their importance in producing flood peaks is diminished by irregular supply of runoff from peaty plateaus above the piped slope and their discharge on to the relatively slow surface runoff regime of valley-bottom mires below the piped slope. Their

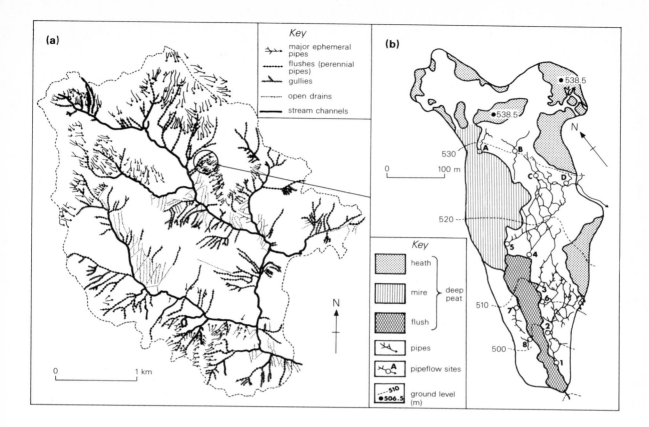

Key
↗ major ephemeral pipes
↟ flushes (perennial pipes)
⊥⊥ gullies
⋯⋯ open drains
━━ stream channels

Key
▓ heath
▦ mire } deep peat
▨ flush
⊡ pipes
⊙A pipeflow sites
510
●506.5 ground level (m)

distribution is irregular, both within the catchment (Fig. 3.9) and on any in-dividual slope (mainly because they form and de-form over quite short periods). By contrast, and returning to freely draining brown earths, Anderson and Burt (1978) have been able to be far more conclusive about the spatial regularity of runoff routes by matrix throughflow into and from hollows.

The major hurdle between the derivation of a conceptual model for upland runoff and its application outside the study area is the identification of both the vertical and spatial distribution of flow routes in the ungauged catchment. Not enough attention has been given to this problem of extrapolation; it means, for instance, that unless the results of research are derived from instrumentation installed around a particular type of widely-available map – topographic, soil or vegetation – there will be little chance of equally widespread applicability for any model. Although topographic maps are widely available, the application of work such as that of Weyman or Anderson and Burt at a scale of 1:25 000 (the best available medium scale) would be difficult; even on the brown earth soils of the upland margins the topographic detail to delimit runoff-producing hollows would not be available. Neither would a purely topographical approach be able to identify subsurface routes of various types.

One of the major handicaps to general applications of process-based models is the relatively small coverage of the country (particularly the uplands) on small-scale soil maps. Only recently has a national-scale map representing a hydro-logical classification of soils been available (Farquarson *et al.* 1978), though there was an earlier attempt through what now appears as the largely inappropriate infiltration approach (Painter 1971). Because of the small coverage by soils maps

Figure 3.9 Soil piping in the Upper Wye (Plynlimon) catchment. (a) Sketch survey of the catchment-scale distribution of soil pipe 'swarms'; (b) detail from one area, showing the relationship with natural vegetation.

73

the distribution of natural vegetation has been found to be both a suitable means of organising field measurements and a potential method of extrapolation (Newson 1976b), using the mapped information described by Coleman (1970).

Nevertheless, the moves towards physically-based models which do require some calibration (but mainly by low cost reconnaissance work from maps or in the field) are becoming clearer. Calver, Kirkby and Weyman (1972) began the trend by suggesting the feasibility of predicting throughflow and surface flow contributions from sideslopes and of using network geometry and hydraulic geometry of channels to route the slope runoff. Beven and Kirkby (1979) have completed a model using the topography of a small upland catchment to calibrate a storage–contributing area relationship together with simple linear channel routing. Although it is conventional to think of channel routing as affecting catchment response timing only at downstream locations, the definition used here for mountain streams (running over waterfalls or through dumps of glacial boulders) has led to the belief that channel routing components should be included in modelling flows from such catchments by research using dilution gauging, hydraulic geometry and flow resistance (summarised by Beven, Gilman & Newson 1979, and Beven 1979). This is most relevant to steep, bedrock-controlled, mountain channels where non-uniformities of flow brought about by falls and pools dominate at low flows. As flow increases, dilution gauging and travel-time curves both indicate a more uniform flow and this effect is manifest in an apparent decline in flow resistance. Many mountain channels are, however, much larger than those studied by Beven and others; Bathurst (1978) has developed a prediction for flow resistance in cobble-bed rivers by collecting measurements from the upper Tees during controlled releases from a major regulating reservoir. He develops the concept of relative roughness to express the changing scale of the cobble bed relative to depth of flow as discharge increases; channel shape is clearly important too. Later, Bathurst, Li and Simons (1979) have gone into far more detail of the drag forces and other losses of energy which explain the resistance process in mountain streams. Although they again indicate declining resistance with increasing depths, i.e. increasing Reynold's number, there are Froude number effects in the appearance of hydraulic jumps. Energy dissipation at the free surface in such rough channels is clearly important.

It is likely, therefore, that the channel phase of runoff in mountain streams will be subjected to more detailed investigation in future, not the least because of the relationship between bed geometry, flow resistance and the critical stresses involved in sediment transport.

Finally, it would be inappropriate to leave even this very brief treatment of runoff process studies in the uplands without reference to peat. Although covering less than 10% of the United Kingdom, peat hydrology has become a widespread interest; in the uplands it clearly controls the hydrology of many of those Welsh, Pennine and Scottish watersheds whose runoff is used for water supply or power generation. Foundations on peat were a contributary cause of the Dolgarrog disaster (see above). It is the substrate for the forester's drive to secure better yields of conifers and the farmer's desire to grow better pasture; there have been attempts to exploit it for fuel. As a direct corollary of development pressures there is concern by nature conservationists that natural wetlands are disappearing fast as a habitat, particularly through drainage. As a further encouragement to research there is the obvious peculiarity of water movement in peats (largely unknown, apparently, to the drainage specialists) and the clarity with which plant species provide a guide to peat hydrology (Ingram 1967).

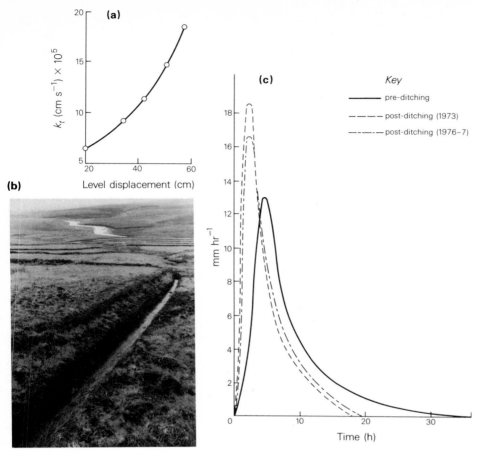

Figure 3.10 Peat hydrology in upland Britain.
(a) The variation of hydraulic conductivity with head, showing the non-Darcian flow properties of peat;
(b) agricultural drains ('grips') dug across moorland in the headwaters of the Tees;
(c) pre- and post-ditching hydrographs for a forestry plantation at Coalburn, northern Pennines.

Although peaty areas can rarely be defined accurately as catchment areas they provide good opportunities for making measurements of rainfall–storage–runoff relationships using raingauges, dip wells and small weirs. In most upland peats a two-fold hydrological division of the vertical profile usually becomes established. Given an average depth of 2 m for upland peats, lateral flows occur down to between 10 cm and 20 cm (Tomlinson 1979) and only vertical movements in response to evaporative loss and rainfall recharge below this 'active layer'. Ingram (1978) prefers the terms **acrotelm** and **catotelm** for the two layers. Obviously they have very different hydraulic conductivities, though values for this variable are difficult to determine experimentally (Rycroft, Williams & Ingram 1975) and appear to be non-Darcian (Fig. 3.10a): there have been attempts to trace the slow water movements over plots using tritiated water and these have determined a range of velocities between 0.5 mm d^{-1} and 10 mm d^{-1} for blanket peat (Knight, Boggie & Shepherd 1972). The type of peat and its conductivity are of key importance to the success or failure of drainage schemes (McDonald 1973). The prevailing view at the time of writing is that upland blanket peats are extremely hard to drain economically below the acrotelm; the effect of surface drains such as those dug for agriculture (Fig. 3.10b) and forestry tends, therefore, to be an increase in the rate of removal of surface water and to increase the magnitude of flood peaks as a result of the reduced times to peak (Robinson 1981). Figure 3.10c illustrates Robinson's 'before and after' study of forestry drainage on peat.

75

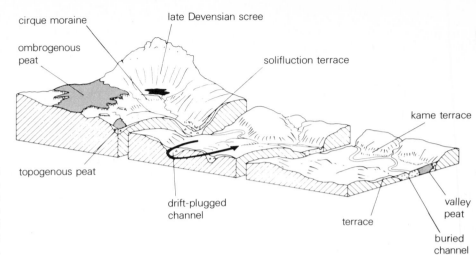

cirque moraine   late Devensian scree

ombrogenous peat

solifluction terrace

kame terrace

Figure 3.11 The Pleistocene legacy in upland geomorphology. Fluvial activity is seen as superimposed on the morphology and deposits of glaciation and periglaciation (after Lewin 1977).

topogenous peat

drift-plugged channel

terrace

valley peat

buried channel

The fluvial geomorphology of British mountain streams

The study of geomorphology in Britain may be said to have been through a morphological phase into a process-study phase but seldom to have re-introduced morphology in order to take the integrated approach. The British uplands are especially difficult from this point of view, having a complicated legacy of morphological remnants including Tertiary planation surfaces, Pleistocene glacial and periglacial activity and Holocene fluvial modifications during changing climate and base level conditions (see Fig. 3.11). Environmental reconstruction of the Quaternary is now armed with as sophisticated a set of techniques as that available to the student of processes. In this respect, palaeohydrological reconstructions laying the basis for integrated contemporary studies deserve more attention than they get (Lewin 1977, Gregory 1979a). The most serious professional outcome of a continuing gap in process-response–historical studies is that of an inability on the part of geomorphologists to explain the physiographic development of an area and predict its future for the benefit of planners and engineers.

Sediment loads in mountain streams

We saw in Chapter 2 that on a world scale the sediment yields of Britain are small. They are often omitted from world surveys (Holeman 1968), perhaps because of the lack of long-term records. As a general point we may echo King's (1953) view that the British landscape is composed of 'arthritic concavo-convex hillslopes, crippled and reduced to impotence beneath a blanket of sod'! In the uplands, however, erosion and sedimentation do create problems, principally in headwater areas, during floods, and often related to land-use developments.

    A major Pleistocene legacy has been coarse superficial deposits, and the activity of postglacial weathering has been to produce finer, cohesive soil layers on top of these (Adams 1974), especially where peat has grown and remains moist. With this binding action ascribable to upland soils it is little wonder that land-use management practices such as drainage (Newson 1980b) and even vegetation changes through burning (Imeson 1974) tend to control erosion rates. What these

(a)   (b)

results point to is that, if the 'sod' of King's quote is removed (or is naturally absent) landscape 'impotence' is not a fair assumption. Morgan (1980), taking an approach through the energy of intense rain storms maps the uplands as liable to soil erosion, although the common stagnogley soils are identified as very stable. The drift materials below British upland soils are, however, seldom fine enough to be unstable if disturbed.

The high residual proportion of coarse materials in British upland channels means that the majority of sediment transport occurs as bedload; quite high thresholds of critical tractive velocity need to be passed before transport occurs and it is restricted largely to periods of flood. Load measurements are expensive to make in such situations and even the bedload traps (Fig. 3.12) which have run for nearly a decade in the Plynlimon catchments have been overfilled twice, requiring estimates of the 'missing' quantities. During long intervening periods no bedload movements are recorded; this also means that bedload research must be long term for averages to mean anything.

The Plynlimon experiment was designed to include an investigation of the bedload yield of grassland and forestry areas in the uplands. As Table 3.1 shows, the forested subcatchment has much higher yields; so too have other catchments in mid-Wales (for which estimates have been prepared) where the ground has been disturbed by cultivation or deep ditching (Newson 1980b).

Further investigation of the distribution of bedload yields in time at Plynlimon shows that sediment *supply* can be limiting. Major floods and, to less extent, frosty/wet or drought/wet sequences of weather release sediments to the bedload system which subsequent flows above the critical threshold can transport; thereafter, yields decline as supply becomes limiting (Newson 1980a). The importance of the weathering and slope processes which are going on during the supply-limited phase points to a need to study the 'recovery period' between floods or between other major releases of sediment. It is interesting to note that sequences of weather types are important to the provision of material; the dry/wet sequence has been separated as crucial to the development of soil pipes (Gilman & Newson 1980), and Lewin, Cryer and Harrison (1974) and Harvey (1974) identify frost or

Figure 3.12 Coarse bedload: how to measure its movement? In the mountain zone a concrete trap on a tributary stream in the Plynlimon catchments: (a) being emptied by excavation; (b) the resulting mound of sediment.

77

snow, followed by rain, as significant to the provision of sediment from bluffs, gullies and channel banks. Bare areas, such as the bluff faces which confine upland meanders are highly significant for sediment supply, especially in winter.

There are signs that delivery ratios of sediments from the locally very erosive uplands to the piedmont reaches of British streams will repay more study, because it is the piedmont zone through which there is an increasing tendency to use river channels to convey water from regulating reservoirs to the consumer in the lowlands. The side-effects of reservoir releases at even one third to one half bankfull during dry periods in summer are likely to be profound on sediment transport (Hey, Thorne & Bathurst 1976) and consequently upon bank erosion and riparian farming or even buildings. As a consequence, there has been an upsurge of interest in these largely gravel-bed rivers (Hey 1975b, Charlton, Brown & Benson 1978). The latter authors made measurements of sediment size, hydraulic geometry and flow conditions on 23 British gravel-bed rivers as a basis for channel design equations. Hey (1978) puts forward nine regime-type equations which form the basis for an extensive data collection programme prior to regression analysis. However, he adds that simulation exercises, rather than regime analysis is the best way to predict changes in flow regime or sediment inputs (because of the feedback controls involved).

If artificial influences on sediment yields in the uplands, such as those reported from mid-Wales (Newson 1980b) are also leading to the supply of more gravel to the piedmont zone the scene is set for extremely complicated river management problems. Comprehensive studies would clearly aid both the river engineer and the farmer who points to a loss of good riparian land or to increased flooding associated with aggradation of river beds as the price of catchment development. Even without the increased outputs of gravel associated with land-use change it is likely that the decline in the use of river gravel for building roads during the last century has already had an impact on upland channels. Clayton (1951) suggests this factor as the major one in creating problems of aggradation in the Lake

Table 3.1 Sediment yields (gravel bedload) from 'natural' and disturbed small catchments in mid-Wales. Catchment areas from 0.25 km² to 13.0 km².

Land-use, catchment	Annual yield ($m^3 km^{-2}$)	
Grassland, undisturbed		
Cyff	2.5	
Cownwy	2.5	
Pen y Banc	9.9	
Maesnant	1.1[a]	
Iago	1.2[b]	
Forested, ditched		
Tanllwyth	8.4–307.7	(main and sub-catchments)
Groes	44.4	
Marchnant	30.9	
Moorland, ditched		
Bugeilyn	57.1	
Hengwm	2.0–17.9	(main and sub-catchments)
Llyn Pen Rhaidr	3.5–38.8	(main and sub-catchments)

[a] From Lewin, Cryer and Harrison (1974).
[b] From Lewin and Wolfenden (1978).

District. In some areas commercial extraction of sand and gravel continues; Fleming (1970) estimates that over 130 000 t of material is removed from the upper Clyde.

The natural gravel shoals of the piedmont zone are also extremely important for fisheries; the Wye in Wales and the Tyne and Tees in northern England are being studied by freshwater biologists alerted by the prospects of river regulation (see Carling 1979). Carling suggests release rules for the new Kielder Reservoir which will not be too low (causing silting or dry shoals) or too high (causing shifting shoals).

Although a high ratio of bed-sediment movements to suspended load has been quoted for the mountain streams of Britain (e.g. 4:1 by Lewin, Cryer & Harrison 1974), the piedmont zone shows a complete reversal of this situation. McManus and Al Ansari (1975) quote a bed–suspended proportion of 0.02 for the Almond in Scotland (Grampian Highlands) and between 0.02 and 0.05 for the nearby Earn. Hall (1967) reports 0.09 and 0.10 for the Tyne and its tributary and Grimshaw and Lewin (1980b) between 0.05 (below a reservoir) and 0.11 in mid-Wales. These are well within the suspended load channel class of Schumm (1963b). The measurement of bedload on these larger rivers is highly problematic. Although the Scottish workers found it possible to use a VUV sampler on the fine gravel bed of the Earn (782 km^2) on the Almond the coarse gravel forced them to use a range of predictive formulae; Grimshaw and Lewin also predicted bedload transport rates. There are also problems of technique in measuring suspended sediments: although the basic sampling procedure of depth-integrating a stream-lined bottle sampler is largely satisfactory the production of a continuous record and, therefore, of total yield figures is dubious (Walling 1977). Two alternatives exist: that of using some form of continuous measurement of turbidity (or a short-interval water sampler) and that of constructing the suspended sediment ratings against discharge for a particular site. Results from the former tend to invalidate the latter because they point, as in the case of bedload, to the operation of supply limitations and variations. For example, arable agriculture begins to replace livestock pastures in the piedmont zone and seasonal cultivation clearly has the effect of increasing supplies of suspended sediment (Al-Ansari, A.-Jabbari & McManus 1977).

Loss of reservoir capacity through sedimentation has yet to be a problem to the water engineer in the British uplands, although there are operational problems. However, reservoir surveys have been used to integrate sediment transport from upland catchments over long time periods (e.g. Hall 1967, Kirkby 1967, Young 1958b, Ledger, Lovell & McDonald 1974). This is time-consuming and demanding work and although there are fewer technical problems than in river sampling, the grossed outputs tend to blur the individual rates of sediment production in tributary catchments which can be diagnostic in curtailing further sedimentation or identifying source areas. River sampling shows variability to be great. Arnett (1979) uses 16 catchments in the North York Moors to illustrate wide ranges of both long-term suspended yield and response to floods within a single upland region. A factor of 32 separated the yield of the most productive from that of the least productive of Arnett's catchments.

The accumulation of sediments in natural lakes has formed a major line of enquiry for the Freshwater Biological Association at its centre in the mountainous English Lake District; the aims of the long study have not been geomorphological, but a summary of rates of sedimentation in 13 British lakes (Pennington 1978) points to a 20-fold variability in current rates of sedimentation and to the accelerated rates of deposition following the agricultural settlements of the Neolithic (1800–1000 BC) and Norse (AD 900) invaders.

Solute loads in upland streams

Returning to King's 'blanket of sod', it is not surprising to find the process of solutional erosion as being important in upland catchments in Britain; weathering of bedrock or drift beneath the soil profile limits both the supply of sediment to channels and the overall rate of slope development and chemical weathering is likely to dominate, spatially at least. However, comprehensive studies are again sparse and the ratios quoted for dissolved and solid loads in streams vary widely (see Table 5.13). Lithology and land use are obviously responsible for much of the variability and the high susceptibility of calcareous rocks is obvious in published work.

Table 3.2 Catchment solute budgeting, (a) as part of ecological studies (Crisp 1966) (Rough Sike, North Pennines, area 0.83 km²); (b) as part of a study of weathering (Waylen 1979) (East Twin, Mendips). The upper basin is the typically upland section of peaty podsols (area 0.1 km²) whilst the lower basin (0.08 km²) is of brown earths. Data are in kg.

(a)	Water (thousands of m^3)	Sodium $(kg\ yr^{-1})$	Potassium $(kg\ yr^{-1})$	Calcium $(kg\ yr^{-1})$	Phosphorus $(kg\ yr^{-1})$	Nitrogen $(kg\ yr^{-1})$
stream water output	1368	3755	744	4461	33	244
evaporation	403	–	–	–	–	–
peat erosion	–	23	171	401	37	1214
drift of fauna in stream	–	0.004	0.011	0.003	0.010	0.118
drift of fauna on stream	–	0.11	0.38	0.07	0.43	4.6
sale of sheep and wool	–	0.16	0.44	1.58	0.98	4.4
total output	1771	3778	916	4864	71	1467
input in precipitation	1771	2120	255	745	38–57	681
difference = net loss for catchment	–	1658	661	4119	14–33	786
net loss per ha	–	20.01	7.97	49.68	0.17–0.40	9.48

(b)	H^+	Ca^{++}	Mg^{++}	Na^+	K^+	HCO_3^-	Cl^-	SO_4^{--}	Si°
Upper basin									
ppt input	8.3	66.0	63.0	204.4	28.6	0.0	438.2	527.7	24.9
net nutrient uptake	−2.6	40.0	16.0		35.0				
basin output	2.3	89.9	93.0	262.0	42.7	143.7	415.6	513.0	102.1
balance	−8.6	63.9	46.0	57.6	49.1	143.7	−22.6	−14.7	77.2
Lower basin									
ppt input	6.3	49.5	47.3	153.3	21.5	0.0	328.6	395.8	18.7
basin output	−2.2	119.1	186.2	201.2	68.5	611.7	372.6	519.7	127.2
balance	−8.5	69.6	139.0	47.9	47.1	611.7	44.0	123.9	108.5
Whole basin									
ppt input	14.6	155.5	110.3	357.7	50.1	0.0	766.8	923.5	43.6
net nutrient uptake	−2.6	40.0	16.0		35.0				
basin output	0.0	209.0	279.2	463.2	111.2	755.4	788.3	1032.7	229.2
balance	−17.1	133.5	184.9	105.5	96.2	755.4	21.4	109.2	185.6

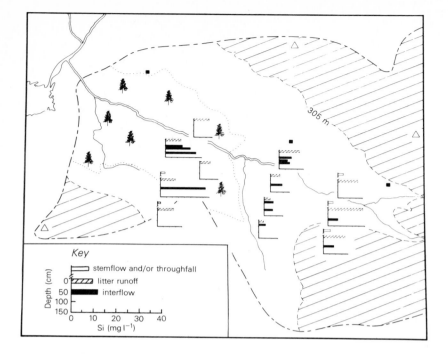

Figure 3.13 The detailed study of an important solute: silica, showing concentrations in stem flow/throughfall, litter runoff and interflow for a small Dartmoor catchment of mixed land-use (after Ternan & Williams 1979).

It is not surprising that the one aquifer of the uplands – Carboniferous limestone – claimed most of the early attention from geomorphologists studying solute loads. In the case of solute loads, the fortunate feature of calcium carbonate is the ease with which quantification is possible through chemical titration; concentrations can also be correlated with electrical conductivity if, as is usually the case in karst areas, there are very low concentrations of other solutes. Because the activity of cavers is important to the collection of samples throughout the limestone stream system the best summaries of the quantitative study of Britain's major karst regions are those in the caving handbooks (Waltham & Sweeting 1974, Smith & Drew 1975, Ford 1977).

In other geologies especially where silica would form the major solute of geomorphological interest there has been surprisingly little detailed work – total dissolved solids being the most common measurement, often via electrical conductivity. Finlayson (1977) used Weyman's study area, the East Twin Brook (Mendip Hills) for such a study, although the main emphasis of his work was on suspended load (Finlayson 1978). Waylen (1979) goes into much more detail in the same catchment, making comparisons between the stream load of a range of ions and their release by weathering, uptake by plants and input from rainfall (Table 3.2). Clearly the amount of solutional *denudation* cannot be simply calculated from stream solute loads. However, much of the East Twin is of brown earth soils and there are few studies of the truly upland situation: Cryer's (1980) study of solutes from soil pipes and peat is a pioneer. Ternan and Williams (1979) are collecting data for dissolved silica from soil pits in a Dartmoor catchment. Their work (Fig. 3.13) illustrates the higher concentrations from throughflow at the base of a forested slope than from grassland throughflow; as with karst, explanations from the relative speed of water movement and the kinetics of solution seem most likely.

Returning to the catchment outlet, an increasing preoccupation in the study of   81 solute loads is with nutrient chemicals, especially nitrogen in the form of nitrate. However, phosphate is likely to be the eventual key to eutrophication if it is to affect upland water bodies and the likely effects of fertilising upland forestry plantations with phosphate have been studied in Scotland (see below). There has been widespread interest in nutrients in the water industry following recent water quality legislation and the realisation that rural development is perhaps a more comprehensive and widespread threat to water quality than is urban industry (MAFF 1976). With this in mind, the study by Oborne, Brooker and Edwards (1980) of the Wye is a useful base-line; it shows very low concentrations of nitrate and phosphate in the upland reaches at present. Downstream increases are linked to land-use and population density. Ecological studies of upland catchments have encouraged the collection of comprehensive measurements to establish mass balances. This involves measuring rainfall inputs (see the papers by Gorham, e.g. 1956a, b). The maritime location of much of the British uplands means a high proportion of stream solutes (especially sodium salts) come from atmospheric input (Cryer 1976) including an important route through dry deposition (White, Starkey & Saunders 1971). Finlayson (1977) also quantifies the atmospheric input of suspended solids. Crisp (1966) pioneered the field of complete ecological balances for a small Pennine watershed, 0.83 km^2 in area. Much of the transport of nutrients from the catchment occurred as organic sediment – i.e. from the erosion of peat (Table 3.2). Crisp and Robson (1979) provide more details of the processes of peat erosion from the catchment. Finlayson (1978) has stressed the presence of quite large amounts of organic matter in suspended sediment loads (20%) and clearly no study of nutrient cycling can discount solid loads, especially in peat areas. Crisp estimated a rate of retreat of a centimetre a year from the bare peat faces. Studies of peat erosion have formed a major topic for investigation in the Pennines, where the rate of loss appears to have increased in the last 200 years (Tallis 1965), either as the result of industrial air pollution from the neighbouring cities, or grazing pressure, or, more recently, tourism. Climatic controls, via frost and drought are however also possible as Tallis (1973) points out. The conclusion that peat and drift erosion have been accelerated or even initiated in the last 500 years has also been reached by Thomas (1956) in the Brecon Beacons; in the Plynlimon area the same author cites sheep grazing as the cause (Thomas 1964).

Studies of channels and channel change

The systematic relationship between process and form in river channels is most often summarised in studies of hydraulic geometry; the engineer's 'regime' equations for dominant flows, the basis of most alluvial channel design (see above in connection with sediment delivery through the piedmont zone), represent the applied side of this field. If, however, the British uplands are paraglacial or post-paraglacial, rather than truly alluvial, how far can the implicit regularities of hydraulic geometry be relied upon? The first complication is the range of channel types. The report by Newson and Harrison (1978) describes irregularities in the relationships between channel cross-sectional area (at bankfull) and the catchment area and in the spacing of riffles and pools in the open channels of the Plynlimon catchments (see Fig. 3.14). The former type of irregularity is in marked contrast to the findings of Park (1975) on Dartmoor. The discrepancy is important because Park's work became the basis of a technique which has been used to assess downstream channel change due to reservoir construction, urban development and mineral extraction (Gregory & Park 1974, Park 1979). Gregory has also used

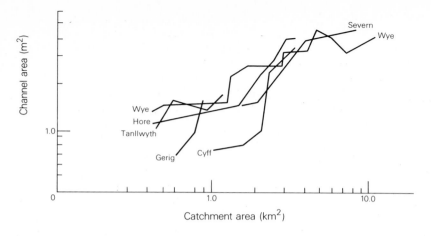

Figure 3.14 Channel capacity and catchment area relationships, showing the irregularity underlying a regression relationship for the Plynlimon catchments when individual rivers are plotted.

the method in another form (1979b) to derive the network power variable for flood prediction. The most likely explanation for the difference in findings is that those who find the channel area–catchment area relationship strong enough to use so confidently have largely worked in the less heavily glaciated or non-glaciated regions of the uplands or where, for other reasons, the sediments are fine enough for regular patterns of flow–sediment interaction to develop.

Turning to irregularities in the planform of upland channels, Milne's study of eleven confined channel reaches in the north of England and Scotland (Milne 1979) suggests that upland meanders are of lower curvature than their lowland counterparts; coarser sediments produce wider, shallower channels and inhibit the full development of secondary flows. The meander forms are very stable at all flows below bankfull but show very variable cross-sectional dimensions. Possibly the hydrograph dimensions of the most recent formative flood are the best explanation for this irregularity: the rapid rise and fall in upland channels may give little opportunity to initiate regular transport and deposition of coarse sediments (cf. the longer duration of flooding and finer sediments of the piedmont and lowlands).

A sedimentological approach to depositional features in piedmont rivers has been undertaken by geologists, especially in Scotland, and confirms that coarse sediments do not travel far, even during floods. Reworking is important; Bluck's (1971) detailed investigation of bar forms and riffles in the river Endrick (Scotland) shows how their stratigraphy and plan represent a process of facies separation between gravel and sand, the gravel areas being stable at most flows. Whittel (1979) suggests very little movement, even over long periods: coarse gravel on the point bars of the river Wharfe in the Yorkshire Dales shows rapid decline in its sandstone and limestone components beyond the downstream limit of those respective lithologies. Wilcock (1967) was early to point out the possible controls on stream channel geometry (mainly slope) exercised by 'residual bedload', i.e. the coarsest material which could only rarely be transported by contemporary flood flows. The presence of substantial quantities of sand, moving through coarser sediments and leading to bi-modal size distributions, appears to be a common feature of Scottish upland and piedmont rivers. Bridge and Jarvis (1976) have studied sand bars at a bend within the uplands in Glen Cova (Grampian Highlands); McManus (1979) suggests methods of depicting the relationship between sand moving as saltation load and gravels moving as bedload in the Tay and Earn (Grampian Highlands). As discovered by other authors, the saltation

83

load is still in motion after bedload is deposited during flood recession and it becomes trapped in the interpebble cavities of the bed.

Measurement of channel planform change by sequential field survey or by comparisons with old maps or aerial photographs has become popular in recent years (see Gregory 1977). However, the majority of such studies have been in the lowland or piedmont zone on British rivers. Two studies by Liverpool University (Hitchcock 1977, Harvey 1974, 1977) have taken the technique into upland headwaters. As already mentioned in connection with bedload movements, flow thresholds must be tripped for change to occur and Hitchcock identifies a discharge which occurs ten times a year as the threshold for change in his Forest of Bowland (Western Pennines) channel.

In their study of a braided piedmont river in Scotland, Werrity and Ferguson (1980) have pointed to *apparent* changes in river morphology when comparing different types of archival plan data; river stage at the time of survey is especially relevant to braided channels. These authors suggest that the selection of braid channels involves thresholds, in that during floods switches in flow direction occur (sometimes to dry channels which are nevertheless at a lower elevation than the pre-flood route). Channel change in coarse deposits is very likely to be influenced by major flood events during which, instead of the local-scale reworking of sediment so often reported, substantial movements occur. However, the influence of a very large event is not always to establish a new and long-lasting channel pattern; Anderson and Calver (1977, 1980) who have studied the recovery of Exmoor streams after the Lynmouth flood of 1952 suggest that valley floor width and sediment availability will be crucial to the effectiveness of a major flood.

Perhaps the simplest way to keep a record of channel change in small upland channels is by repeated photography using marked features, such as trees, as a camera position, or by taking the 'before' photograph into the field when taking the 'after' shot. Photography during the recovery period from floods which cross the threshold of change is equally important to that done immediately after the event (Newson 1980a). This has already shown, for example, how depositional forms stabilised by key boulders, vegetation, or by other obstructions can become unstable after quite small events (Fig. 3.15).

Desolate hills? Applications of research in upland catchments

It was suggested above that it was the urbanisation of the lowlands during the Industrial Revolution which forced the rapid development of Britain's upland water resources. The Victorian ethic of public health made great play of the purity of water from the desolate hills, supplied through an enclosed pipeline from a castellated masonry dam, the whole reservoir ringed by impressive wrought iron to keep out sheep and the few visitors.

There has been a revolution in our attitude to the use of reservoirs for recreation and conservation since the Second World War (Douglas & Crabb 1972) but an even greater one is foreseen in relation to the use of land in reservoir catchment areas. Development may well test the sensitive hydrological and geomorphological regime of the uplands referred to at several points in this chapter. Since the First World War it has been the British Government's aim to make the country more self-sufficient in timber by utilising large areas of the uplands for subsidised coniferous afforestation. However, upland agriculture is not static; following the Second World War farming, too, became government-subsidised in the uplands.

Upland livestock production has proved successful and techniques are improving in the development of hill pastures; these techniques include quite heavy applications of fertiliser (Munro, Davies & Thomas 1973). Also an increase in personal mobility has put tourist and recreational pressure on even the most remote upland areas.

To consider the likely impact of afforestation, the catchment study results gathered by the Institute of Hydrology at Plynlimon (see Table 3.3 and Fig. 3.16a) have been extrapolated, using process studies of rainfall interception, to the important reservoir catchment areas of Britain (Calder & Newson 1979 and Fig. 3.16b). The obviously serious water resource implications of a doubling of the present forest area are now being assimilated by the water and timber industries alike (see Centre for Agricultural Strategy 1980). Clearly there is conservation of mass in the hydrological cycle and the extra evaporation from a forested catchment will fall as rain elsewhere. However, this extra input has yet to be detected, whereas any loss to a reservoir upsets its design calculations and operating rules, especially in the case of smaller reservoirs where refilling during autumn and winter following a single drought summer is critical: this would be the period most

(a)

(b)

Figure 3.15 Sequential photography and small-scale change: (a) showing the incorporation of freshly-deposited cobbles (left) by vegetation only a year after (right) a major flood; (b) showing approximately 5 m^3 of gravel dammed behind fallen trees during a flood (left), released by rotting of the vegetation only 6 months later (right).

influenced by interception. The importance of the interception process means that it is only the upland catchment with its typically long duration, low-intensity rainfall which will be significantly affected by afforestation; in the lowlands transpirational losses dominate.

Reductions of flow in any upland stream are likely to promote subtle changes in, for instance, fish life and in the dilution of pollutants, even within the upland

Figure 3.16 Artificial influences on upland hydrology, afforestation and water yield. (a) Catchment losses from the Plynlimon experiment. The Severn is afforested; the Wye, rough pasture. (b) Predictions of the percentage increase in loss from major reservoirs catchments after afforestation, based on a simple interception model. The assumed forest cover is 50% canopy cover, 75% land area cover.

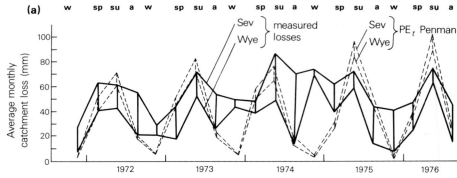

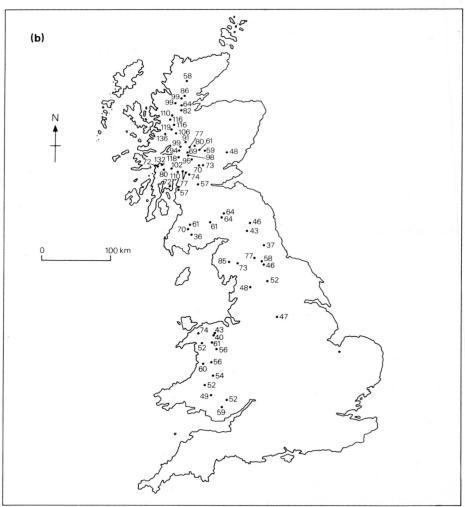

Table 3.3 Annual values of *P*, *Q* and *P−Q*: Wye and forested area of the Severn catchment only, years 1970–77 (units: mm).

| | P: precipitation | | Q: streamflow | | P−Q: losses | | Difference in losses |
	Wye	Severn	Wye	Severn	Wye	Severn	(Severn−Wye)
1970	2869	2485	2415	1636	454	849	+395
1971	1993	1762	1562	797	431	965	+534
1972	2131	2124	1804	1342	328	782	+454
1973	2606	2380	2164	1581	442	799	+357
1974	2794	2703	2320	1785	474	918	+444
1975	2099	2035	2643	1213	456	822	+366
1976	1736	1645	1404	921	332	724	+392
1977	2561	2573	2236	1638	325	935	+610
1978[a]	2356	2367	2128	1668	228	699	+471
Mean	2349	2230	1964	1398	385	832	+447

[a] Significant snow recorded.

boundary (for instance where rainfall is polluted from industrial sources outside the uplands). If one adds to this the increased flashiness of runoff after forest drainage, the increased yield of gravel bedload, and reduced summer water temperatures it is not surprising that the popular impression is of significant reductions in fish numbers within extensively afforested areas. Provisional surveys at Plynlimon indicate a far more numerous, healthy population of Brown Trout *Salmo trutta* in the grassland Wye than in the forested Severn; electro-fishing at seven stations in the Wye resulted in a catch of 95 fish, while at nine stations in the Severn only seven fish were caught (Crisp, Cubby & Robson 1980).

Both forests and improved pastures require fertiliser applications. Harriman (1978) has reported increased nutrient runoff from forestry but concludes that in Scotland the effect is not long-lasting or a serious threat to water quality except in small lochs and reservoirs. There is perhaps more concern about nitrate runoff from improved grassland; a lysimeter study at Plynlimon has, however, demonstrated a similar recovery (following a pulse of nitrate runoff) to enhanced equilibrium levels (far below the limits for human potability).

The likely effect of land-use change on floods and droughts in upland areas is likely to be less than on average flows, with the exception of the local impact of cultivation and drainage on floods of moderate return period. The scale of land-use change and land management practices is at present insufficient to cause alarm. However, there is strategic value in deriving methods of extrapolating the small catchment studies (referred to above) to take account of future developments. Progress towards a flood hydrograph model which can be applied from maps, or a brief field reconnaissance using simple techniques is, however, bound to be slow during an era in which empirical techniques appear to be satisfactory. A case in point is in the regulation of the river Dee in North Wales, where an empirical method (Lowing, Price & Harvey 1975) has been preferred to a hydrological model based on detailed soil survey (Rudeforth & Thomasson 1970).

Is the prospect any better for the direct application of upland geomorphology? Already the piedmont zone of river regulation is receiving attention as has been described. Here, however, much of the interest in altered sediment dynamics concerns the river as a habitat for fish, rather than as a geomorphological system for its own sake and there are signs that both legislation and water resources practice react favourably towards river fisheries. The engineering response to geomorphological activity tends to be piecemeal and structural. Although it may be fairly claimed that there is insufficient information upon which to base a whole-river structural approach (via regime) it would be better, in most cases, to refrain from structural intervention in the meantime. The point is particularly relevant to channel maintenance in the piedmont zone. The most likely opportunities for the future in applying our, albeit scanty, knowledge of upland hydrology and geomorphology lie, therefore, in developments in land-use which are extensive enough to raise interest in *non-structural* solutions to environmental problems.

Conclusions

At various points in this chapter it has been concluded from published results that the natural environment in the uplands is changing; while subtle climatic or even endogenetic changes may be the cause, the most popular explanation is the influence of man. Upland development from Neolithic and Norse deforestation to the afforestation plans of modern governments, sheep grazing, river regulation, and fertiliser applications: all have been suggested as the cause of changes in the rates of runoff, gullying, sediment yields, channel migration and fish breeding. Indicative of the change in our perception of environmental change is the title chosen for the book by Gregory and Walling (1979), *Man* and environmental process; it follows but six years after their, *Drainage basin form* and process.

Despite a general word of protest in this chapter at the lack of attention paid by researchers to the mountains and uplands of Britain, it has amassed quite a reference list! Does this mean that future development of mountain streams by man will occur against a well-documented base-line of 'natural' process studies? Unfortunately, whilst the individual studies of aspects of hydrology and geomorphology are of excellent quality there is a marked tendency for them to be too detailed, too local in scale and too unco-ordinated to make them of direct applied value. Attempts to bring together the quantitative results of the work already completed on erosion in an attempt to confirm or refute this impression is dogged by the variety of units of measurement and technique; cursory inspection does, however, reveal that *for areas identified as sediment sources* in the British uplands, rates of erosion are high. What has yet to be done effectively is to identify and calibrate the sediment sinks (into storage) which result in those few published figures for the contribution of sediment from British rivers to their estuaries being low in the world rankings.

Despite their extensive area, the British uplands are regarded as marginal for economic activity and suitable for only low-output enterprise such as forestry or livestock farming. As a result, research on upland hydrology and geomorphology is only occasionally patronised by resource agencies; elsewhere it falls strictly under the heading of strategic research but this tends to be of short duration and intensive. There are many practical problems with longer-term instrumentation and management: those who work on the rain-swept acres of Plynlimon or Moor House know this only too well! (It is also a matter for concern that neither of these two research centres is in Scotland and that the future of Moor House is very uncertain.)

Although this chapter has attempted to identify the need for further field

research in hydrology (extrapolation of models, channel flow processes) and
geomorphology (long-term stream load/morphological monitoring, flood studies, slope studies), the uplands are worthy of a wider and more integrated ecological approach. The importance of the uplands as wilderness means that it may be of more benefit to put forward the study of mountain streams as part of strategic work involving ecologists and freshwater biologists as well as hydrologists and geomorphologists. The Institute of Terrestrial Ecology has already set about reconciling different scales of approach and different disciplines of enquiry in its land-use survey of upland England and Wales (Countryside Commission 1978); however, the report finds presaging the future of upland development extremely hard, especially in the light of possibly far-reaching changes in the availability of energy and finance by the year 2000.

Perhaps, however, climate will have the last word since, as Parry (1978) has identified, man's hold on the uplands and mountains of Britain and Scandinavia is tenuous; the margin has moved extensively during the last 500 years, suggesting that the socio-economic system is as sensitive as the ecological one with which it interacts or interferes. Since energy availability may be crucial to future movements of the margin it is ironic that the latest developments in mid-Wales are diametrically opposed: Ashby (1979) suggests 163 tributaries of the River Dovey as suitable for hydropower generation on a small scale, developing 33 megawatts, while in the same area farmers are obstructing the efforts of geologists seeking safe dumping grounds for the waste from nuclear power plants! Both groups have expressed keen interest in the mountain stream.

4 Channel form and channel changes

R. I. Ferguson

Introduction

British rivers vary considerably in character. There is no whitewater canoeing or salmon fishing in East Anglia, and no punting or rowing in the Scottish Highlands. Much of this diversity of character stems from differences in streamflow and its erosional and depositional effects, as already discussed in Chapters 1 and 2, but the most immediately obvious characteristics of any river are the size, three-dimensional shape, and valley setting of its channel. No British river is as wide as the Rhine let alone the Mississippi; none shifts its course as actively as the monsoon-swollen Brahmaputra of Bangladesh or the icemelt-fed outwash rivers of New Zealand's South Island; none is as spectacularly hemmed in by rock walls as many rivers in the European Alps and other young mountain ranges. But although small, stable, and unspectacular by world standards the channels of British rivers display considerable diversity in size, shape, setting, and activity and this diversity is of importance in understanding the natural environment and managing it for man's use.

A conceptual framework is necessary if river channels are to be discussed systematically. That adopted here is to isolate significant characteristics of channel form and relate them to environmental conditions, especially hydrology. Rather than attempt to describe directly the three-dimensional subtleties of channel form we can concentrate like an architect or draughtsman on three separate two-dimensional views in turn: river longitudinal profile and slope, as seen from the side if the landscape were sectioned; channel cross-section shape and size; and channel pattern as seen from the air. A coherent picture of the functional inter-relationships of channel profile, section and plan can then be sketched by noting how each is affected by the others and by external factors.

As well as describing the characteristics of British rivers in relation to their geographical location this chapter attempts to demonstrate the extent to which channel form can be explained in terms of environmental controls. Specifically, channels are viewed as the outcome of a continuous struggle between the erosive potential of the river and the resistive forces of the valley-floor setting, and useful generalisations are sought about interrelationships between form, flow and floor.

Rivers exist to carry water to the sea and they develop channels able to contain their normal flow. The form of the river channel affects the flow of water in it and, through erosion and deposition, the flow modifies the form. The channel (and if it migrates, the whole valley floor) acts as a jerky conveyor belt for alluvium moving intermittently seawards. In this way the hydrological and geological cycles are meshed together, and it is inevitable that the form of the interface represents some kind of balance between water power and geological resistance. Under stable climatic conditions, geomorphologists and engineers have reasoned, river channel geometry must be in regime or equilibrium with prevailing streamflow characteristics and local valley-floor slope and sediment type, not forgetting also such complications as bank vegetation and valley constrictions. Some of these controls vary downstream with catchment area, some depend on geographical location, others appear random. Statistical analysis of river properties shows that correlations do exist between channel characteristics and these inferred controls, at both reach and catchment scales, and some relationships have been confirmed by controlled experiments with miniature rivers.

This chapter seeks to place the channel geometry of British rivers in this generalised theoretical perspective. Three complications must nevertheless be recognised at the outset. First, streamflow outside the laboratory is never constant for long so if rivers are in any kind of equilibrium it must be a dynamic rather than static one, with channel processes and forms perpetually adjusting and readjusting to fluctuating imposed conditions.

Second, rivers suffer from historical hangovers. The equilibrium channel geometry established from scratch in particular environmental conditions might not be attainable by a river whose channel slope and materials had already been modified to suit a vanished climate. It is increasingly clear that many British rivers have transformed themselves in the 10–15 000 years since the last glaciation; some may well retain features inherited from this time which, although stable in present conditions, have not and would not have evolved under them. Persistent passive disequilibrium of this kind may be widespread in the channel patterns of British rivers.

The third complicating factor is man. We have already seen that dam construction, mine waste disposal, urban growth, and many other economic activities disturb the natural equilibrium of any river whose catchment is affected and this may lead to channel changes, possibly drastic ones.

Channel long profile and gradient

The longitudinal profile of a river is the graph of height against distance downstream along the main course. As water flows downhill the profile drops continuously except where lakes have built up behind reverse gradients. Since rivers occupy the lowest parts of basically saucer-shaped water catchments their long profiles tend to be concave upwards and channels thus tend to have progressively gentler gradients from the headwater areas near the divide to the lowlands near the river mouth. However, the degree of concavity varies and abnormal long-profiles with major convexities can and do occur. Average slopes also vary greatly, and this has consequences for stream power which is an important control over channel behaviour and pattern.

Long profiles can also be examined at much finer scale. Many British rivers possess a closely spaced alternation of relatively deep and shallow reaches – the 'pools' and 'riffles' of fishermen and fluvial geomorphologists – whose effects on channel processes have an important bearing on both channel shape and channel pattern.

Long profiles

Until recent years, long profile studies by British geomorphologists, and of British rivers, focused entirely on compound profiles (with several concave reaches separated by convex steps) and their supposed genetic significance in deciphering long-term landscape history. Some geographers and geologists in the early part of this century went to the lengths of fitting mathematical equations, by hand, to river profiles and terrace fragments with a view to estimating former sea levels by down-valley extrapolation of the fitted curves (e.g. Jones 1924).

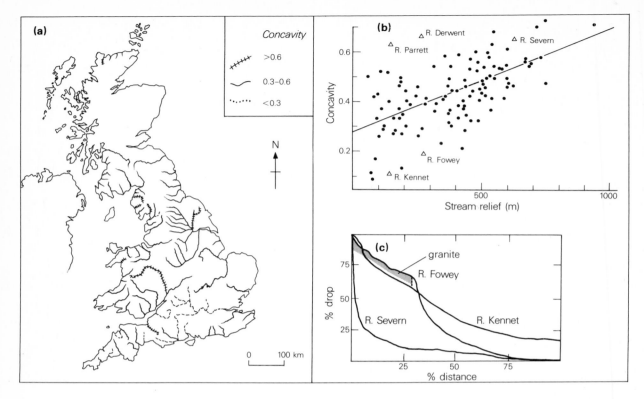

Figure 4.1 River long profiles: degree of concavity, its relationship to relief, and examples of under- and over-concavity (after Wheeler 1979a, b).

That such attempts did not become popular owed more to anti-quantitative feeling than to any thorough demonstration that the method is unreliable. Only recently has the variability of long profile form in Britain been demonstrated by a comprehensive empirical investigation (Wheeler 1979a, b). Wheeler's analysis of 115 British rivers took two parts, statistical comparison of the goodness of fit of long profile curves proposed by different workers and statistical analysis of profile concavity. The curve-fitting exercise showed not surprisingly that equations with a greater number of adjustable parameters fitted better on the whole, but otherwise did not reveal any clear 'best' curve.

The alternative approach utilised a concavity index based on the maximum departure below a constant gradient of the % drop – % distance profile. Concavity was found to vary from less than 0.1 to over 0.7, almost the full possible range, with some fairly clear geographical patterns (Fig. 4.1a). In general, rivers in the more mountainous northern and western parts of Britain have more concave profiles. There is a strong positive correlation between concavity and total drop (Fig. 4.1b), which Wheeler explains by an extension of Gilbert's argument that increased discharge allows reduced slope. Since rainfall in Britain is heavier on higher ground, it is here that rivers experience the greatest rate of downstream increase in discharge and thus the most rapid reduction in slope, giving highly concave profiles. A further factor may be the tendency for larger drainage networks to be more elongated (Shreve 1974), again leading to reduced increments of discharge per extra kilometre along the river.

The scatter about this tendency is considerable but plausible explanations can be found for most of the apparently anomalous rivers. 'Over-concave' rivers that plot well above the trend in Figure 4.1b have had their courses lengthened mainly in late Quaternary times. Examples include the Parrett in Somerset which now

92

extends over Holocene marine sediments, the Yorkshire Derwent whose path to the North Sea was blocked by moraines and replaced by a much longer inland route, and the Severn (Fig. 4.1c) which has been diverted southwards through the Ironbridge meltwater gorge. In each case nearly all the river's drop is concentrated in less than half its length, giving a highly concave profile.

Under-concavity in British rivers is of two main kinds. Some rivers have compound long profiles with major convex knickpoints separating individually concave profile segments. Often the convexity is associated with a lithological boundary, a good example being the River Fowey in Cornwall (Fig. 4.1c) which steepens considerably on leaving the granite batholith of Bodmin Moor. Hard-rock knickpoints also occur on some larger rivers, for example at Aysgarth Falls on the Ure and Bonnington Linn on the lower Clyde, but with less effect on the concavity index since this is defined as a fraction of total drop along the river.

The second type of under-concave river has a low gradient almost from its headwaters and consequently a rather straight profile. The Kennet in Berkshire (Fig. 4.1c) is but one of several under-concave rivers in the chalklands of southern England. Again the explanation may lie in the downstream rate of increase in discharge, abnormally low in these spring-fed rivers.

Channel gradient

River long-profiles with the same degree of concavity may have very different overall gradients. A general impression of the regional distribution of river slope in Britain is given by the map of Figure 3.2b above, compiled by the Institute of Hydrology as part of its floods study (NERC 1975a). This map is based on mean gradients between points 10% and 85% along individual rivers (hence the abbreviation S1085), and shows clearly the obvious tendency for rivers rising in the more mountainous north and west to have steeper profiles, but it is generalised on the basis of what is only a weak correlation between channel slope and catchment rainfall and it conceals quite substantial local variations in gradient. This is apparent from Figure 4.2 which maps S1085 for individual rivers. There are tenfold differences in the average gradient of neighbouring long profiles in such areas as South Wales (compare the Rivers Usk, Taff and Tawe) and Strathclyde.

Differences in slope exist first of all because rivers are not all of the same size. The concavity of the typical long-profile means that average gradient, as well as local channel slope, decreases with the length of river considered. Geological and hydrological differences between river basins ought also to influence stream gradients. Geomorphologists, geologists and engineers have long assumed that river slope is delicately graded to the value necessary for the available discharge to transport the sediment load supplied from upstream. If the slope is insufficient aggradation will raise it, if too great incision will lower it. This is not the whole story, for an imbalance in sediment throughput can be rectified by adjustments to channel shape and pattern without alteration to valley slope; and valley slopes in Britain owe much to Pleistocene glaciation and proglacial alluviation. But even if the functional linkages between slope, discharge, and sediment supply are not quite as clear-cut as traditionally assumed, the statistical interrelationships of these variables are of considerable practical and theoretical interest.

The pioneering statistical study of stream gradients was Hack's (1957) analysis of long profiles in the Appalachian states of the US. Hack measured channel gradient S and median bed material size d for a total of 62 reaches on 15 small streams, and used catchment area A as a measure of discharge. Simple correlations

93

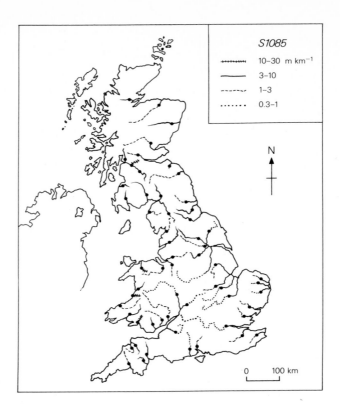

Figure 4.2 Average mainstream gradient of major British rivers. Gradient varies both between and within regions.

Figure 4.3 Relationship of stream slope to median bed material size and catchment area in South-East England (after Penning-Rowsell & Townshend 1978).

between logarithms of S and d, and S and A, were respectively positive and negative as expected but both were weak. The multivariate relationship $S = 6(d/A)^{0.6}$ (with S in m km^{-1}, d in mm, A in km^2) gave a much better fit. Stream gradient therefore depends not on grain size alone or discharge alone but on the balance between them; and streams of given size on different types of rock may differ in slope according to the coarseness of *in situ* weathered material in the stream bed or the rate of attrition of transported material. Thus Hack found long profiles of similar-sized streams tended to be progressively steeper on limestone, shale, sandstone, and igneous rock.

No countrywide test of this interrelationship has yet been attempted for British

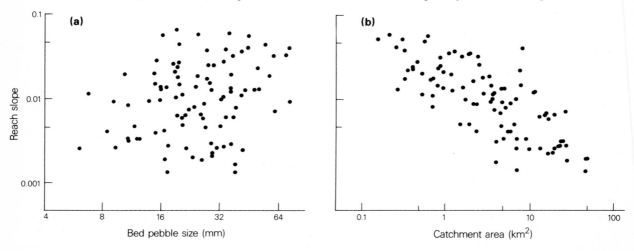

rivers but two local investigations support Hack's conclusions. Wilcock (1967) found an insignificant correlation between gradient and bed material size for 21 reaches of the River Hodder in the Bowland hills near the Lancashire/Yorkshire boundary, but a strong one between gradient and d/A, with the same 0.6 exponent that Hack had found. Slopes along the Hodder were also found to correlate well with the median size of residual bed material, i.e. that too coarse to be moved by present-day bankfull flows. This suggests the river is graded to conditions that are probably a legacy of the Pleistocene, and that Hack's equation here describes adjustment of active bedload to an imposed slope, not vice versa.

More recently Penning-Rowsell and Townshend (1978) have described a correlation study of stream slopes in South-East England, beyond the limit of Pleistocene glaciation. Slope and median pebble size were measured in 96 reaches on three different geological formations dominated lithologically by clay, sandstone and mudstone. Reach slopes estimated from contour maps were predicted very poorly by sediment size but more accurately by catchment area as a surrogate for discharge (Fig. 4.3). Multiple correlation using both variables gave a further improvement in predictive ability, though regrettably Penning-Rowsell and Townshend do not quote regression coefficients that would enable the relationship to be compared with those found by Hack and Wilcock.

Stream power

An important but neglected river property which is highly dependent on gradient is the rate of energy supply at the channel bed for overcoming friction and transporting sediment. A river of discharge $Q \, m^3 \, s^{-1}$ flowing down a slope S loses potential energy at the rate $\Omega = \rho g Q S \, W \, m^{-1}$ (watts per metre) where $\rho = 1000 \, kg \, m^{-3}$ and $g = 9.8 \, m \, s^{-2}$. This gross stream power corresponds to a specific power, or energy availability per unit area of bed, of $\omega = \Omega/W = \tau V \, W \, m^{-2}$ where W is width, V mean velocity, and τ the mean bed shear stress.

The specific power ω appears to determine bedform type given sediment size (Simons *et al.* 1965) and bedload transport rate given relative roughness (Bagnold 1977); and aspects of channel morphology have been explained in terms of the availability of gross or specific power (Bull 1979, Ferguson & Richards 1981) or the minimisation of gross or unit power (Chang 1979, Yang 1971).

Maps of stream power at bankfull discharge in reaches of various British rivers show a striking range of values (Fig. 4.4). To the extent that slope decreases as discharge rises gross power should be a conservative quantity, yet it has a thousand-fold range (Fig. 4.4a). Since high runoff and steep slopes go together in Britain the geographical pattern shows the familiar division discussed in Chapter 3 between lowlands to south and east and highlands to north and west, though with a tendency for larger rivers in any area to be more powerful. Dividing by channel width to give specific power (Fig. 4.4b) almost eliminates this scale effect – as many rivers show a downstream decrease in power as an increase – but there is still a huge lowland–highland range, exemplified by the difference between the Cam and the Spey. The significance for channel pattern of energy availability is discussed later.

Pools and riffles

Although the typical river long profile is smoothly concave it is often found that the channel bed is undulating with relatively deep pools at intervals of 3–10 **95**

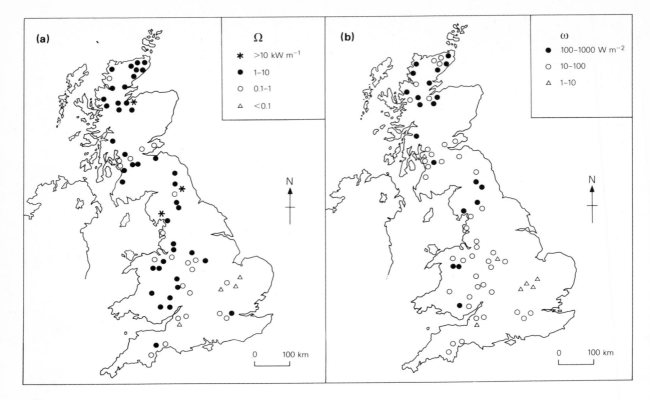

Figure 4.4 Stream power at bankfull discharge in some British rivers (data from Nixon 1959, Charlton *et al.* 1978, Riddell 1980). The pattern of power per unit channel length (Ω) and per unit channel area (ω) is broadly similar.

channel widths. The pools are separated by topographic highs extending partly or completely across the channel, obliquely or transversely, with steep downstream faces over which the river spills in a turbulent 'riffle'. At low discharges the contrast between still deep pools and shallow fast-flowing riffles is an obvious feature of many British rivers, especially those whose bed material has a median size in the gravel or cobble range (2–256 mm). The contrast between pools and riffles provides varied ecological niches for aquatic life and is well known to fishermen, canoeists, and all others who paddle in rivers for duty or pleasure.

Deep pools are especially associated with meander bends, where they form by scour beneath the concave bank at and past the apex of the bend. In actively meandering rivers, therefore, there is usually a pool at each bend and an intervening riffle where the current spills across the diagonal continuation of one point bar into the next on the opposite side of the channel (Fig. 4.5). The pool to pool or riffle to riffle spacing is thus half the meander wavelength. In straight or gradually curving reaches pools are not specifically related to bends. Riffles may then be central features around which flow divides, they may be attached to alternate banks as incipient point bars, or several in a row may be on the same side of the channel around the inside of a gradual bend.

Some of these variations on the pool and riffle theme are illustrated from pebbly upland streams in Figure 4.6. The Kingledoors Burn in the Scottish Borders is a small sinuous stream partially confined by valley bluffs. The downstream part of the reach mapped in Figure 4.6a is actively meandering with pools on the outside of the two eroding bends and diagonal riffles joining successive point bars. The upper part of the same reach is less regular with three pools and two riffles round the outside of a gradual bend, a major riffle where a terrace bluff is undercut, two more pools around the next bend and another in the straight reach leading to the

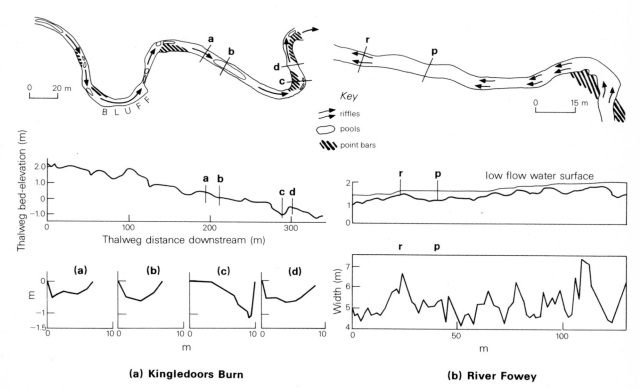

Figure 4.5 Pools, riffles and point bars in an actively meandering pebbly stream: the Kingledoors Burn in the Scottish Borders. Flow is from right to left.

Key

➤➤ riffles
⬭ pools
▨ point bars

(a) Kingledoors Burn

(b) River Fowey

Figure 4.6 Pool–riffle morphology in upland streams: the partly meandering Kingledoors Burn and the mainly inactive River Fowey in Cornwall (after Milne 1980, Richards 1976a). The Kingledoors reach includes the bends of Figure 4.5. Associations between plan, profile and cross-section form are discussed in text.

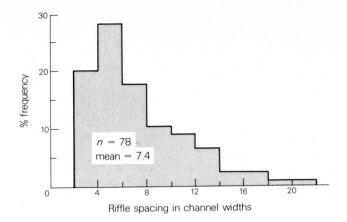

Figure 4.7 Pool–riffle spacing
in relation to channel width in
upland streams in the northern
Pennines and Scottish Borders
(after Milne 1980).

active S-bend. The long-profile shows that the amplitude of bed undulation is greatest in the most sharply curved parts of the channel, and the cross-sections demonstrate the tendency for pools and riffles to be fairly symmetric in straight reaches but not in meandering ones.

The River Fowey in Cornwall is a straighter stream with tree-lined banks. At bends pools tend to be offset and riffles are diagonal, as at the top of the reach shown in Figure 4.6b, but the straighter reach just downstream is more typical with its central riffles, sometimes compound, around which flow diverges causing bank erosion and channel widening (Richards 1976a).

Despite these differences in location within the channel pattern the mean spacing of riffles (and pools) tends to be fairly constant when expressed as a multiple of mean channel width. It is approximately four widths in the Kingledoors meander, five in the rest of the Kingledoors reach (Fig. 4.6a), and between three and seven in the Fowey (Fig. 4.6b) according to how many separate riffles are distinguished. Pools and riffles studied by Milne (1980) in 11 upland streams in the northern Pennines and Scottish Borders had a modal spacing of 4–6 bankfull channel widths (Fig. 4.7) which agrees with that found for US streams by Leopold, Wolman and Miller (1964, p. 203) and Keller and Melhorn (1978). In a study of three small meandering streams of quite different character in southern England, Harvey (1975) found a virtually linear relationship between riffle spacing and channel width with spacing again approximately five times width.

Explanations for this characteristic scale of bed undulation in pebbly channels

Figure 4.8 Relationship of
mean depth and velocity to
discharge (90% to 60%
duration) in a pool and riffle of
the River Fowey, at the lower
end of the reach of Figure 4.6
(after Richards 1977).

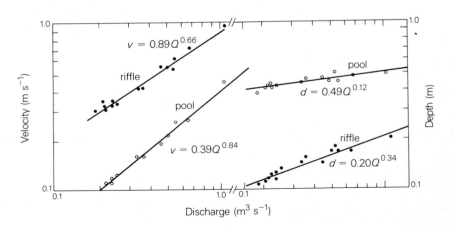

are rather speculative as is clear from the review by Richards (1976b), but once a pool–riffle sequence has been established its maintenance appears to be assured by the effects of bed undulations on flow in the channel. At low discharges each riffle acts as a broad-crested weir ponding up water in the pool immediately upstream, as illustrated by the low-flow water surface profile in Figure 4.6b above. Water depths in pools are consequently much greater than in riffles but velocities much lower; coarse bedload cannot move through pools and may even be partially buried by sand deposition. With rising discharge the water surface profile flattens over riffles but steepens over pools, where rapidly increased shear stress leads to bed scour and entrainment of pebbles from the riffle face through the pool to the head of the next riffle.

The mechanism of high-flow sediment transport through pools and low-flow storage on riffles has been confirmed by measurements by Richards (1976b) in the River Fowey and Ashmore (1977) in Kingledoors Burn. Figure 4.8 shows how as discharge rises hydraulic conditions in pools and riffles tend to converge with extrapolated bankfull velocities in pools almost as high as in riffles (Richards 1976b) and shear stresses slightly higher (Ashmore 1977). Floods may therefore scour out pools, but sedimentation will occur on the falling stage and it is commonly found that surface sediment is finer in pools than riffles.

Channel size

River channels vary greatly in cross-section shape but are mostly bounded on one or both sides by a fairly well defined bank separating channel from floodplain or valley side. The bankfull dimensions of a channel together with a depth–velocity relationship such as the Manning equation determine the discharge it can convey. Channel dimensions are not arbitrary but appear to be adjusted by erosion and deposition so that the channel can contain all but the highest flows it experiences; the typical river overtops its banks at most a few times a year, and maybe only once every few years.

Estimated return periods of bankfull discharge in British rivers range from 4 months to 5 years in Scotland (Riddell, pers. comm.) and 1.3 to 14 years in Lowland England (Harvey 1969); the duration of overbank flooding in England and Wales is from 1 day in 3 years to 11 days a year (Nixon 1959) with a mean of 2 days a year. Variability in the frequency of bankfull discharge can be rationalised in terms of hydrological regime (Harvey 1969). A flashy river may cut and fill its bed and banks several times a year and thus adjust its capacity to a flow that occurs relatively frequently, whereas a baseflow river may erode only in rare floods and preserve its enlarged form over intervening years or decades, unless aquatic vegetation induces rapid sedimentation.

Relationships between channel dimensions and streamflow volume have been analysed in several rather different ways. In the late 19th and early 20th centuries, design rules for irrigation canals in India and elsewhere were established by what came to be known as regime analysis: the fitting of fractional power laws between bankfull dimensions and design discharges of canals that were stable or 'in regime'. The size of natural river channels was first investigated thoroughly by the US Geological Survey (Leopold & Maddock 1953) under the title of downstream hydraulic geometry, which involved fitting power–law relationships between wetted channel dimensions at different sites and either mean streamflow or gauged flows of a chosen frequency. These two methods were combined by Nixon **99**

(1959) who fitted fractional-power relationships between the bankfull dimensions and discharges of some British rivers. More recently, one school of British geomorphologists has used catchment area as a surrogate for discharge in power laws for bankfull channel dimensions in a truly downstream approach.

Any of these approaches yields powerful quantitative generalisations about more than just the width and depth of the channels studied. To the extent that good fits are found, relationships can be extrapolated to other rivers or used to interpolate along a single river. Differential increases in width and depth with increasing discharge or catchment area define a trend in the width/depth ratio and thus in channel shape as well as size. Increases in width and depth together define the rate of increase in cross-section area, and if expressed as functions of discharge they also define the downstream trend in velocity since discharge is the product of velocity and area. Systematic discussion of channel dimensions thus poses and to some extent answers questions about channel shape, velocity, and adjustment to hydrologic regime as well as size alone.

Regime analysis

'Downstream' hydraulic geometry as originally conceived described the variation between sections on the same or different rivers in wetted width, depth and velocity at a specified flow frequency. This is of value in flood routing and pollution studies (see, for example, Stout 1979) but is not especially informative about bankfull channel dimensions. Low to medium discharges are contained well within most channels and prediction of bankfull width, depth and velocity from low-flow values requires a knowledge of the rate of increase of each variable with discharge at the particular cross-section: the 'at a point' hydraulic geometry of Leopold and Maddock (1953). This is not without scatter at a site, and very variable between sites because of differences in cross-section shape and local hydraulic conditions, so it is treated in this chapter as a consequence of channel morphology rather than a means by which to understand or predict it. Attention is concentrated instead on investigations in which bankfull channel dimensions are measured directly and related to bankfull discharge in what may be termed the regime analysis approach.

A preliminary difficulty with regime analysis is that bankfull dimensions and discharge are not always easy to define even for a river with steep banks. Opposite banktops may be at different levels and each may fluctuate in height along the river. Sandy or gravelly banks, especially meander point bars, are seldom steep and may not have well defined tops. Different objective definitions of the bankfull stage exist (see Richards 1977, Williams 1978 for reviews) but commonly it is taken as that at which the width:depth ratio is least, which typically means the top of the steepest part of the steeper bank. Vegetation limits may provide additional guidance, or a generalised banktop surface may be defined by instrumental levelling along both banks.

Estimation of bankfull discharge is problematic because, being infrequent, it is unlikely to be observed except at a permanent gauging station. Here it will be obvious as the inflexion point on the stage–discharge rating curve, and nearby sections can usually be levelled in to the gauge site; but in ungauged rivers or reaches bankfull discharge can only be estimated by indirect means such as the Manning equation.

These problems of estimating bankfull stage and discharge are one obvious source of scatter in regime relationships. The other is the varying nature of bed and bank materials and vegetation which might be expected to influence channel erodibility and thus channel dimensions.

Nixon (1959) was the first to analyse bankfull dimensions and discharges of British rivers. Dimensions of 27 channels in England and Wales with flow capacities ranging from under 10 to over 500 m³ s⁻¹ were well represented by fractional-power relationships of classic canal regime form: in SI units,

$$W = 2.99 \, Q^{1/2}$$
$$D = 0.55 \, Q^{1/3}$$
$$V = 0.61 \, Q^{1/6}$$

where W is banktop width, D mean depth and V mean velocity. Least-squares regressions fitted to Nixon's data (Fig. 4.9) have exponents 0.49, 0.27 and 0.24, the last of which is just significantly different at the 5% level from Nixon's fractional value. Nixon noted that the scatter is least about the width relationship, suggesting width is the most easily adjusted channel dimension, and cited in support examples of rapid width adjustment to engineering interference. The velocity relationship shows a slightly greater increase with discharge than was found for US rivers by Leopold and Maddock (1953), but as in that study Nixon's data do not show consistent downstream increases in all rivers.

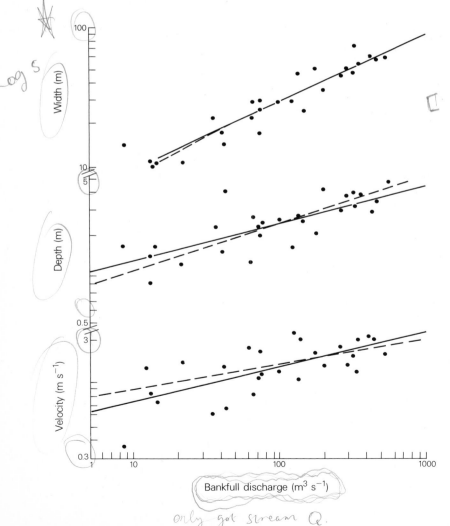

Figure 4.9 Variation of width, mean depth and mean velocity with bankfull discharge in English and Welsh rivers (data of Nixon 1959). Dashed lines are fractional-power regime equations, solid lines are least-squares regressions.

Rather surprisingly Nixon's pioneering work was not extended to other British rivers until recently. A study of gravel-bed rivers in England and Wales by the Hydraulics Research Station (Charlton, Brown & Benson 1978) confirmed that width is the most closely predictable channel dimension, with a best-fit relationship

$$W = 3.74\ Q^{0.45}$$

for 23 rivers with gauged bankfull discharges from 3 to 550 m³ s⁻¹. Depth–discharge and velocity–discharge relationships were not published but can be calculated from the listed data as

$$D = 0.31\ Q^{0.40}$$
$$V = 0.86\ Q^{0.15}$$

with correlations as good as the preferred design equations based on Shields' competence criterion and an empirically calibrated friction law.

J. Riddell (pers. comm.) has measured channel geometry at 17 Lowland and 17 Highland sites in Scotland with bankfull discharges between 2 and 350 m³ s⁻¹. The width relationships in the two samples are very similar with exponents 0.53 and 0.52, but the depth and velocity relationships show some divergence with

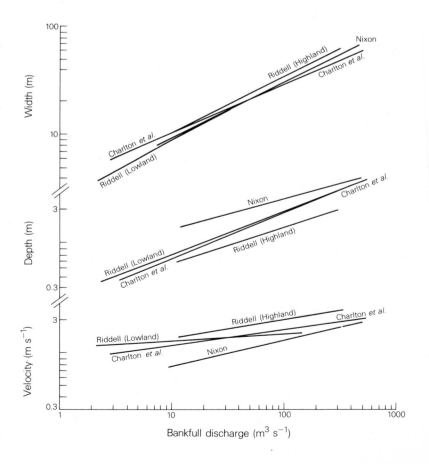

Figure 4.10 Regime relationships for rivers in England and Wales (data of Nixon 1959, Charlton *et al.* 1978) and Scotland (Riddell 1980). Lines are least-squares fits over the range of discharge indicated.

$D \propto Q^{0.32}$, $V \propto Q^{0.16}$ for the Highland streams but $D \propto Q^{0.40}$ and $V \propto Q^{0.07}$ for the
Lowland sample.

Comparison of the trends found in these different investigations (Fig. 4.10) shows width–discharge relationships are strikingly similar in different samples and environments. The depth–discharge relationships have similar slopes but an almost twofold range in intercept, and the same is true of velocity whose relationship to discharge is of course determined by the width and depth equations since $Q = WDV$. In general mean channel depth for a given discharge appears to be lower, and mean velocity higher, in upland rivers. This shallow swift character is to be expected because of the generally steeper slope of such rivers. There is no obvious way in which gradient should affect the width–discharge relationship and the appropriate partial correlation was insignificant in the Hydraulics Research Station work.

Confirmation that the general increase in width, depth and velocity with discharge between rivers also applies along many individual rivers comes from several studies of downstream hydraulic geometry for individual rivers using assorted flow frequencies, from the mean annual flood down to the median discharge. Regime exponents found by Wilcock (1971), Knighton (1974) and Richards (1976b, 1977) do not differ systematically from the bankfull ones just discussed but they are more variable: 0.33–0.61 for width, 0.16–0.55 for depth, and 0.02–0.30 for velocity. This variability is probably due to differences in at-a-station hydraulic geometry along and between rivers which are certainly to be expected and could also explain the tendency for the exponent of width to fall, and the exponents of depth and velocity to rise, with increasing flow frequency.

Differences in cross-section shape are also a major source of scatter about the bankfull relationships shown in Figure 4.10. Sections that are narrower and deeper than average for their discharge will evidently plot below the general trend of width and above that of depth. Channel width:depth ratio is a simple but effective index of shape and may vary for a variety of reasons. It is often regarded as a function of boundary sediment cohesion, following the work of Schumm (1960), but discharge too affects channel shape since the faster downstream rise of width than depth means W/D increases as about $Q^{1/6}$. Evidence from British rivers lends only limited support to Schumm's findings in the very different environment of the American Great Plains. Analysis of Nixon's (1959) data shows some tendency for rivers with cohesive banks to have low width:depth ratios for their size (Fig. 4.11a) and Richards (1979) has found a significant dependence on bed and bank mud percentage, albeit a weak one and not the same as Schumm's. Knighton (1974) concluded bank cohesion affects at-a-point more than downstream hydraulic geometry, through the angle of the banks; and Charlton, Brown and Benson (1978) found no significant correlation between width and any sediment variable. As they note, sediment properties in river banks show great vertical and lateral variations and a single average figure for a quantitative property is unlikely to mean very much. What did prove significant in their study was the protective effect of bank vegetation: channels with grassy banks averaged 30% wider, but tree-lined ones up to 30% narrower, than the overall width–discharge trend would suggest (Fig. 4.11b).

Bankfull width and depth also vary systematically with channel pattern. Divided sections tend to be wider than single ones and bends wider (at bankfull stage, not low flow) than straight reaches because of differences in channel shape that in turn relate to secondary flow as discussed later. Most studies of channel dimensions have avoided this source of scatter by restricting attention to straight reaches, or   **103**

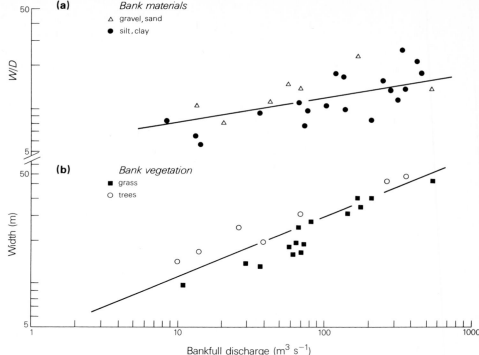

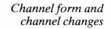

Figure 4.11 Effect on
bankfull channel form of bank
materials (from data of Nixon
1959) and bank vegetation
(after Charlton *et al.* 1978).
Lines are overall regime trends
for points shown.

to crossovers rather than bends in meandering rivers. In small streams the local variability in channel size can be very high. Milne (1980) in a study of 11 reaches of partially confined meandering streams found coefficients of variation of width and depth ranged as high as 32% and 84%. Some of this variation related to pool–riffle sequences, some to inputs of coarse sediment from terrace bluffs or silt from infilled channel traces. The pool–riffle sequence was also identified as a possible cause of width fluctuations in small streams by Hamlin and Thornes (1974), and Richards (1976a) found riffles in the River Fowey to be 15% wider on average than pools. Cursory inspection of air photographs suggests pattern-related fluctuations in the width of large British rivers may be of the same order.

Downstream analysis

Although the regime analysis of width, depth and velocity is known to geomorphologists and geologists as 'downstream' hydraulic geometry the sections compared do not necessarily form a true downstream sequence and may indeed belong to different river systems, as in all the bankfull studies just discussed.

For single catchments, studied in particular by K. J. Gregory and his associates, bankfull channel dimensions may be plotted against catchment area or a drainage network measure such as total channel length. In a humid environment any such variable is a surrogate for discharge so this approach has affinities with regime analysis while avoiding the problematic estimation of bankfull discharge. Figure 4.12 shows the downstream variation in bankfull width, depth and cross-section area or channel capacity along the River Dart in east Devon (Park 1975, 1976).

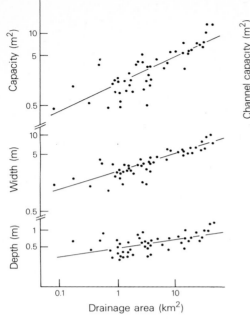

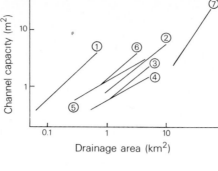

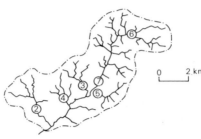

Figure 4.12 Downstream changes in channel dimensions in the River Dart, Devon (after Park 1975, 1976). Channel width, depth, and capacity generally increase downstream but there are differences between sub-catchments.

The 46 measured sections receive runoff from areas rising from about 0.1 to 40 km². Width increases as the 0.32 power of drainage area, depth as the 0.16 power, so that channel capacity increases as $A^{0.48}$. Channel dimensions at any point in the network can thus be predicted simply by estimating on a map the area draining to that point.

In the absence of velocity measurements at bankfull stage it is not possible to compare these downstream trends directly with regime-type relationships but the more rapid increase in width than depth is as expected. The lower exponents compared to a regime analysis can be explained by a downstream decrease in bankfull discharge per square kilometre, as seems reasonable for a river flowing from wet uplands to drier lowlands. Since this effect will vary from catchment to catchment it is not surprising that other downstream analyses show diverse results with the channel capacity exponent ranging from 0.33 to 1.02 in Devon alone (Park 1978).

Differences in bankfull discharge per unit area may also explain why the downstream tributaries and lower mainstream of the Dart plot lower in Figure 4.12 than do the headwaters. Such shifts seriously impair the value of catchment area as a predictor of channel dimensions but better results can be obtained using total channel length (Petts 1977), or indeed any other network property that is better than area as a predictor of flood discharge since it is mainly through this that catchment properties affect channel morphology.

The general conclusion from this discussion of channel dimensions must be that the dominant control is the volume of streamflow carried by the channel during floods which cause bank erosion and deposition. Properties of the banks, and flow non-uniformity associated with bedforms and channel pattern development, are secondary controls with locally more variable effects. In general width, depth, width:depth ratio, and mean velocity all increase with discharge and thus, in the absence of complications, downstream.

105

Channel pattern

After size the most obvious characteristic of a river channel is its planform or pattern. Verbal description of channel pattern can convey strong clues to cross-section shape and river processes, and an airphoto stereopair is undoubtedly the best indication of river character for many purposes (Kellerhals, Church & Bray 1976).

There are several classifications of channel pattern but most of them are ill-suited to British conditions. In particular the well known division into straight, meandering and braided channels (Leopold & Wolman 1957) is only satisfactory for reaches shorter than a few channel widths. Over longer stretches of valley floor these traditional descriptive terms are neither mutually exclusive nor exhaustive. Channel division or braiding may be superimposed in varying degree on straight or meandering patterns (Kellerhals, Church & Bray 1976) and straight and meandering channels are themselves end-members of what is really a continuum of patterns of differing sinuosity and irregularity (Schumm 1963a, Ferguson 1975). For example many British rivers have a zigzag pattern, sinuous but irregular, with long straight or gently curved reaches separated by occasional sharp bends.

An alternative approach to pattern classification focuses on features within the channel rather than the latter's blue-line pattern on a map. The USSR State Hydrological Institute (Popov 1964) distinguishes several 'channel processes' characterised by the type and arrangement of sand or gravel bars in the channel and the extent to which the channel is constrained by valley walls. As well as mid-channel bar (braided), freely meandering, and embedded (incised non-meandering) patterns Popov (1964) recognised limited (confined) meandering, the side bar (alternate riffle) process, and incomplete meandering (with chute cutoffs). The 'channel process' of a river is a good guide to its general level of activity and mobility, whereas classification by sinuosity can lump together actively braided with passively straight rivers, and active and inactive meanders.

An attempt is made here to classify British rivers in a very general way using both sinuosity and activity as criteria. Sub-groups and examples are discussed and different patterns are tentatively related to distinctive combinations of streamflow and valley environment.

First, a substantial minority of British rivers are actively meandering. The term is used to denote rivers that are perceptibly eroding the outsides of bends and depositing point bars at the insides, with no implication of especial sinuosity or regularity of pattern.

Second, a lesser number of rivers have actively changing channels in which erosional and depositional activity is not concentrated at bends and point bars are uncommon. These rivers are of low sinuosity, generally with braiding tendencies.

Finally, a large number of British rivers have channels that are not perceptibly migrating and do not contain many, if any, exposed point or braid bars at ordinary low flow. This group includes fairly regularly sinuous channels as well as irregular and straight ones.

Classic statistical and experimental work, mostly American, on river channel patterns suggests that different types of pattern occur in distinct combinations of environmental conditions. Leopold and Wolman (1957) noted a tendency for braiding to occur at greater bankfull discharges and/or channel slopes than meandering. Sand-tank experiments (notably those of Ackers & Charlton 1970 and Schumm & Khan 1972) have confirmed that initially straight channels meander only beyond a certain critical slope for given discharge and discharge for

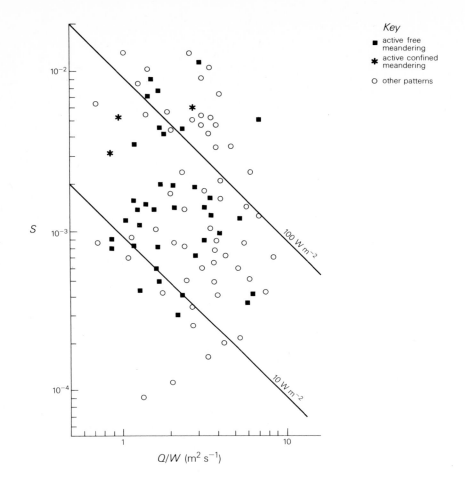

Figure 4.13 Channel slope and bankfull discharge per unit width of some British rivers (data of Nixon 1959, Charlton *et al.* 1978, Riddell 1980). Diagonals are lines of equal specific power in watts per square metre. Active meandering occurs over a wide range of power.

given slope, and braid only beyond a further threshold. Since discharge and slope are the two variable quantities in stream power these results imply a pattern sequence from straight to meandering to braided with increasing power. The other obvious control over channel pattern, channel materials or sediment supply, has been stressed by Schumm (1963a) who found that, in the semi-arid midwestern US, meandering was associated with cohesive sediments and washload, braiding with sandy channels and bedload transport.

In relating this conventional wisdom to British rivers we have to keep several points in mind. Schumm specifically excluded gravelly channels, which predominate in Britain; Leopold and Wolman's 'straight' patterns, again common in Britain, were widely scattered in their discharge-slope diagram; and most British rivers occupy much more densely vegetated valleys. Moreover, the Postglacial increase in vegetation cover coincided with a marked decline in discharge and sediment supply so that rivers must have become much less active. Adjustment to Postglacial environmental change may well not have created the same channel patterns as would have developed from scratch in modern conditions as in a laboratory experiment. Finally, many lowland rivers have been straightened at one time or another or had their meander pattern stabilised by the construction of levées. Clear relationships between channel pattern and modern environmental conditions are thus hardly to be expected.

107

Active meandering

Channel migration through lateral erosion at bends occurs mainly in alluvium and requires that the stream is sufficiently powerful to erode its banks. It is reasonable to assume that more powerful rivers can erode more resistant bank materials, and certainly meandering occurs in Britain not only in a wide range of alluvial sediments, from silt to gravel, but also at a wide range of stream powers as Figure 4.13 shows. Meandering is not restricted to lowland rivers, indeed many such rivers although sinuous are not migrating today; but upland channels are so frequently confined by valley-sides or terraces that fully developed meandering is uncommon.

In unconfined alluvial meandering bank erosion is complemented by point bar deposition on the inside of each bend as the meander loop grows or migrates (Figs 4.5, 4.14). On average deposition just keeps pace with erosion, since otherwise the channel would be growing or shrinking, but local imbalances are possible and individual cross-sections often experience erratic or progressive change in channel shape and flow properties.

A well documented example is Knighton's (1972, 1974, 1977) study of straight, curved, and divided sections on the meandering rivers Bollin and Dean in Cheshire. One actively meandering reach with examples of each kind of section is shown in Figure 4.15. The bend section changed particularly rapidly during the 18-month period of observation, with intermittent bank retreat totalling over 1 m or 15% of the channel width and deepening of the pool by about 0.5 m during a major flood. Migration of an unchanged cross-section does not alter hydraulic geometry but the deepening of the pool in this case led to greatly increased mean depth, reduced mean velocity, and slightly lower surface width for any given discharge (Fig. 4.15, M).

The straight section in contrast has a characteristically different, almost rectangular, shape and was stable throughout the period of study (Fig. 4.15, S). With both banks steep a rise in discharge is accommodated almost entirely by increased

Figure 4.14 Meandering in a sandy channel: the River Endrick near Drymen, Central Scotland. Flow is left to right over riffle in foreground. Sheep are on gooseneck with river flowing rightwards again in front of row of trees. Note step from point bar to floodplain.

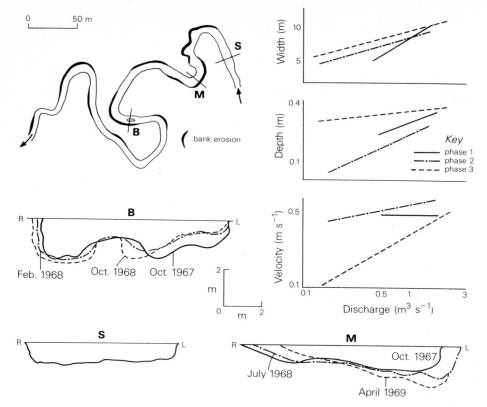

Figure 4.15 Channel form and channel changes in straight (S), curved (M) and divided (B) sections of the meandering River Dean near Adlington Hall, Cheshire (after Knighton 1974, 1977).

depth and velocity, without however leading to erosion because with no bend immediately upstream there is no impingement of flow more on one bank than the other. The divided section a little way downstream shows the more active situation at a meander crossover where although the channel is locally straight secondary flow exists and bank erosion occurs. The result here (Fig. 4.15, B) was for the right-hand channel to take progressively more of the flow and for the riffle bar which initially divided the section to be trimmed and gradually incorporated into the point bar extending downstream into the left bank of the section.

The morphology of meander point bars has been discussed in Chapter 2 and the only aspect that needs reiteration here, since it affects cross-section shape and the nature of channel change, is that the lateral slope of point bars varies with sediment size. To some extent this can be explained from hydraulic principles (Bridge 1976). Sandy point bars rise relatively steeply and are often separated from a fine-grained floodplain top by an inner accretionary bank whereas gravelly point bars are flatter and often merge into the floodplain (compare Figs 4.5, 4.14). During floods they are readily overtopped and may be dissected by chute channels, leading to incomplete meandering and possibly the cutting off of the original bend. Cutoffs in sandy meanders are more likely to be of the neck variety.

Rates of bank erosion in meander bends depend on streamflow variations, bank conditions and channel geometry as discussed in Chapter 2 so they are highly variable in space and time when estimated directly over 1–2 years using erosion pins. Amounts of channel migration between successive maps, air photos or ground surveys (Lewin & Hughes 1976, Hooke 1977) are perhaps a surer guide to long term average rates of bank erosion. Bigger rivers tend to erode faster so rates are best compared in dimensionless form as channel widths, or % channel area, per year (Lewin, Hughes & Blacknell 1977, Hooke 1980). In Wales, actively meandering channels are migrating at rates of 0.1–5.5% per year at randomly selected reaches (Lewin, Hughes & Blacknell 1977) though locally faster rates are known.

If meander bends escape truncation they may grow and deform almost at will, but some modes of development seem commoner than others in British rivers. Hooke (1977) reported that of 444 eroding bends on rivers in Devon, 55% were either translated downstream, extended laterally, or both, generally in a gradual consistent fashion. Other changes such as longitudinal enlargement, rotation, or the development of multiple lobes were less common and cutoffs were infrequent. These results imply that meander chord wavelength, L, remains approximately constant while bends migrate or grow, in the latter case leading to an increase in the along-channel wavelength λ. Continued growth is thus incompatible with a constant pool–riffle spacing unless additional pools and riffles form along the limbs of the enlarged meander (Keller 1972), a position in which they are in fact found (Lewin 1972, and see Fig. 4.6a).

Geometric variations between low- and high-sinuosity bends are in broad agreement with this evolutionary model. Hey (1976a) found that the ratio of chord length to channel width, $L/2W$, in 57 bends of the Rivers Tweed and Wye is not constant but decreases with angle of turn, in such a way that the arc length ratio $\lambda/2W$ is approximately constant (at 2π, as for pools and riffles). However, Ferguson (1973a) found that arc length increased with sinuosity of individual bends even though the mean arc wavelengths of different rivers were independent of sinuosity.

Neither Hey nor Ferguson found any constancy in bend tightness (radius of curvature R divided by channel width W); rather, it increases with the angle of turn. It may however have a limiting value as suggested by Bagnold (1960) and Hickin (1974): Hey found no bends with $R/W < 2$ and Ferguson only a few.

The relationship of meander wavelength to river size has attracted much attention ever since Dury's (e.g. 1958) use of it to reconstruct palaeo-discharges of valley meanders but there is still no theoretically-based wavelength formula that fits river data and can be used for prediction without detailed knowledge of the channel concerned. Of the available empirical formulae, Dury (1964a, 1976) has at various times advocated Inglis's Indian relationship $L = 54\ Q^{1/2}$ (SI units), Leopold and Wolman's (1957) $L = 7.0\ W^{1.1} \approx 11\ W$, and his own best-fit relationship for mainly American data, $L = 32.9\ Q^{0.55}$. The rule of thumb $L/W = 10$ to 14 certainly seems to work in Britain but only for well-defined meander bends. Lowland rivers with zigzag or gently sinuous patterns, and upland ones with confined meanders, often have a very irregular planform whose wavelength is difficult to define and even free meanders are less regular than commonly supposed (Ferguson 1975).

One approach to this problem is to treat the pattern as a series of direction or direction-change (curvature) values and use spectral analysis to identify the dominant oscillatory period. Wavelength spectra of sinuous (not necessarily actively meandering) rivers in Britain are broad but generally do have a single dominant peak (Ferguson 1975), and are consistent with a disturbed periodic model (Ferguson 1976) that allows varying degrees of irregularity, presumably due to distorted meander migration.

Wavelengths obtained in this way are somewhat higher than those estimated by eye, which tend to represent the smallest scale of oscillation and are of course

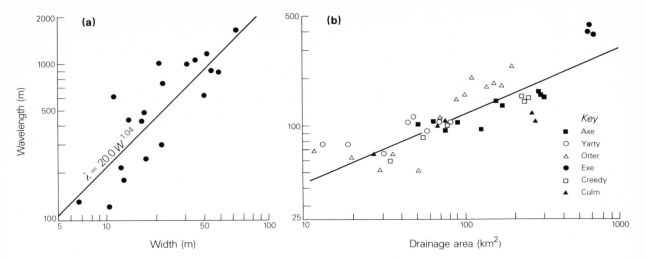

Figure 4.16 The relationship of meander wavelength to channel width (English and Scottish data of Ferguson 1975) and catchment area (Devon rivers, after Hooke 1977).

measured across bends rather than around them as with spectral analysis; hence the different constant in the best-fit relationship $\lambda = 20.0\,W^{1.04}$ for 19 English and Scottish rivers (Ferguson 1975, Fig. 4.16a). The scatter about this equation is very wide, from approximately 0.4 to 2.4 times the predicted value, perhaps because of the inclusion of inactive meanders whose wavelength may reflect past rather than present hydrologic conditions.

Since channel width is empirically proportional to about the square root of discharge, as already discussed, meander wavelength also varies as $Q^{0.5}$. Discharge in turn increases with catchment area, somewhat less than linearly, so wavelength is loosely proportional to catchment size to the 0.3–0.4 power (Dury 1958, Park 1975, Hooke 1977 and Fig. 4.16 here).

Confined meandering

The observations and analyses discussed so far relate primarily to free alluvial meandering. Many British rivers, from small upland streams to stretches of such major rivers as the Tyne and Wye, flow in narrow valleys that restrict the scope for meander development and lead to confined patterns, first discussed in detail by Lewin and Brindle (1977).

That deepened valleys are so widespread is another legacy of the current Ice Age. Research on Pleistocene fluvial sediments in Britain and their palaeohydrologic implications is in its infancy but it is increasingly clear that many valleys have been deepened and terraces formed through internal readjustment of river long-profiles since the last glaciation, rather than because of regional base-level change, even though interglacial to glacial sea-level lowering must have had a major impact on British rivers at an earlier time. In some areas, both lowland and highland, the coarse-grained valley fills of periglacial or proglacial braided rivers have been terraced by Postglacial meandering rivers which presumably experienced a greater reduction in sediment supply than in discharge during the climatic amelioration and plant succession that followed the most recent deglaciation. Elsewhere straight or winding valleys cut into soft bedrock or glacial deposits mark the former channels and floodplains of lateglacial or early Postglacial rivers whose shrunken successors are constrained by the valley walls.

Some of the distinctive morphologic features and changes associated with confined meandering are illustrated from Welsh rivers in Figure 4.17. The three reaches shown are confined by different media: the Tywi by a railway embankment built in the 1840s, the Rheidol partly by its valley sides and partly by gravelly terrace bluffs, and the Monnow by the rock-cut sides of a valley which is itself meandering. In each case confinement has led to local restriction or prevention of what were identified above as the normal processes of meander development, i.e. downvalley translation and lateral extension, and the channel pattern is consequently distorted.

Several characteristic features can be identified in confined meanders although not all are necessarily present in any one reach. First, restricted lateral growth means downvalley migration is relatively more important and perhaps faster in absolute.terms. In a valley which is narrower than the river's potential meander belt width, and fairly straight, a rather regular sequence of restricted bends may develop which creeps downvalley without much distortion. The bends have a typically box-shaped or square-wave form with maximum curvature at the points of impingement against, and out-turn from, the valleyside. This boxed pattern is visible at the points labelled B in the map of the Monnow (Fig. 4.17). A frequent consequence of enforced downvalley migration is the creation of a long backwater slough in the wake of the migrating pool at the bend apex (points labelled S on the Tywi and Rheidol in Fig. 4.17). Sloughs of this kind tend to be transient features, either reactivated following cutoffs or gradually infilled by fine-grained sediment brought in by backwaters, overbank floods, and groundwater seepage through floodplain gravels.

In many confined valleys some loops of the river become ensconced in the valley sides or terrace bluffs, either at irregularities in these or because the river is sufficiently powerful to start cutting into the confining walls but then becomes unable to remove the large quantities of coarse sediment released from undercut bluffs. Lewin and Brindle (1977) have described the effects of this type of confinement. One distinctive feature is the gradual overtaking of an ensconced bend by a more freely migrating loop on the other side of the valley. This transforms an S-bend into a Z-shape lying across, not along, the valley with a hairpin bend at the point of confinement and a long central limb in which the river flows diagonally

Figure 4.17 Confined meandering of some Welsh rivers: the Monnow at Grosmont, Rheidol at Glanrheidol, and Tywi at Golden Vale (after Lewin & Brindle 1977). Labelled features are discussed in text.

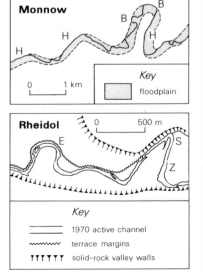

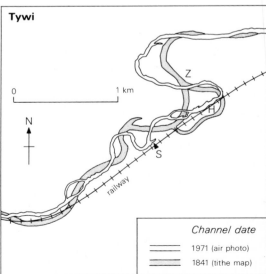

112

upvalley. The sites labelled Z on the Tywi and Rheidol in Figure 4.17 show
well-developed examples in which the rivers are well on the way to neck cutoffs.
The incipient stages are also visible on the Rheidol where the ensconced bend E is
becoming increasingly box-shaped with two separate loci of erosion and is
beginning to be overtaken by the more freely developing bend upstream. This site
and the better developed Z-bend on the Tywi also illustrate the characteristic
development of midchannel bars and islands because of the influx of coarse
sediment from undercut confining walls. Similar tendencies were found by Milne
(1979, 1980) in the Scottish Borders where channels at and just downstream of
bluffs are particularly likely to have abnormal cross-sections.

A final characteristic feature of confined meanders is a tendency to hug one or
other valley wall for substantial distances. This is especially common where the
valley itself is winding, as with the Monnow in Figure 4.17. At valley bends the
river tends to cross the valley floor and impinge on the concave wall from which it
is unable to turn away (sites labelled H in Fig. 4.17). Long scour pools often
develop in such situations, as alongside the railway embankment which confines
the Tywi at location H. Channels may also hug valley walls in straight valleys, but
normally only for intermediate angles of incidence: a channel impinging very
obliquely is free to turn away from the valleyside and one impinging almost
perpendicularly will usually become ensconced.

Active low-sinuosity channels

Many British rivers with coarse bed materials display free or confined meandering
but others are relatively straight while still actively modifying their channels. In
these rivers bank erosion is not restricted to bend migration opposite growing
point bars but is a more haphazard accompaniment of the evolution of midchannel
bars during floods when bedload transport is widespread. At lower discharges
bars may emerge and divide the flow, giving a locally braided channel pattern. At
reach scale, however, the river is generally either straight or sinuous: occupation
of an entire valley floor by an intricate network of dividing and recombining
channels, as in some proglacial areas, is almost unknown in Britain.

Local channel division is quite common in small streams in all upland parts of
Britain. A typical boulder-bed torrent that is sufficiently active to have destroyed
a tarmac road in 1978 is shown in Figure 4.18. It drains an area of 15 km^2 and has
an exceptionally steep 8% gradient. During summer cloudbursts this stream
creates boulder bars, divides around them, and floods over its valley floor
uprooting vegetation, depositing sand and gravel, and cutting additional channels.
Upland catchments of similar size but gentler gradient often support straight or
meandering streams whose channels divide around occasional cobble bars. Such
channels may be transformed in major floods, or even choked by bedload and
abandoned for a new course cut into another part of the valley floor (Anderson &
Calver 1980). Channel changes are particularly likely at bends where chute cutoffs
and distributary formation near the apex occur (Hitchcock 1977).

Channel division is much less common in larger British rivers. The vegetated
islands known as aits or eyots in the Thames and other rivers in lowland England
are not active bedforms, although those not of artificial origin may well represent
ancient channel bars. Fairly extensive active braiding is restricted to one major
British river, the Spey, and a few smaller rivers draining catchments of 50–500
km^2. No examples of this size are known to the writer from outside central Wales

Figure 4.18 An active low-sinuosity boulder channel: the Allt Mhor in the northern Cairngorm mountains, Scotland. View is looking downstream one day after a summer flood.

and the Scottish Highlands, though smaller ones can be found in the Southern Uplands, Pennines, and Lake District.

All these rivers have gravel or cobble beds and their valleys have fairly wide floors that are not densely wooded. Their banks are therefore not only weak, hence readily eroded, but also low so that lateral erosion does not supply the river with more bedload than it can remove as at some confined meander bends. These are probably preconditions for extensive braiding in a humid environment, but the crucial requirement is that the river be sufficiently powerful to create mid-channel bars and erode and remove substantial quantities of coarse bank material. Bagnold (1977) has shown that bedload transport increases with specific power and is more efficient in channels that are shallow in relation to the size of bed material. High bed mobility is thus likeliest in steep rivers. Worldwide data collected by Leopold and Wolman (1957) show that rivers of a given bankfull discharge tend to braid only beyond a certain slope, in SI units

$$S = 0.013\, Q^{-0.44} \approx 0.015\, Q^{-1/2}$$

which corresponds to a power of about 50 W m^{-2} in rivers of average width for their discharge ($W \approx 3Q^{1/2}$ as suggested by Fig. 4.10 above).

A plot of channel slope against bankfull discharge per unit width for British rivers (Fig. 4.19) supports the idea of a threshold power for braiding but suggests it is 2–3 times higher than 50 W m^{-2}. This is not implausible for there are theoretical reasons why the threshold should vary according to sediment type and many of Leopold and Wolman's braided rivers have sandy channels that should be more mobile than the gravel or cobble beds of British examples. Active mountain torrents such as the Allt Mhor (Fig. 4.18) with a fairly low discharge but very high slope again have bankfull power in excess of 100 W m^{-2} so it seems justifiable to conclude that braiding and allied forms of low-sinuosity activity are characteristic of rivers with high specific power.

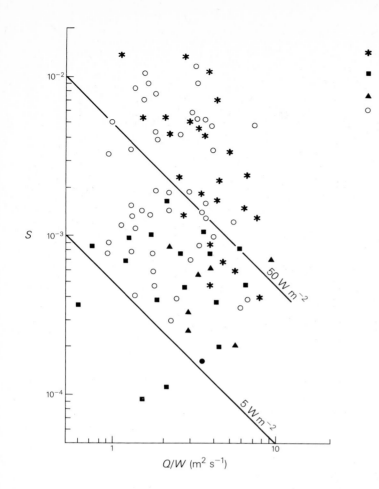

Key

* inactive incised or confined meanders
■ inactive straight or winding channels
▲ underfit meanders
○ active channels

Figure 4.19 Channel slope and bankfull discharge per unit width of some British rivers (data of Nixon 1959, Charlton *et al.* 1978, Riddell 1980). Active low-sinuosity channels occur only at high stream powers.

The morphology and behaviour of divided channels in Britain is by no means totally dissimilar to that of active meanders. For example, the reach of the lower Spey mapped by Lewin and Weir (1977) has a gently sinuous overall pattern (Fig. 4.20) with channel bars concentrated in complexes at the insides of bends, and the only slightly less braided reach near the Boat O'Brig gauging station a little further upstream was analysed as a low-sinuosity (1.13) meander pattern by Ferguson (1975). But the bar complexes in such patterns differ in form and origin from point bars. At bend A in Figure 4.20 a complex lateral bar (Bluck 1976) of rhomboid shape has developed by downvalley riffle migration and bar platform growth, with the channel migrating away from the growing bar and a slough forming on its inner side. Further downstream, at B in Figure 4.20, the more comprehensively divided pattern of channels is evidence of another braiding process, the dissection of bar heads and platforms at intermediate to low discharges.

These and other aspects of braiding have also been investigated in an unconfined reach of a tributary of the Spey, the River Feshie which drains 110 km² of the Cairngorm mountains (Werritty & Ferguson 1980). The river is flashy and transports cobble-sized traction load not only within its channels but also at times over vegetated floodplain areas. Channel alignments change from year to year (Fig. 4.21a) but tend to be gently sinuous with midchannel and lateral bars. Repeated surveys of one sub-reach (Fig. 4.21b) show how bars advance downstream with consequent migration of riffles, bank erosion below these and where the main

115

current is deflected outwards, and backwater overspill leading to new riffles or occasionally distributaries. Annual bank erosion averages 17% of channel area and a major switch of course occurred in 1976–7.

The degree of braiding apparent in rivers such as these tends to decrease with stage as channel bars are drowned, though during major floods this is offset by the reactivation as distributaries of normally dry channels. This stage-dependent appearance makes it harder to assess channel changes from historical maps or air photographs but Lewin and Weir (1977) concluded that the lower Spey has reworked about half its valley floor since the 1880s, despite a definite reduction in the degree of braiding due perhaps to partial bank protection works and floodplain afforestation. The Feshie too has changed considerably since its first mapping by

Figure 4.20 Morphology of a river with braiding tendencies: the Spey near its mouth showing channel bars and overall sinuosity (from an original diagram by J. Lewin & M. J. C. Weir). Sites A, B are discussed in text.

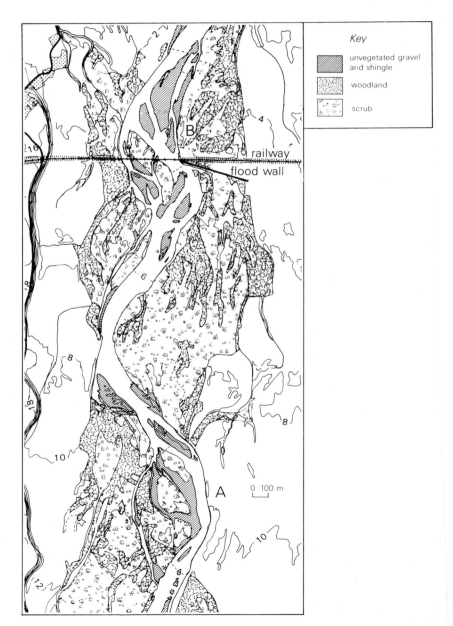

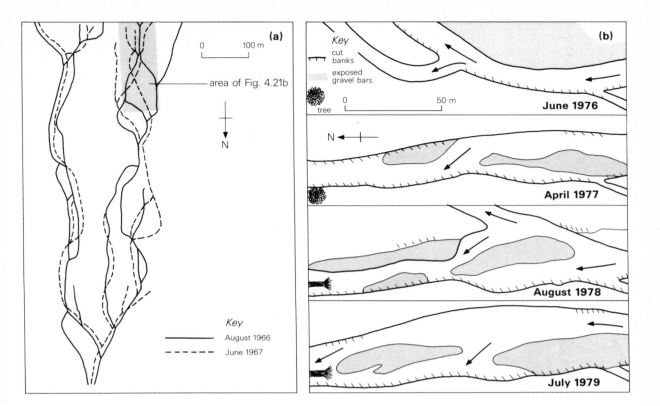

Figure 4.21 Channel changes in the braided river Feshie: (a) switching and migration in the reach; (b) surveyed bar growth, bank erosion and distributary formation in the area stippled in the main map.

the Ordnance Survey in 1869 (Werritty & Ferguson 1980) and post-1946 air photos suggest something of a cycle of change: major floods transform the channel pattern into chaotic and unstable braiding which over the next few years is rationalised and stabilised into a less divided and more sinuous pattern.

Inactive channels

The actively meandering and braided rivers whose channel patterns have been discussed so far in this chapter are reworking substantial parts of their valley floors each century. The majority of British rivers, however, have not changed their courses measurably since the first accurate surveys in the late-19th century. The rates of river migration quoted above from Lewin, Hughes, and Blacknell's (1977) work in Wales were for those rivers which showed measurable change: 75 out of 100 randomly selected reaches did not. Similarly, Hooke's study of channel pattern changes in Devon (1977) showed migration along up to 40% of the length of some rivers but this still means the majority of reaches have not shifted perceptibly this century. The stability of many British rivers, especially in lowland areas, is often evident in their heavily-vegetated banks and sometimes in the survival of medieval or Roman riparian buildings.

In many lowland rivers and a few upland ones channels have been artificially stabilised this century by local bank protection measures by landowners or river boards, or longer ago by the raising of levées to restrict a river to a particular course or at least a confined meander belt. But many other British rivers are naturally inactive, which must mean either that there is no secondary circulation tending to form bars and undercut banks or that the river is insufficiently powerful

117

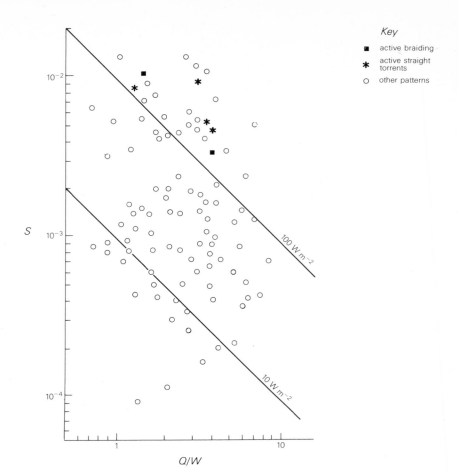

Figure 4.22 Channel slope and bankfull discharge per unit width in some British rivers (data of Nixon 1959, Charlton *et al.* 1978, Riddell 1980). Unconfined inactive patterns occur only at low to moderate stream powers.

to overcome the resistance of its banks to erosion by secondary currents. Since many inactive rivers are not straight it must be presumed that secondary currents exist and channel stability is the result of insufficient stream power in relation to bank erodibility. When inactive unconfined channels are plotted on the graph of channel slope against bankfull discharge per unit width (Fig. 4.22) they are seen to be occupied by relatively feeble rivers: those plotted as underfit, straight or irregular have bankfull powers from little over 1 to about 60 W m^{-2}, with a median of about 15 W m^{-2}. In contrast, active free meanders range in power from 5 to 350 W m^{-2} with a median of about 30 W m^{-2}. More powerful rivers with apparently inactive patterns are all incised or confined.

There is clearly a spectrum of types of inactive channel in Britain but most cases can be described as either rock-bound channels, tree-lined gravelly rivers, or clay lowland rivers.

Rock-cut channels are uncommon in Britain outside the upland headwaters discussed in Chapter 3. Only in a few areas are long stretches of river incised into raised tablelands; examples include the River Wye in the Welsh borders and the Dove and Wye in Derbyshire. The incised meanders of these rivers are of generally low sinuosity and the gorges are mostly fairly open in character so that the channels are as often bounded by boulders as bedrock.

True rock-walled channels occur for short distances along these rivers, at knickpoints in otherwise alluvial rivers (for example High Force on the Tees,

Bonnington Linn on the Clyde, Aysgarth Falls on the Ure), and where modern
rivers occupy glacial meltwater channels cut in hard rocks (as at Rumbling Bridge
on the River Devon east of Stirling and Corrieshalloch gorge on the Broom near
Ullapool). Channels at such sites tend to have a stepped profile over one or more
falls or rapids separated by deep bouldery pools that have been extended upstream
by waterfall recession. Cross-sections tend to be rectangular and are often wider
in pools than at falls where the low-flow channel may be notched into a wider
gorge of rectangular or trapezoidal section which may be a relic of greater
discharges in the past but could in most cases also be explained by valley-side cliff
collapse and retreat. In all cases the detailed morphology of rock-cut channels is
closely adjusted to rock jointing and bedding and the characteristically rectangular
geometry suggests that joint block removal is a more effective process of erosion
than gradual abrasion.

The second type of inactive channel in Britain is far more widespread. The
middle courses of many upland rivers and the headwaters of some lowland rivers
flow on intermediate slopes with very often a pebbly bed and stony soil-covered
banks on which trees flourish. Tree-lined gravel channels of this type generally
appear to be inactive whether or not they occupy confined valleys.

Valley-floor woods are now uncommon in Britain but many rivers are lined by
trees that may represent the last vestiges of an extensive cover that was cleared
centuries or millennia ago for pasturage or cropping; and even a single line of trees
along a river's banks can have an important stabilising effect on the channel. As
noted above Charlton, Brown and Benson (1978) found that tree-lined gravel
channels averaged some 30% narrower than expected from their bankfull
discharges. The protective influence of trees is probably due to both the direct
mechanical strengthening of banks by root binding and a variety of indirect
effects. Leaf fall promotes organic soil development and thus more cohesive bank
sediment; interception of rainfall and uptake of soil moisture may help prevent
saturation of fine-grained banks with consequent mechanical weakening; and if
bank scour does succeed in exposing tree roots they tend to trap bedload and
create eddies in which washload settles out, usually preventing further erosion.
Moreover, although local bank erosion may occur between trees the systematic
undercutting of long stretches of concave bank opposite growing point bars is
likely to be prevented.

The channel pattern of inactive gravel rivers of this kind may be virtually
straight, gently winding, or irregular with straight reaches and occasional fairly
sharp bends. Low-sinuosity winding patterns may represent incipient meandering
and certainly small point bars are to be seen on such rivers. In other cases sinuosity
may be inherited from early Holocene times when rivers may have been more
active because of higher discharges, sparser valley-floor vegetation, or both.

The final type of inactive channel in Britain is again common and geographically
widespread. Clay lowland rivers are found locally on glaciolacustrine and glacio-
marine sediments in northern and western Britain but are particularly associated
with East Anglia and the Thames basin, where low regional slopes and a small
rainfall surplus over evaporation combine to give low stream powers but river
banks, derived from soft bedrock or drift, are fine-grained and cohesive. The
combination of low stream power and high bank resistance explains the absence of
perceptible channel migration in such rivers. Nevertheless they are not always
straight. Some have a zigzag pattern with occasional bends linking straight or
gently curved reaches, and many have underfit meander patterns with a wavelength out of proportion to the modern river.

The widespread occurrence of underfit meanders in England (and other temperate lowlands) was first recognised by Dury (e.g. 1958) who proposed a universal origin in river shrinkage due to postglacial climatic change; individual cases had previously been explained only by appeal to special circumstances such as river capture.

There are two main types of misfit meanders. A manifestly underfit river is one whose modern meanders are superimposed on larger bends, either of the meander belt (as in some tributaries of the upper Thames) or of a confining valley (as with the River Monnow in Fig. 4.17 above). Dury explained the larger meanders as formed at a time when bankfull discharges were around 50 times greater than now, judging by the wavelength ratio of modern and valley meanders, and attributed the subsequent shrinkage to reduced precipitation and increased evapotranspiration between 12 000 and 9000 years ago.

The other type of misfit meandering is termed Osage underfitness after an American river whose sinuous pattern is simple, not compound, but of anomalously high wavelength for the present channel width. On the River Severn near Shrewsbury, for example (Dury, Sinker & Pannett 1972), a manifestly underfit reach separates two reaches whose meander wavelength is very high at about 40 channel widths but whose pool–riffle spacing is nearer 7 W, as in simple meanders with the 'normal' wavelength of 10–14 W. Again an order of magnitude reduction in discharge is inferred. Dury and his co-workers considered this channel pattern to be disharmonious with modern hydrometeorological conditions but it is entirely logical that a river which has reduced its slope by meandering, and then suffers a considerable reduction in discharge too, should no longer be powerful enough to erode its banks in order to create shorter meander bends even though it is still able to scale down its bed undulations. As Richards (1972) noted this part of the Severn has a valley slope (and thus stream power) less than half that of more actively meandering reaches nearby, and in Figure 4.19 other underfit meanders of both kinds plot consistently in the lower range of stream powers. Table 4.1 compares hydraulic properties of two lowland rivers with clayey banks and similar bankfull discharges, but on different regional slopes. The Weaver near Ashbrook in the Cheshire plain is several times steeper and more powerful than the Great Ouse at Bedford, and this is reflected in its gravelly instead of fine-grained bed, higher mean velocity, and actively meandering instead of inactive manifestly underfit pattern.

Although Geyl (1976) has presented arguments for an estuarine origin of certain underfit meander patterns in East Anglia and Somerset there seems little

Table 4.1 Bankfull properties of active and inactive clay lowland channels (data from Nixon 1959).

	River	
	Weaver	*Great Ouse*
pattern	meandering	underfit
discharge ($m^3 s^{-1}$)	71	74
power ($W\ m^{-2}$)	39	7
bed material	gravel	sandy silt
width (m)	18	26
mean depth (m)	2.4	2.5
mean velocity ($m\ s^{-1}$)	1.7	1.2

doubt that Dury's explanation is the most widely applicable. However, the magnitude of the discharge reduction he invokes can be questioned. As Geyl and others have pointed out, a 30–60-fold increase in discharge would put many misfits well above the threshold for braiding (Leopold & Wolman 1957). Braiding is not necessarily incompatible with large scale sinuosity, as the example of the Spey shows (Fig. 4.20 above), but if wavelength depends primarily on width and braided channels are unusually wide for their discharge then they will have unusually high wavelength too. Thus some 'valley meanders' could represent the traces of former braided rivers whose discharges were not quite so much larger than today (Ferguson 1973b). This explanation seems all the more plausible in the light of recent sedimentological evidence for braiding of the Thames, Kennet and Nene during the last glacial (Briggs & Gilbertson 1980, Cheetham 1976). Whatever the history, the hangover remains in the inactivity of so many lowland rivers in England.

The effects of man

Throughout this chapter the changes involved in the adjustment of river channel form to environmental conditions have been stressed. Even Osage underfits have modified their channel width and pool–riffle spacing, and more active rivers may transform their cross-sections and patterns within years or decades. Efforts to restrict natural channel changes by bank protection measures have already been touched on, but paradoxically human activity also induces many channel changes and these merit separate discussion even though they operate through natural processes of erosion and deposition.

An urban and industrial society such as Great Britain interferes with river behaviour in a number of ways and to an ever-increasing extent. Direct engineering works along channels include diversion, straightening and conduiting as well as bank protection. Perhaps less obvious but more important are the various indirect effects on channel behaviour of man's interference with the hydrological cycle.

An understanding of the consequences of direct or indirect interference with river channels is increasingly important for water managers, planners and engineers. Awareness of how man's intervention modifies the natural controls of channel behaviour should be the key to avoiding embarrassing, expensive or even dangerous consequences. This requires a marriage between knowledge of natural river behaviour and case-study investigations of induced channel changes in individual rivers.

Channel straightening

Few non-tidal rivers in Britain have been used for inland shipping since the canal-building period of the Industrial Revolution, so channels have not been affected by extensive navigational improvements. Short reaches of some rivers in Yorkshire and Lancashire have been canalised as links between the inland canal system and navigable estuaries, and several rivers draining to the Wash were straightened by Dutch engineers in the draining of the Fens in the 18th century, but otherwise channel straightening has been local and occasional.

In the past century channel realignment has probably most often been carried

121

out for the protection of railway and road embankments from flooding and erosion. Less often, improved evacuation of flood waters and sediments from headwaters has been the motive. In major construction projects new channel alignments are carefully designed and banks are thoroughly protected so that the new course is completely stable, but this has not always been the case in more modest works on smaller rivers.

Straightening an actively meandering river, and thus increasing its slope and power, without protecting its banks is a recipe for accelerated erosion and the question is not why but how rapidly the channel will adjust. Lewin (1976) has described the initiation of asymmetric gravel bars and alternate bank erosion following the straightening in 1969 of a reach of the River Ystwyth in mid-Wales. The channel had already reverted once to a meandering pattern after being straightened in 1864 to run clear of a railway track and Lewin's observations showed that the process begins very rapidly in a fairly powerful river with unprotected banks. After a single winter with a total of only 75 hours of competent flows, talweg sinuosity had risen to nearly 1.2 and bank erosion equivalent to 50% of the original channel area had taken place.

Renewed meandering of artificially straightened reaches has also been revealed by comparison of modern and historic maps of rivers in Devon (Hooke 1977). Several reaches near old mills and weirs were straight until *c.* 1900 but are now meandering following the lapse into disuse and disrepair of the weirs. The damped oscillatory pattern of some of these reaches today suggests the propagation downstream of a wave of secondary circulation induced by the partially collapsed weir.

Flow regulation

Britain has many small reservoirs but none to compare with Lake Mead or Lake Nasser, and the sediment loads of British rivers with their mostly armoured gravel beds are far lower than in the Colorado and Nile. The two best known effects of reservoirs on river channels, clearwater erosion below the dam and backfill in the channel above the reservoir, are not therefore significant problems in Britain. But even if long-profile changes can be ignored, channels below both abstracting and regulatory reservoirs are liable to alter in size and possibly channel pattern.

The first demonstration of such changes in Britain was Gregory and Park's (1974) downstream analysis of the River Tone above and below Clatworthy reservoir in Devon. Channel cross-sections below the dam are frequently compound with an active inner channel that is separated from older pre-reservoir river banks by vegetated berms or benches of fine sediment on one or both sides. Flow regulation by the reservoir since it was completed in 1959 has thus led to a drop in channel capacity. By plotting bankfull cross-section areas of both inner and outer channels against catchment area, Gregory and Park showed that the reduction in capacity is substantial immediately below the dam, but becomes progressively less marked downstream as the fraction of the catchment controlled by the reservoir decreases.

Subsequent studies of rivers below other small reservoirs controlling catchments of up to 50 km² have shown quite complex patterns of channel change which are reviewed by Petts (1979). Channels below reservoirs may passively accommodate reduced peak flows or they may adjust in any of three ways: clearwater degradation, aggradation, or pattern metamorphosis. The last has not been reported from Britain but clearwater erosion is indicated by channel capacities more than 30% greater than expected immediately below two of the 14 reservoirs investigated. Inferred reductions in capacity of at least 30% were found immediately below six dams and at one or more sections further downstream on all 14 rivers, the maximum reduction in capacity being 75% which is about the same as the maximum reduction in peak flows (Petts & Lewin 1979).

The general downstream pattern is illustrated from the River Rede in Northumbria in Figure 4.23 but the magnitude and nature of the aggradational response to flow regulation varies between as well as along rivers. Many coarse-bed reaches with well vegetated banks do not appear to have changed since reservoir construction, presumably because reduced peak flows have not reached the competent threshold and are passively accommodated within a misfit channel. Actively meandering reaches appear to adjust more readily with fairly consistent reductions in width. The other main locus of channel change is below tributary junctions where reduced mainstream flows are unable to flush away tributary sediment inputs. Several channels which are apparently unaltered immediately below a dam are suddenly reduced in capacity by 30–50% below the first major tributary by the formation of benches like those described from the River Tone, but this effect diminishes further away from the dam as non-regulated tributary discharges come to dominate channel behaviour. Both in meander belts and below tributaries aggradation is mainly of fine sediment trapped by encroaching vegetation; some bedload deposition may also occur but in general width:depth ratios are reduced. Richards and Wood (1977) have pointed out that preferential narrowing is consistent with the downstream pattern of hydraulic geometry, as discussed earlier in this chapter, and it has also been found to ensue from water abstraction to mills along some rivers in lowland England (Dury 1974).

Most of the reservoirs considered by Petts (1979) are less than 20 years old and channel adjustment downstream may not yet be complete. Petts speculates that over a century or more there will be some evening out of the complex downstream response as rare floods redistribute sediment over longer distances.

The cases investigated to date are all of channels in which peak flows have been reduced by regulation or abstraction. If interbasin transfers of water become more commonplace the question will arise of channel response to an increase in mean, and possibly peak, discharge. Hey (1976b) and Richards and Wood (1977) have discussed this in general terms but for practical guidance it may be necessary to turn to other countries. Experience in Canada (Kellerhals, Church & Davies 1979) suggests the nature of channel adjustment depends on geomorphic setting as well as the extent of hydrological change.

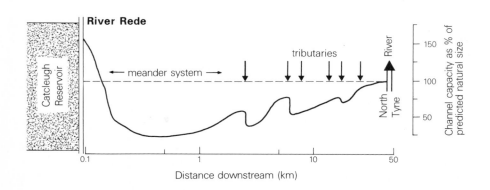

Figure 4.23 Channel capacity fluctuations below Catcleugh reservoir, River Rede, Northumbria (after Petts 1979).

Land use changes

Many regions of Great Britain are heavily urbanised and the continued spread of residential suburbs in particular has had clear effects on catchment hydrology and stream behaviour. The consequent impairment of water quality is discussed in Chapter 5 but channel changes also ensue.

Gregory and Park (1976a) found that channel capacities at 12 sites within the garrison town of Catterick in North Yorkshire were up to 150% higher than those predicted by extrapolating the well defined relationship between channel capacity and basin area for rural tributaries of the same streams. The mean enlargement ratio was 1.7, increasing to 2.6 for five sites below the built-up area. A comparable 70% increase in channel capacity was inferred for West Sussex by Hollis and Luckett (1976). Even greater increases were inferred by Knight (1979) in and below Stevenage and Skelmersdale New Towns, where channel capacities rise to respectively over twice, and three to four times, those for nearby rural streams draining catchments of the same size.

These are striking channel changes but they are for small streams draining catchments of less than 50 km^2 with a high paved fraction (55% at Stevenage). Large rivers, with much smaller proportions of their catchments affected, would be unlikely to show much if any adjustment to urbanisation even if they were not generally canalised where they flow through towns and cities.

Suburban expansion has also been suggested as the most likely explanation for a change since the 1930s in the activity of a meandering reach of the River Bollin south of Manchester (Mosley 1975). Map and air photo evidence shows the sinuosity of the channel decreased slightly from 2.41 in 1872 to 2.34 in 1935, mainly as a result of a single chute cutoff; elsewhere bend migration did not exceed 10 m or about one channel width. Since 1935 there have been seven cutoffs, the sinuosity has fallen to 1.4, channel migration has exceeded 30 m in several places, and the mapped channel width has increased from about 8 m to 13 m. The pace of change appears to have accelerated in the 1960s and streamflow records since 1956 show a significant increase in annual maximum floods. Rainfall records since 1912 reveal no clear trends in mean precipitation or heavy falls, so it appears the channel is adjusting to a flashier regime due primarily to suburban growth but also to the renewal of tile drains in the agricultural majority of the catchment.

A final type of land use that may have implications for river channel behaviour is the disposal of mining waste. The evidence from British rivers is circumstantial but convincing. In a study of the effects of 19th-century lead and zinc mining in mid-Wales Lewin, Davies and Wolfenden (1977) noted that an unusually braided reach of the River Ystwyth is immediately downstream from a spoil tip and crushing mill. Toxic metals from these have been redistributed across the floodplain, killing vegetation and thus accelerating channel activity. A second example is Richard's (1979) study of channel adjustment to sediment pollution by the china clay industry in Cornwall. Turbid waste waters from hydraulic mining, and runoff from spoil tips still containing large amounts of clay, have polluted local rivers continuously since the 1770s with the result that washloads are exceptionally high and kaolin is deposited on channel banks. Surveyed dimensions of polluted and unpolluted channels show a significant difference in downstream trend (Fig. 4.24): polluted channels tend to be narrower and deeper in approximate proportion to the silt and clay content of their banks, as found by Schumm (1960) for natural channels in the American midwest.

124 Man's effects on rivers in Britain are less dramatic than in many other countries

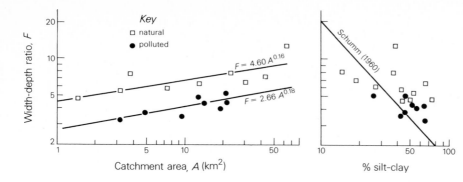

Figure 4.24 Channel adjustment of Cornish rivers to china-clay pollution (after Richards 1979).

(cf. Schumm 1971, Shen 1973, Kellerhals *et al.* 1979) and so are the costs associated with natural erosion, deposition and channel changes. This is no coincidence. Induced channel changes are simply accelerated versions of adjustments that can occur naturally given the same changes in hydrologic regime, sediment supply, channel slope or bank vegetation. British rivers are small by world standards and in a generally subdued and well-vegetated landscape they are for the most part naturally stable and quite well buffered against human interference. The study of channel changes is nevertheless of obvious applied value to the river engineer and environmental planner as well as of interest to geomorphologists and geologists for what it tells about river behaviour today and in the past. The geomorphological study of British rivers really only began in the late 1960s, but has already begun to contribute to the wider needs of Earth scientists and environmental managers.

5 Water quality

D. E. Walling and B. W. Webb

Introduction

The discussion of the hydrological characteristics of British rivers presented in Chapter 1 was concerned with the *quantity* aspects of river flow and behaviour and must be complemented by an examination of river water *quality*. Just as it is possible to examine characteristic values and the spatial variability of such parameters as annual runoff depth and flood and low-flow magnitude, so it is possible to analyse the dominant water quality characteristics of British rivers. An analysis of this quality dimension could indeed be viewed as particularly important in view of the growing interest of hydrologists in the quality component of the hydrological cycle (e.g. Walling 1977c), the increasing relevance of quality criteria in the optimum development of limited water resources and the current concern for environmental quality.

The precise context in which the term water quality is interpreted will, however, depend upon the perspective of the individual. For example, to the water supply engineer the term must primarily connote a consideration of water potability and associated standards, whereas the focus of a public health engineer might be on effluent standards and the capacity of a particular river system for effluent disposal, that of the freshwater biologist on turbidity and dissolved oxygen status, and that of the geomorphologist on the transport of material in solution and in suspension. It is perhaps the physical hydrologist who is best able to provide a broad-based and objective view closely equivalent to that generally adopted for the quantity dimension. Through his eyes, water quality can be viewed independently from considerations of potential water use by man or aquatic life and it is this approach which is adopted here.

Table 5.1 reproduces a representative selection of water quality statistics for a number of major rivers in Britain, and further analysis and discussion may be structured to develop a number of themes. First, it is necessary to examine the nature, extent and spatial distribution of significant water pollution, because this is an important control on the water quality of British rivers and accounts for the major contrasts in the levels of such determinants as dissolved oxygen, biochemical oxygen demand (BOD) and ammoniacal nitrogen listed in Table 5.1. Second, attention must be given to what is frequently referred to as background water quality, because the effects of pollution are superimposed upon a pattern of water quality behaviour which itself reflects considerable spatial and temporal variation in response to essentially natural controls. The major emphasis has been placed on this topic, since, although water pollution is a serious problem in Britain, it must be recognised that nearly 90% of the total length of non-tidal water courses in the country with a mean flow exceeding 0.05 m^3 s^{-1} may be considered as essentially unpolluted. For convenience, the discussion of background water quality has been organised under the major headings of dissolved material or solute levels, water temperatures and suspended sediment. The first relates primarily to the *chemical* quality of river water whilst the last two are essentially measures of *physical* quality.

Table 5.1 A sample of water quality statistics for selected sites in the Harmonised Monitoring Scheme for the United Kingdom, 1977[a].

River	Sampling point	Determinants[b]									
		pH	Conductivity $\mu S\ cm^{-1}$	Dissolved oxygen $mg\ l^{-1}$	BOD $mg\ l^{-1}$	Ammoniacal nitrogen $mg\ l^{-1}\ N$	Nitrite $mg\ l^{-1}\ N$	Nitrate $mg\ l^{-1}\ N$	Chloride $mg\ l^{-1}$	Total alkalinity $mg\ l^{-1}$ $CaCO_3$	Ortho-phosphate $mg\ l^{-1}\ P$
Ribble	Samlesbury	7.7	431	10.34	3.0	0.192	0.07	4.12	33.3	102.5	0.286
Tyne	Wylam	7.7	266	10.78	2.4	0.279	0.02	0.75	17.9	68.1	0.029
Trent	Yoxall	7.7	1039	10.66	4.0	0.229	—	9.28	127.5	164.3	1.170
Severn	Haw Bridge	7.8	555	11.62	2.8	0.172	—	6.28	43.9	123.8	0.552
Don	Doncaster	7.5	1185	7.60	6.5	5.700	0.68	6.91	219.9	128.7	0.488
Bedford Ouse	Earith	8.0	815	9.46	3.1	0.182	—	11.33	60.7	177.1	0.856
Thames	Teddington Weir	8.0	554	10.53	2.9	0.192	—	7.97	37.6	186.6	0.768
Exe	Thorverton Road Bridge	7.4	161	11.13	2.1	0.078	—	2.81	16.5	38.6	0.069
Dee	Iron Bridge	7.4	264	10.20	1.6	0.153	0.03	2.11	26.5	55.1	0.131
Clyde	Glasgow Green	7.6	427	8.94	5.9	1.188	0.24	2.60	66.5	97.7	0.423

[a] Taken from DOE (1978a).
[b] Values represent annual mean concentrations.

Consideration of non-point pollution, and more particularly the loss of nutrients from agricultural land, has been included within the treatment of background water quality since the controlling processes are more closely related to the natural hydrological system than to the discharge of effluent from point sources. Similarly, discussion of thermal pollution has been included in the general review of river water temperatures in terms of the modification of natural temperature regimes.

River pollution

For many individuals, discussion of the water quality of rivers in a densely populated and highly industrialised country such as Britain must evoke a picture of widespread pollution. Although this view would be misleading if not qualified by a recognition of the large proportion of the country which is not significantly affected by water pollution, it is clear that any meaningful attempt to describe the water quality of British rivers must consider the magnitude and distribution of river pollution. Information on the nature and extent of water pollution in Britain is collected at several levels. The individual regional authorities are responsible for documenting the pollution status of rivers within their jurisdiction and employ routine surveys, sampling above and below effluent outfalls, investigations of specific complaints and more specialised studies for this purpose. Their emphasis is on local river management, but a degree of national co-ordination has been imposed by the Harmonised Monitoring of River Water Quality Scheme which has been developed by the Department of the Environment through co-operation with the regional authorities (Price 1975, Simpson 1978). This scheme aims to provide nationally consistent information on the quality of major rivers and, more particularly, on the concentrations and loads of material passing the tidal limit. Samples are taken at nearly 250 locations and Table 5.1 provides a sample of the wide range of statistics available for sites within the Harmonised Monitoring network. However, these measurements primarily relate to the mouths of major rivers and information on the extent of pollution at the national scale must be sought from other sources. Fortunately, these are to be found in a number of national river pollution surveys which provide a valuable basis for any attempt to consider the magnitude and distribution of pollution in British rivers.

In England and Wales, countrywide river pollution surveys, co-ordinated by the Department of the Environment, have been carried out in 1958, 1970, 1971, 1972 and 1975 (DOE 1971, 1972, 1978b). Equivalent surveys of Scottish rivers have been undertaken in 1968 and 1974 (Scottish Development Department 1972, 1976), and the most recent compilation of water quality information for Northern Ireland relates to the summer months of 1978 (Department of the Environment for Northern Ireland 1978). These national surveys have been concerned with a chemical classification of significant water courses and results are reported in the form of statistical digests and colour-coded maps. A wide range of different sized streams are included and for England and Wales all rivers between an upstream limit where flow reaches $0.052 \, \text{m}^3 \, \text{s}^{-1}$ and a downstream limit corresponding to the seaward boundary of controlled waters were surveyed in 1975 (DOE 1978b). Categories defining the degree of river pollution used in the surveys have been based on both objective measurements and subjective assessments, and criteria employed include BOD and dissolved oxygen levels, the occurrence of polluting discharges, turbidity, the absence of fish life, the presence of toxic substances, the existence of smell and the frequency of complaints.

Four chemical classes of rivers have been recognised by the river pollution surveys of England and Wales and of Scotland (Table 5.2a) but recent information for Northern Ireland is based on a more detailed classification (Table 5.2b) which is to be more widely adopted for surveys in Britain during the 1980s (National Water Council 1978). Other attempts to refine the classification of river pollution in the United Kingdom have involved derivation of water quality indices (Scottish Development Department 1976) and the development of biological classifications (DOE 1971, Scottish Development Department 1972, 1976). The latter approach has been adopted because plant and animal communities, especially benthic invertebrate faunas (Woodiwiss 1964, Mellanby 1974), are considered to reflect long-term quality conditions in river reaches and may also indicate the occurrence of pollutants undetected by chemical sampling (Hawkes 1978, Hellawell 1978). However, lack of knowledge concerning riverine ecology and the great diversity of biological environments in British rivers have hampered the development of a satisfactory nationwide biological classification and, despite recent advances in sampling methods (e.g. Rabeni & Gibbs 1978) and use of new groups (e.g. McGill *et al.* 1979, Wilson 1980), employment of faunal evidence has been temporarily discontinued in the pollution surveys of England and Wales (DOE 1978b).

Table 5.3 presents the most recent national statistics concerning the degree and extent of river pollution available for Britain, and Figure 5.1, which is based on the latest maps produced by the countrywide surveys, summarises the spatial distribution of pollution in the major rivers of Britain. More than 75% of the total length (*c.* 39 000 km) of rivers surveyed in England and Wales during 1975 was classified as being unpolluted or recovered from pollution (Class 1), whereas for Scotland in 1974 and for Northern Ireland in 1978 more than 95% of the surveyed

Table 5.2 Chemical classification employed in pollution surveys of England and Wales and Scotland (a), and suggested classification of river water quality employed in recent surveys of Northern Ireland (b).

(a) Class	Description
1	unpolluted and recovered from pollution
2	doubtful quality and needing improvement (fairly good in Scotland)
3	poor quality requiring improvement as a matter of some urgency
4	grossly polluted

(b)[a] Class	*Limiting criteria* (95 percentile)
1A unpolluted	DO saturation $> 80\%$, BOD ≤ 3 mg l^{-1}, $NH_4 \leq 0.4$ mg l^{-1}, EEC A_2 category, non-toxic to fish
1B high quality	DO saturation $> 60\%$, BOD ≤ 5 mg l^{-1}, $NH_4 \leq 0.9$ mg l^{-1}, EEC A_2 category, non-toxic to fish
2 doubtful quality	DO saturation $> 40\%$, BOD ≤ 9 mg l^{-1}, EEC A_3 category, non-toxic to fish
3 poor quality	DO saturation $> 10\%$, BOD ≤ 17 mg l^{-1}, not likely to be anaerobic
4 grossly polluted	inferior to Class 3 and likely to be anaerobic at times
X insignificant watercourses	DO saturation $> 10\%$

[a] Based on National Water Council (1978).

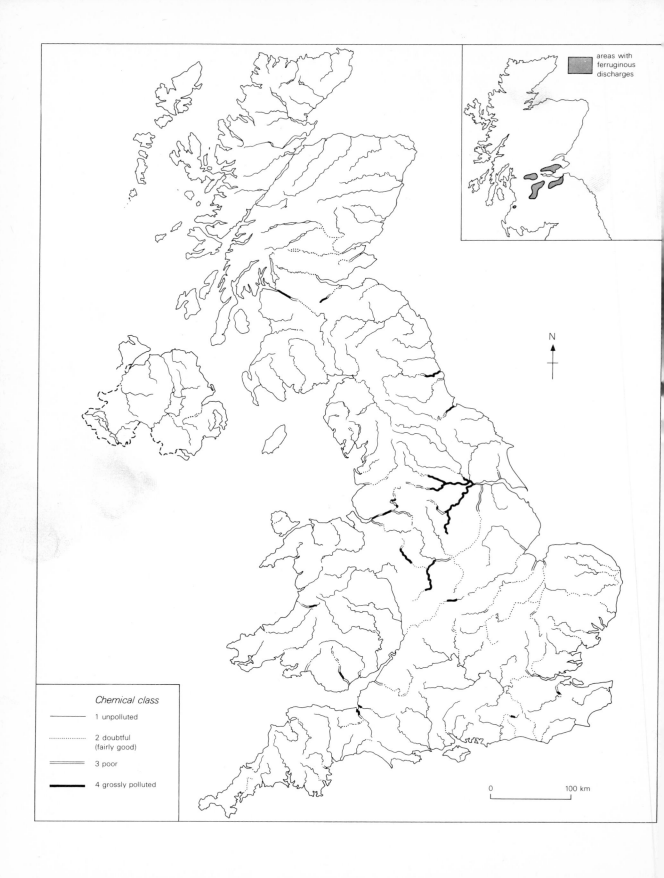

areas with
ferruginous
discharges

N

Chemical class

———————— 1 unpolluted

·················· 2 doubtful
(fairly good)

════════════ 3 poor

━━━━━━━━━ 4 grossly polluted

0   100 km

river lengths (*c.* 45 500 and 1000 km respectively) were found to be in Class 1 (Table 5.3). Rivers of poor quality (Class 3) and grossly polluted watercourses (Class 4) accounted for about 9% of the total surveyed length in England and Wales. In Scotland and Northern Ireland, the occurrence of rivers in Classes 3 and 4 is much more restricted (Table 5.3), and reflects the lower population density, the more restricted industrial and urban development, and the greater extent of undisturbed land use in these areas. Table 5.3 further indicates that the tidal reaches of many British rivers are frequently classified as polluted.

Table 5.3 Statistics of river pollution in Britain.

Area	Year	Chemical class								Total
		Unpolluted		Doubtful[a]		Poor		Grossly polluted		
		km	%	km	%	km	%	km	%	
England and Wales										
total rivers	1975	29 459	75.6	6178	15.8	1873	4.8	1479	3.8	38 989
non-tidal	1975	28 037	77.6	5458	15.1	1449	4.0	1178	3.3	36 123
tidal	1975	1422	49.6	720	25.1	424	14.8	301	10.5	2866
Scotland										
total rivers	1974	45 407	95.1	1728	3.6	438	0.9	199	0.4	47 772
non-tidal	1974	45 084	95.3	1627	3.4	407	0.9	161	0.4	47 279
tidal	1974	323	65.5	101	20.5	31	6.3	38	7.7	493
Northern Ireland[b]										
non-tidal rivers	1978	953	95.9	31	3.1	10	1.0	0	0.0	994

[a] 'Fairly good' category used in Scottish surveys.
[b] Northern Ireland survey is based on a more recent chemical classification.

Figure 5.1 illustrates the general reduction in water quality from source to mouth evident along many of the main British rivers. Some catchments, such as those of the Tyne and the Clyde, exhibit a systematic deterioration from unpolluted streams in the headwaters, through reaches of doubtful and poor quality, to grossly polluted environments near the river mouth. This downstream progression reflects the increasing influence of agricultural, domestic and industrial pollution. The greater volume of the lower river reaches is clearly highly significant in terms of pollutant loadings, and the need to relate the quality and the flow magnitude of polluted rivers has been recognised in the latest national survey of England and Wales (DOE 1978b). The maps produced by this investigation retain the four-fold chemical classification, but also employ different line thicknesses to depict the mean flows of individual reaches as one of ten classes ranging from less than 0.31 m^3 s^{-1} to more than 80 m^3 s^{-1}. Reduction of these classes to five categories and calculation of the percentage of non-tidal rivers in different chemical classes for each flow division (Table 5.4) emphasises the more frequent occurrence of poor quality and grossly polluted reaches with increasing mean discharge.

Figure 5.1 *(opposite)* The degree and extent of river pollution in major British rivers, based on DOE (1978b), Scottish Development Department (1976), and Department of the Environment for Northern Ireland (1978). Inset depicts the distribution of ferruginous discharges in the Central Valley of Scotland based on Scottish Development Department (1976).

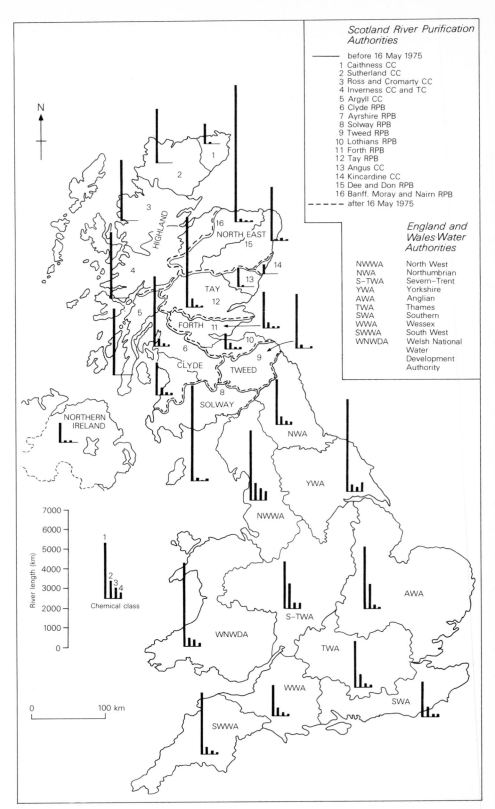

Figure 5.2 Lengths of rivers in various chemical classes for Regional Authority areas in Britain. Data refer to water courses with a mean flow exceeding 0.05 m³ s⁻¹, and are based on DOE (1978b), Scottish Development Department (1976), and Department of the Environment for Northern Ireland (1978).

Scotland River Purification Authorities

before 16 May 1975
1 Caithness CC
2 Sutherland CC
3 Ross and Cromarty CC
4 Inverness CC and TC
5 Argyll CC
6 Clyde RPB
7 Ayrshire RPB
8 Solway RPB
9 Tweed RPB
10 Lothians RPB
11 Forth RPB
12 Tay RPB
13 Angus CC
14 Kincardine CC
15 Dee and Don RPB
16 Banff, Moray and Nairn RPB

after 16 May 1975

England and Wales Water Authorities

NWWA   North West
NWA   Northumbrian
S-TWA   Severn–Trent
YWA   Yorkshire
AWA   Anglian
TWA   Thames
SWA   Southern
WWA   Wessex
SWWA   South West
WNWDA   Welsh National
        Water
        Development
        Authority

N

HIGHLAND

NORTH EAST

TAY

FORTH

CLYDE

TWEED

SOLWAY

NORTHERN IRELAND

NWA

YWA

NWWA

S-TWA

WNWDA

TWA

AWA

WWA

SWA

SWWA

River length (km)

7000
6000
5000
4000
3000
2000
1000
0

1

2
3
4

Chemical class

0   100 km

Table 5.4 Percentages of non-tidal rivers in various quantity and quality classes for   *River pollution*
England and Wales, 1975.

Chemical class	Flow class[a]					
	I	*II*	*III*	*IV*	*V*	*Total*
1	77.6	78.7	74.7	75.4	79.4	77.6
2	15.7	14.0	14.8	15.0	14.7	15.1
3	4.1	3.6	4.8	1.8	5.2	4.0
4	2.6	3.7	5.7	7.8	0.7	3.3

Based on DOE (1978b).
[a] Mean flows ($m^3 s^{-1}$): I, <0.62; II, 0.62–5.0; III, 5.0–20; IV, 20–40; V, >40.

Figure 5.1 also reveals that certain major river systems in Britain are more seriously affected by pollution than others, and this aspect of spatial variation is further demonstrated if comparisons are made between areas under the jurisdiction of different regional authorities in Britain (Fig. 5.2). Extensive pollution of rivers is caused by discharges of domestic sewage and industrial effluents from the major urban and industrial areas. Catchments in the North West, Northumberland and Yorkshire Water Authority areas and in the Central Valley of Scotland (Figs 5.1 and 5.2) are strongly influenced by this source of pollution. The Trent similarly provides an example of a river system which has been strongly contaminated by urban and industrial effluents (Lester 1967) and problems of pollution in this catchment are particularly acute because industry and population are concentrated in its headwaters. The main river is unusual in exhibiting a downstream improvement in water quality, and this amelioration occurs mainly through the influence of unpolluted inflows from the Dove and Derwent tributaries (Fig. 5.1).

Industrial processes generate a wide range of contaminants (Klein 1962) and some industrial activities, such as mining operations, are capable of causing

Table 5.5   Total lengths of all rivers in various chemical classes in different surveys.

(a) England and Wales

Chemical class	1958		1970		1971		1972		1975	
	km	*%*	*km*	*%*	*km*	*%*	*km*	*%*	*km*	*%*
1 unpolluted	24 660	70.3	28 758	74.1	29 236	75.4	29 514	76.1	29 459	75.6
2 doubtful	5544	15.8	5972	15.4	5927	15.3	5702	14.7	6178	15.8
3 poor	2460	7.0	2209	5.7	1919	4.9	1949	5.0	1873	4.8
4 grossly polluted	2411	6.9	1869	4.8	1720	4.4	1637	4.2	1479	3.8
totals (km)	35 075		38 808		38 802		38 802		38 989	

(b) Scotland River Purification Boards

Chemical class	1968		1974		1968	1974
	km	*%*	*km*	*%*	*%[a]*	*%[a]*
1 unpolluted	4049	80.6	30 288	92.8	79	78
2 fairly good	620	12.3	1713	5.3	14	16
3 poor	193	3.8	438	1.3	4	4
4 grossly polluted	165	3.3	199	0.6	3	2
totals (km)	5027		32 638		4986	

[a] Based on lengths common for both surveys.

pollution in both industrial and rural areas. Strongly acid and highly turbid drainage from underground workings and surface waste tips of coal mines intensify the problems of river pollution in the main industrial regions of England and Wales and in Scotland, where ferruginous discharges (Scottish Development Department 1976) are widely distributed through the Central Lowlands (Fig. 5.1 inset). In predominantly rural areas, such as Cornwall, discharges from china clay (Nuttall & Bielby 1973) and tin workings may cause gross pollution of local streams, whereas rivers in mid-Wales are still suffering from the legacy of historic metalliferous mining (Grimshaw *et al.* 1976).

Rivers draining agricultural land are generally less polluted than those affected by industrial and urban conurbations, but increased use of fertilisers (Tomlinson 1970), improvements in land drainage (Davis & Slack 1964), discharges of farm wastes and domestic effluents from small towns (Oborne *et al.* 1980) have promoted considerable deterioration in the water quality of rural rivers in Britain over the last 25 to 30 years (Rodda *et al.* 1976). In regions of intensive agriculture, such as East Anglia, a substantial proportion of the streams are of doubtful quality (Class 2, Figs 5.1 and 5.2), and the rivers are susceptible to eutrophication and attendant imbalances in plant and animal communities (Edwards 1973a, 1974).

Some information on temporal trends in the extent of river pollution may be obtained by comparing national surveys from different years (Table 5.5). Results for England and Wales from 1958 and 1975, and for Scotland from 1968 and 1974 cannot be directly compared because of the very much greater lengths of river investigated in the most recent surveys. However, comparison of reaches which are common between individual surveys (Tables 5.5b and 5.6) indicates recent reductions in the total length of grossly polluted and poor quality streams, but also reveals a diminution in the extent of high quality stretches (DOE 1978b).

Despite these changes, evidence from water quality investigations in Britain demonstrates that the great majority of rivers are unpolluted. This general cleanliness however does not imply that British rivers are uniform in chemical and physical composition. Indeed, spatial variations in background water quality represent an important, but perhaps less widely appreciated, aspect of water quality in the United Kingdom.

Table 5.6 Net changes in length (km) of rivers in various chemical classes between 1972 and 1975 for England and Wales.

Chemical class	Net change[a]	%[b]
1	−200.5	0.52
2	+439.4	1.13
3	− 82.6	0.21
4	−156.3	0.40

Based on DOE (1978b).
[a] Based on 38 751.6 km in 1975 common to 1972.
[b] Net change expressed as percentage of total common length.

134

National patterns

Discussion of the background water quality of British rivers can usefully commence with a consideration of solute levels and their countrywide variation in response to hydrometeorological and physiographic controls. The data produced by the Harmonised Monitoring network (e.g. Table 5.1) afford an insight into the contrasts evident between major rivers, and, by selecting those largely unaffected by pollution, some indication of the variation in this facet of background water quality may be obtained. However, data collected from large rivers provide only an aggregate measure of water quality in the area upstream and are unable to provide a detailed representation of the countrywide variation in solute levels. Information must be obtained from small- and medium-sized streams where quality will reflect that of runoff from a local source area. There is no direct equivalent to the national pollution survey in this context, and the number of research investigations in small catchments which might provide data is limited (e.g. NERC 1979a). In the absence of other relevant published work, the authors have attempted to make use of the water quality data collected by regional authorities from small- and medium-sized streams during routine surveys, in order to derive countrywide maps of background solute levels.

These routine surveys involve sampling at either monthly, fortnightly or occasionally weekly intervals at a large number of sites throughout the country. The precise rationale underlying the design of the sampling network varies according to the regional authority concerned, but the essential purpose is to provide data on the quality of individual water courses and on pollution problems. There are several limitations to the use of these data to study national patterns of background water quality, because the sites are chosen primarily to monitor pollution, sampling frequencies vary from region to region, and individual authorities report different sets of determinants which are in turn mainly related to an assessment of pollution status. Nevertheless, a detailed countrywide analysis was considered worthwhile.

Data relating primarily to the period 1977–9 were collected from the regional authorities and information for sites on small tributaries, classified as unpolluted by the national pollution survey, were selected. Because of the lack of consistency in the determinants reported for different regions, attention was restricted to specific conductance and pH levels and to chloride and nitrate–nitrogen concentrations. These were widely available and together provide a worthwhile representation of background solute levels. In some instances it was necessary to estimate specific conductance levels from hardness and alkalinity values and to assume that total oxidised nitrogen measurements were equivalent to nitrate–nitrogen concentrations in unpolluted streams. Mean values of these determinants were calculated, and it is proposed that they provide a reasonable approximation of the values that would be obtained from a more intensive sampling programme. A computer-based system was used for data storage and retrieval and for automated classification and plotting of over 1500 individual measuring points by grid reference on a map of Britain. The sites were classified according to the magnitude of the solute value being mapped and the final choropleth maps (Figs 5.3–5.6) were produced manually. This has necessarily involved generalisation according to dominant values in particular areas but the patterns shown provide a meaningful representation of the countrywide patterns

135

depicted on the original plots. However, in certain areas such as the Highlands of Scotland the maps must be viewed as tentative in view of the limited availability of sampling sites.

These maps represent the first attempt to depict countrywide variation of background solute levels known to the authors. They show the solute levels representative of small streams and therefore of source runoff, which may be directly related to the hydrometeorological and physiographic characteristics of the immediate vicinity. Inspection of the four maps (Figs 5.3–5.6) demonstrates that the measures of background solute level portrayed exhibit marked variation across the country, and that both the extent and precise pattern of variation varies between the individual parameters in response to different controls.

Specific conductance levels provide an indication of the total dissolved solids concentration of stream water and mean values encountered for individual sites ranged between less than 35 μS cm^{-1} to greater than 1200 μS cm^{-1}. The generalised pattern depicted on Figure 5.3 exhibits an 8-fold range in specific

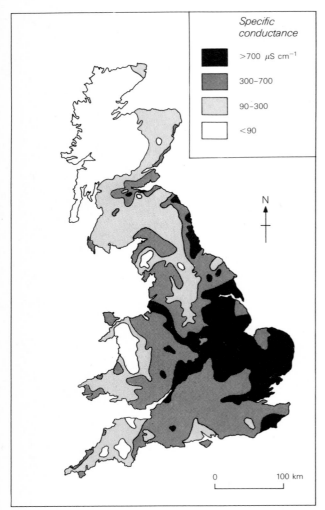

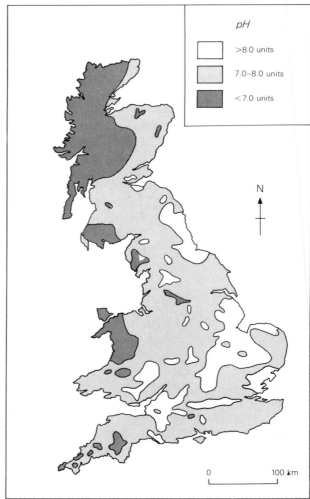

Figure 5.3 Countrywide variations in background levels of specific conductance in streams. Mean levels, based primarily on data collected in the period 1977–9, are shown.

Figure 5.4 Countrywide variations in background levels of pH in streams. Mean levels, based primarily on data collected in the period 1977–9 are shown.

conductance levels between <90 μS cm^{-1} and >700 μS cm^{-1} for British rivers. In detail the pattern reflects the influence of a number of factors including the concentration of dissolved material in precipitation, the relative magnitude of precipitation and runoff totals, and the intensity of chemical weathering and other mechanisms of solute production. Rock type and lithology exert a particularly strong influence on the countrywide pattern of specific conductance levels, because they provide the dominant control on chemical weathering and associated solute release. Thus an important distinction may be drawn between the low specific conductance levels characteristic of upland areas developed on resistant rocks (e.g. Dartmoor, Central Wales, Snowdonia, Lake District and Highlands of Scotland) and the much higher levels found on the younger less resistant rocks to the east of the Tees/Exe line. Further details of the pattern reflect the precise nature of the underlying rocks and, for example, the relatively low values (<300 μS cm^{-1}) associated with the New Forest area may be accounted for by the solute-deficient sandstone lithology of that location and the high (>700 μS cm^{-1}) values found in Norfolk may be ascribed to the presence of calcareous drift deposits overlying soluble bedrock. Table 5.7 provides an insight into the general relationship between rock type and specific conductance levels by listing the levels characteristic of a number of rock types outcropping over large areas of Britain. The close correspondence between areas of low relief and soft solute-rich strata serves to accentuate the pattern outlined above, since lowland areas are typically areas of low annual runoff and intensive agricultural activity, factors which are themselves also conducive to increased solute levels.

Table 5.7 Characteristic specific conductance levels in streams draining major rock types in Britain.

Rock type	Characteristic specific conductance levels (μS cm^{-1})
granite and metamorphics	<40–90
resistant Palaeozoic sandstones, slates and shales	40–300
Carboniferous Limestone	200–500
Permo-triassic, Mesozoic and Tertiary sedimentaries	>300
chalk	400–800
boulder clays over Mesozoic sediments	>700

Average pH levels represented in the national data-base ranged between 5.0 and 8.5 but the generalised map of countrywide variation of this water quality parameter indicates that values between 7 and 8, and therefore in the range neutral to slightly alkaline, are typical of most British rivers. In simple terms, the pH of stream water may be viewed as controlled by the pH of incoming precipitation and the ability of the vegetation, soil and rock in a drainage basin to modify these levels. The pH of precipitation over Britain is typically of pH 4–5 (e.g. Cawse 1977) and is buffered by ion exchange before reaching the stream. Acid stream waters (pH<7.0) are therefore to be expected in areas with low base exchange capacity and their correspondence on Figure 5.4 with such areas as Dartmoor, Snowdonia, Central Wales, the Lake District and the Southern Uplands and Highlands of Scotland may be related to the highly-leached base-deficient soils and to the peat cover found in these locations. Streams with a pH in excess of 8.0 on Figure 5.4 are associated with additional sources of alkalinity such as provided by outcrops of Carboniferous and Jurassic limestones (e.g.

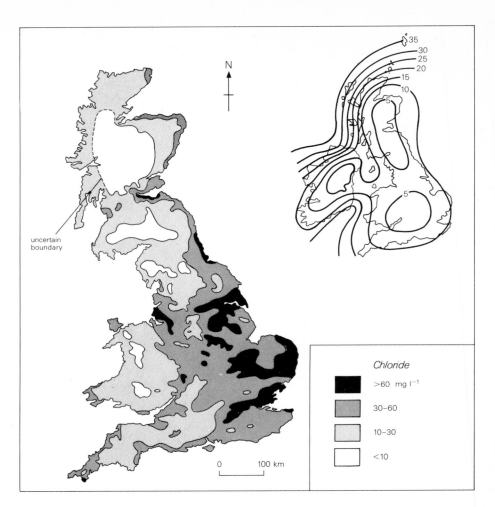

Figure 5.5 Countrywide variations in background concentrations of chloride in streams. Mean concentrations, based primarily on data collected in the period 1977–9, are shown. Inset depicts annual chloride medians of rainfall over Britain from Stevenson (1968).

Northumberland and Durham and the Bristol region), the chalk (e.g. the Chilterns) and the boulder clay of Eastern England.

Chloride concentrations documented in the national data-base ranged from less than 5 mg l^{-1} to in excess of 200 mg l^{-1} and the countrywide pattern depicted in Figure 5.5 exhibits a number of contrasts when compared to the previous maps. In the absence of pollution, this ion is generally accepted as reflecting an atmospheric source derived from oceanic aerosols (e.g. Gorham 1961, Holden 1966) and concentrations in stream water can be expected to reflect the concentration of chloride in precipitation and the runoff:precipitation ratio of a drainage basin, rather than the underlying geology. The high concentrations of this ion found in streams in coastal areas may be readily ascribed to the proximity of the oceanic source because Stevenson (1968) has shown how the median chloride concentrations of rainfall over Britain tend to decrease from approximately 10 mg l^{-1} in coastal locations to less than 5 mg l^{-1} in inland areas (Fig. 5.5 inset). Particularly high rainfall concentrations in excess of 30 mg l^{-1} have been documented for the exposed north-west coast of the country. The resultant pattern of streamwater concentrations will also be influenced by the water balance of a specific location because a low runoff:precipitation ratio will serve to increase chloride levels in streamflow by an evaporation or concentration effect.

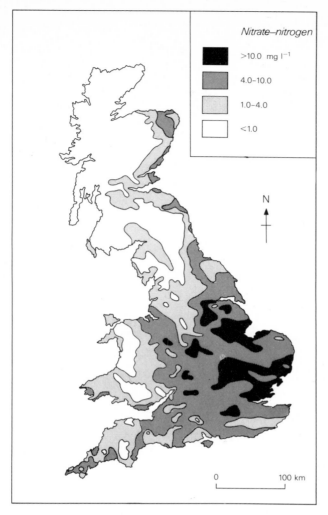

Figure 5.6 Countrywide variations in background concentrations of nitrate–nitrogen in streams. Mean concentrations, based primarily on data collection in the period 1977–9, are shown.

The low chloride concentrations associated with streams draining inland upland areas on Figure 5.5 (i.e. mid-Wales, Snowdonia, the Lake District, and the Southern Uplands and Highlands of Scotland) may therefore be accounted for in terms of high precipitation totals and low evapotranspiration. The progressive increase in chloride levels as one moves eastwards across the country is similarly controlled by the decreasing runoff:precipitation ratio. Concentrations in excess of 30 mg l^{-1} are typical of most lowland areas and values rise as high as 60 mg l^{-1} or more in such areas as Lincolnshire, Essex, Norfolk and Suffolk. Here runoff: precipitation ratios approaching 0.15 could be expected to produce stream water concentrations more than six times higher than those found in precipitation. Local anomalies in chloride levels apparent on Figure 5.5 may frequently be related to geological sources of chloride in the underlying rocks, as found in the Triassic strata of the Cheshire basin.

Nitrate concentrations in stream water can again be expected to reflect different controls to those influencing the solute parameters considered previously. The source of this ion is predominantly within the soil, and concentrations in runoff have been shown to be closely related to the intensity of agricultural activity (e.g. MAFF 1976), since both the rate of mineralisation of organic nitrogen and the application of fertiliser–N tend to increase with increased cropping and cultivation. Atmospheric inputs of nitrate in precipitation and the biological fixation of atmospheric nitrogen may also be significant, but non-point pollution from agricultural activity probably provides the major source. The countrywide pattern of nitrate–nitrogen concentrations in streamwater shown in Figure 5.6 may therefore be viewed as reflecting the magnitude of non-point pollution from agricultural sources and its interaction with overall runoff magnitude, because a dilution effect must operate in wetter areas.

At the national level nitrate–nitrogen concentrations in stream waters range from $0.1 \, mg \, l^{-1}$ to in excess of $15 \, mg \, l^{-1}$ and a clear distinction is apparent between upland Britain where levels are generally less than $4.0 \, mg \, l^{-1}$ and lowland regions where concentrations are considerably greater. Within upland Britain, the highland areas of Dartmoor, Exmoor, the Brecon Beacons, central Wales and Snowdonia, the Lake District, the Pennines and the Southern Uplands and Highlands of Scotland stand out as areas with concentrations less than $1.0 \, mg \, l^{-1}$, a feature which may be attributed both to the high rainfall and to the relatively undisturbed land use. In lowland Britain, concentrations increase eastwards in response to both a decreasing runoff:precipitation ratio and the increasing intensity of agricultural activity. Values in the range $4–10 \, mg \, l^{-1}$ are typical of many regions including the east coast of Scotland, but concentrations rise to more than $10 \, mg \, l^{-1}$ in East Anglia and adjacent counties. Certain areas of poorer soils and reduced agricultural activity such as the Weald and the New Forest in Southern England stand out as local inliers of lower concentrations.

Solute loads

The general dilution effect associated with areas of high annual runoff has been shown to exert an important influence on the countrywide pattern of variation in solute concentrations. It is therefore important to consider the spatial variation of solute loads ($t \, km^{-2} \, yr^{-1}$), in order to illuminate the precise interaction of runoff volumes and solute concentrations. For example, solute loads could exhibit little spatial variation if increases in concentration were entirely offset by decreases in runoff volume. Furthermore, information on solute loads is of value in studies of nutrient cycling, chemical denudation and related topics, and it is appropriate to

Table 5.8 Yields of major cations in selected British catchments.

Catchment	Load ($t \, km^{-2} \, yr^{-1}$)				Source
	Ca	Mg	Na	K	
East Twin	1.2	1.6	2.6	0.6	Waylen (1976)
Maesnant	1.1	0.9	4.4	0.1	Cryer (1976)
Rough Sike	5.4	—	4.5	0.9	Crisp (1966)
Duddon	7.4	—	7.7	0.5	Sutcliffe and Carrick (1973)
Cynon	9.9	6.7	23.1	2.7	Hughes and Edwards (1977)
Frome	62.1	—	9.5	1.5	Casey (1969)
Yare	30.2	1.2	7.3	0.9	Edwards (1973a)
Tud	20.4	0.8	4.4	0.6	
Severn	17.2	4.6	6.7	1.5	Brookes (1974)
Wye	19.6	2.8	4.4	1.3	
Usk	23.1	3.3	4.9	1.2	

Catchment	Load (t km⁻² yr⁻¹)				Source
	Ca	Mg	Na	K	
Bristol Avon Catchments					
Chew Stoke					
Stream	23.3	7.6	2.4	1.6	
Chew	20.4	3.6	2.7	1.3	
Wellow Brook	65.5	8.0	20.4	4.2	
Midford Brook	46.1	5.6	13.1	2.9	
Frome	34.6	2.5	5.0	2.4	Brookes (1974)
Semington Brook	26.8	1.6	4.5	2.4	
Marden	46.7	1.9	6.5	2.7	
Gauze Brook	47.3	2.6	3.5	1.6	
Avon	38.0	2.2	5.8	2.1	
Sussex Catchments					
Balcombe	9.0	2.3	12.3	2.6	
Billingshurst	14.1	4.9	10.7	2.2	
Clayhill I	5.7	1.3	4.7	1.2	
Fulking	100.0	5.6	33.3	44.4	
Nutley	10.5	3.5	9.3	5.8	Collins (1973)
Winterbourne	6.8	0.3	2.4	0.3	
W. Adur	10.3	2.3	13.0	2.9	
Ouse	11.2	2.8	14.6	3.1	
Cuckmere	9.4	2.3	10.1	1.8	
Wye Catchments					
1	3.2	1.8	8.0	0.5	
2	4.1	1.7	6.1	0.6	
3 Elan	0.5	0.4	2.0	0.1	
4 Ithon	11.7	2.7	5.6	1.1	
5 Irfon	7.4	2.8	6.2	0.7	Oborne *et al.* (1980)
6	9.4	2.8	14.3	1.1	
7	15.6	1.8	5.3	1.0	
8 Lugg	27.7	3.6	5.7	1.6	
9	13.0	4.4	5.2	1.5	
Wye	15.5	3.1	5.3	1.2	
Exe Catchments					
Quarme	5.8	2.0	4.5	0.7	
Black Ball Stream	0.9	1.0	5.4	0.5	
Haddeo	4.8	2.0	5.0	1.2	
Upper Exe	4.7	1.9	4.6	0.9	
Barle	3.3	1.7	5.6	0.8	
Exe, Stoodleigh	5.8	2.5	5.8	1.2	
Dart	5.2	3.3	6.3	3.5	
Exe, Thorverton	6.0	2.5	6.0	1.7	

include a discussion of this theme in a review of the background water quality of British rivers.

The assessment of solute loads is not included in the water quality monitoring activities of regional authorities and although it is intended that the Harmonised Monitoring scheme will eventually produce load estimates for major rivers, such data are not currently available. It is therefore necessary to turn to the results of individual research investigations in order to provide information on the solute loads characteristic of British rivers, and Tables 5.8 and 5.13 present the annual loads of a number of ions and of total dissolved solids for a representative selection of rivers. However, these compilations provide little indication of the precise nature and extent of countrywide variation and the authors have attempted to extend the analysis of the data used to derive the national maps of solute concentrations in order to provide corresponding maps of solute loads.

This has been achieved by assuming that the values of average concentration available for individual sites afford worthwhile estimates of the long-term discharge-weighted mean concentration. Annual solute loads have been calculated as the product of this concentration and an estimate of mean annual runoff for the catchment above the measuring point. Runoff estimates for individual measuring sites were derived from available hydrological maps using a computerised grid-square interpolation procedure. Although the limitations of the data and method employed must be recognised, Figures 5.7, 5.8 and 5.9 are presented as provisional maps of countrywide variations in the chloride, nitrate and total dissolved solids loads of local runoff. Total dissolved solids (*TDS*) loads

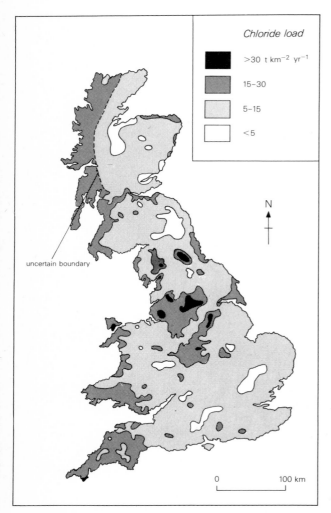

Figure 5.7 National pattern of annual chloride loads in streams.

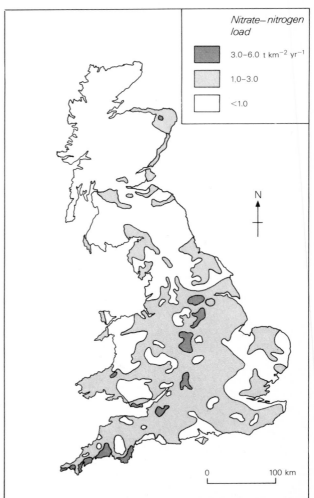

Figure 5.8 National pattern of annual nitrate–nitrogen loads in streams.

have been evaluated using a relationship between *TDS* concentration and specific *Solute levels* conductance (*SC*) of the form:

$$TDS \text{ concentration} = 0.65 \, SC$$

Significant countrywide variations are apparent in the annual loadings of each of the three solute parameters considered. The importance of runoff volumes in influencing load values is clearly demonstrated in that maximum loadings are rarely coincident with the areas of highest stream water concentrations. Chloride loads within the range 5–15 t km^{-2} yr^{-1} are typical of large areas of Britain, although higher loads between 15 and 30 t km^{-2} yr^{-1} are evident in western coastal areas and in the Midlands, and values less than 5 t km^{-2} yr^{-1} are to be found in areas of low annual runoff such as Hampshire and Essex.

The nitrate–nitrogen loadings depicted on Figure 5.8 may be viewed as largely excluding contributions from sewage effluent and therefore represent contributions from land runoff and non-point pollution from agricultural sources.

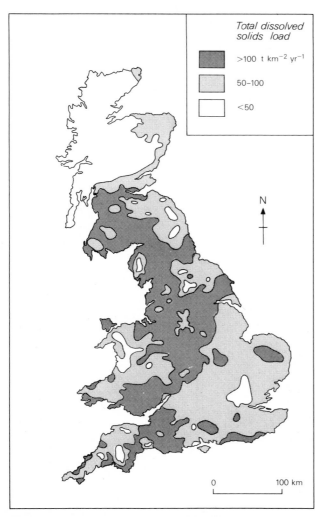

Figure 5.9 National pattern of annual total dissolved solids loads in streams.

Values of 1–3 t km^{-2} yr^{-1} (10–30 kg ha^{-1} yr^{-1}) are characteristic of large areas of the country. Lower values are found both in highland areas (e.g. Dartmoor, Snowdonia, the Lake District and the Highlands of Scotland), where they may be related to low concentrations (Fig. 5.6) and in areas of very low annual runoff such as Lincolnshire, Essex, Suffolk, Norfolk and Hampshire, where concentrations are, nevertheless, amongst the highest in Britain. Higher values (3–6 t km^{-2} yr^{-1}) are associated with regions where both concentrations and runoff volumes are sufficiently high to produce sizeable loadings, as for example in coastal areas of South-West England and parts of the Midlands.

Total dissolved solids loadings calculated in this analysis ranged between 10 and 400 t km^{-2} yr^{-1} and the pattern of countrywide variation illustrated in Figure 5.9 essentially reflects the interaction of runoff volumes and geological controls on total solute concentrations. Areas with low specific conductance levels or low total solute concentrations (Fig. 5.3) are commonly encountered in upland regions which also exhibit high annual runoff, whereas higher solute concentrations in much of lowland Britain are offset by low annual runoff. The overall range of solute loads is therefore less than that of specific conductance, but geological controls are still important since areas of low total solute load (50 t km^{-2} yr^{-1}) mainly correspond with areas of resistant solute-deficient rocks (e.g. Dartmoor, North Wales, the Lake District and the Scottish Highlands).

This discussion of countrywide variation in solute concentrations and loadings has been limited by the restricted number of solute parameters considered, which in turn has been constrained by data availability. However, the individual parameters discussed have been shown to reflect different controls and it is proposed that the discussion of the significance of underlying geology, runoff magnitude, runoff:precipitation ratios, precipitation chemistry and land-use activity must be equally relevant to many other solute species. It must also be recognised that the maps presented reflect a large degree of generalisation and that considerable regional and local variation may be apparent within areas mapped as essentially uniform at the national scale.

Regional and local patterns

Information on the concentrations of major cations in streamflow collected by the South West Water Authority during their routine monitoring surveys may be used to introduce consideration of additional chemical constituents as well as to high-light the nature and extent of local variation in background solute levels. A cation triangle (Fig 5.10a) has been used to portray the average cation composition, in terms of reacting values, of samples collected from 212 (Fig. 5.10b) relatively small and unpolluted streams in South-West England. This diagram evidences the wide range of water chemistry to be found within the South-West Peninsula. Streams dominated by calcium, sodium and magnesium are encountered, and there are many streams possessing a more balanced composition.

Many factors are likely to contribute to regional variations in water composition, but classification of the sampling sites according to the geology of the upstream catchment (Fig. 5.10c) indicates that rock type exerts a strong

Figure 5.10 *(opposite)* Cation triangle depicting water composition of streams in South-West England (a). Location of sampling sites (b) and cation composition (c) are shown in relation to major rock types in South-West England. Data presented in (a) to (c) were kindly made available by the South West Water Authority. Chemical composition of waters draining geologies typical of upland and lowland Britain (d) based on data presented in Rodda *et al.* 1976.

influence on the cation content of stream water in South-West England. Streams draining granite uplands exhibit a cation composition dominated by sodium, whereas drainage originating on the younger sedimentary rocks in East Devon are rich in calcium, and runoff from the metamorphic rocks of the Lizard district is dominated by magnesium (Fig. 5.10c). Of the older sedimentary units, Carboniferous rocks are associated with Ca–Na and Na–Ca waters, whereas runoff from Devonian strata in the north and south of the peninsula is characterised by a wide range of cation composition. Variations in the geochemistry, mineralogy and textural and structural characteristics of major rock types in South-West England account in detail for contrasts in cation content, whereas the range of water

Solute levels

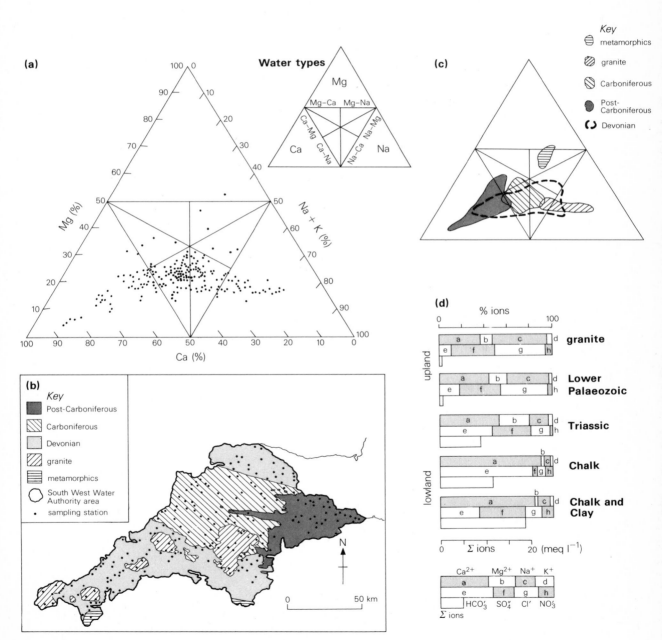

composition associated with drainage from a single stratigraphic unit may be related to lithological contrasts and the magnitude of total solute concentrations. In the latter context, the composition of runoff containing low dissolved solids concentrations will be highly susceptible to minor changes in the content of the major cations, and the wide range of water types associated with Devonian rock types in the South-West Peninsula may reflect this influence.

In view of the considerable geological diversity evident in Britain, a wide range of water composition can be expected in other regions. Contrasts may be particularly well developed between the rock types typical of upland Britain, which have drainage dominated by sodium, chloride and to a lesser extent sulphate, and strata characteristic of lowland areas, which yield runoff containing higher proportions of magnesium, calcium and bicarbonate (Fig. 5.10d). The last two solute species completely dominate water composition in chalk and limestone districts, whereas nitrate, chloride and sulphate make significant contributions to the anion content of streams in clay lowlands (Fig. 5.10d). However, it should be noted that land use, climate and other physiographic factors can strongly influence the chemical composition of drainage in the lowland zones of Britain.

Investigation of local variation in solute levels may usefully supplement information collected at the national and regional scales by allowing more detailed mapping of background water quality and by providing a better understanding of the complexity of the environmental controls which influence stream solute levels. Surveys of a single river system undertaken during a period of stable flows facilitate direct spatial comparisons of solute levels, and results from one such exercise in the catchment of the River Exe (1462 km^2) in Devon are presented in Figure 5.11. In this survey, samples were collected from approximately 270 sites in less than three days during a period of stable baseflow in June 1979. Sampling sites were located on small streams in order to investigate the quality of runoff at source, and the sampling network was designed both to give a good spatial coverage of the basin and to isolate drainage from different terrain types.

Examples of the resultant maps of spatial variation of solute levels relating to the parameters already considered at the national level are provided in Figure 5.11, and it is clearly apparent that local investigations may provide a more complex perspective of solute variations than is available from the archives of regional authorities. It is beyond the scope of the present chapter to comment in detail on the spatial patterns depicted on Figure 5.11. However, attention may be directed to the contrasting distributions associated with the individual parameters which in turn reflect the influence of different assemblages of controlling factors. In addition, the range of variation apparent serves to emphasise that local variations in background solute levels in many parts of Britain are likely to be considerably greater than has hitherto been generally appreciated.

Temporal variations

Mapping of solute concentrations and of solute loadings emphasises the spatial variation of background solute levels in Britain, but some consideration of the nature and extent of temporal variation in stream water chemistry and in solute transport is also necessary if the water quality of British rivers is to be fully documented. Investigations of temporal patterns of solute response should ideally be based on records from continuous monitoring equipment or from intensive sampling exercises at specific sites (Walling 1975). Considerable effort has been invested in the development of continuous monitoring equipment for use in

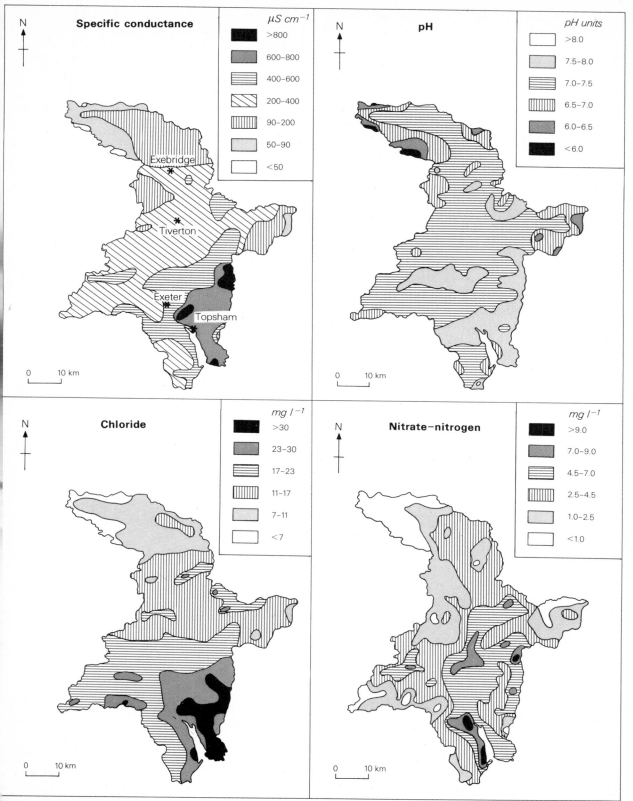

Figure 5.11 Local variations in baseflow solute levels recorded in the Exe Basin, Devon, in June 1979.

British rivers (e.g. Water Resources Board 1969, Briggs 1972) and a sophisticated computer-based telemetry system is now in operation in the River Lee catchment (Rodda *et al.* 1976). However, apparatus of this type is primarily orientated to the detection of parameters relating to river pollution rather than to background water chemistry, and the provision of measuring stations is by no means extensive or equally distributed across the country. Data collected in the Harmonised Monitoring scheme and in other routine sampling activities of regional authorities does provide some information on quality fluctuations through time, but these programmes seldom provide for sampling of discharge extremes, when changes in solute levels may be most marked. Furthermore, intensive monitoring by regional authorities is frequently concentrated on the downstream reaches of major river systems rather than on upstream tributaries. A data-base detailing temporal variations of solute levels, equivalent to that employed in mapping national patterns of solute concentrations and loads, is not available for Britain.

This lack of information is, however, partly offset by the considerable research interest in stream solute fluctuations shown by biologists and Earth scientists based in academic institutions and other establishments in Britain. Associated field investigations have primarily focused on the response of solute concentrations to changing flow conditions and solute concentration–discharge relationships have been documented at more than 60 sites in the United Kingdom. Although the information produced from these studies is to some extent restricted by the short duration of many data collection programmes and by inconsistencies in sampling strategies and monitoring periods between different studies, it does provide some insight into the character of temporal patterns of solute response in British rivers.

Figure 5.12a provides frequency distributions of the slope exponents and correlation coefficients associated with dissolved solids concentration–discharge relationships recorded at 60 sites in Britain. These relationships are of the form:

$$C = aQ^b$$

where C = specific conductance or total dissolved solids concentration, Q = discharge, a = constant and b = exponent. It is clear from the frequency histograms that solute concentrations in British rivers are characteristically diluted in increasing flows. Similar behaviour has been documented in many studies throughout the world and is readily accounted for by the varying origins of runoff during low and high streamflow conditions (Gregory & Walling 1973). More specifically, total solute concentration–discharge relationships in British rivers are characterised by strong correlations ($r > 0.8$) and by slope exponents in the range -0.09 to -0.12, and the rating plot for the River Barle at Brushford, Somerset (Fig. 5.12b) represents a conductance–streamflow relationship typical of those recorded in Britain. However, Figure 5.12b also provides examples of conductivity rating relationships which deviate from the common response both in terms of the degree of scatter and the existence of a positive rather than a negative relationship.

The concentration–discharge relationships associated with individual ions evidence considerable variation in response both between particular solute species and individual stations. For example, Figure 5.12c illustrates, in standardised form, the range and average response of the major cations at 12 stations in the Middle and Upper Exe Basin, Devon. Magnesium concentrations tend to be more strongly diluted with increasing flow than calcium or sodium levels, and it has been noted in several British studies (e.g. Imeson 1970a, Edwards 1973b, Brookes 1974, Spraggs 1976) that sodium generally exhibits a relatively limited range of temporal fluctuation. Potassium levels in many tributaries of the Middle and Upper Exe Basin (Fig. 5.12c) increase during high streamflow. A similar response has been recorded in other British streams (e.g. Waylen 1976, Foster 1977) and may be explained by the importance of vegetation leaching as a source of this ion during storm runoff events.

More complex solute concentration–discharge relationships have also been recorded in some British rivers. Walling (1971), for example, has reported that the rating curve for total dissolved solids may exhibit a compound form when runoff from contrasting terrain types contributes to streamflow at the catchment

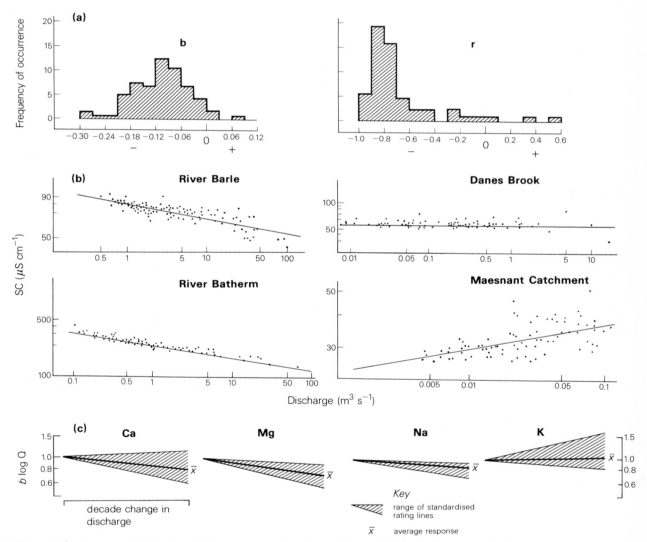

Figure 5.12 Frequency distributions of slope exponents, *b*, and correlation coefficients, *r*, associated with dissolved solids concentration–discharge relationships recorded at 60 sites in Britain (a). Conductance discharge rating plots recorded in 4 British rivers (b), and the range and average response of cation concentrations in the Middle and Upper Exe Basin, Devon. The latter are presented in standardised form which plots the change in *b* log *Q* over a one decade change in discharge (*Q*). Results presented for the Maesnant catchment (b) are based on Cryer (1978).

outlet (Fig. 5.13a). Quadratic rating relationships have been recorded for the River Chew, Avon (Brookes 1974), where calcium concentrations become virtually constant in low flows (Fig. 5.13b) and for the River Batherm, Devon, where calcium levels change very little at high discharges (Fig. 5.13c). A higher order polynomial has also been employed to describe the total dissolved solids response of the East Twin catchment, Mendip (Finlayson 1977), where solute concentrations react to the extremes of discharge, but are buffered over the greater part of the streamflow range (Fig. 5.13d).

In the rating plots for many British streams (e.g. Brookes 1974, Foster 1977, Cryer 1978) it is possible to distinguish samples collected at different times of the

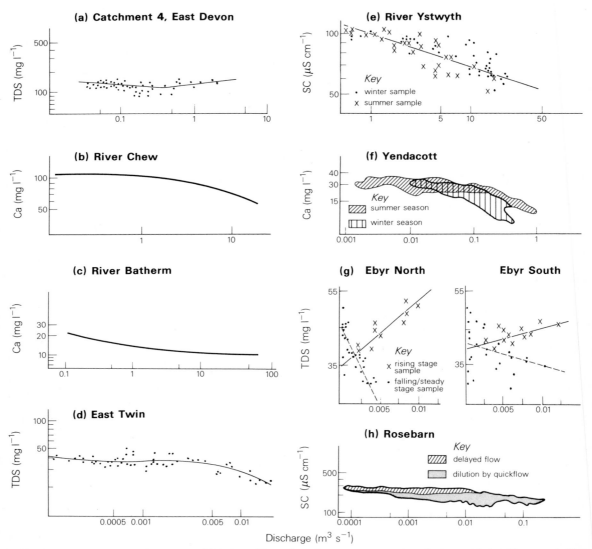

Figure 5.13 A selection of compound (a) and curvilinear (b to d) solute concentration–discharge relationships recorded in British rivers. Examples of rating plots in British catchments for which samples have been distinguished according to season of the year (e and f), stage conditions (g) and flow components (h). Results from the River Chew are based on Brookes (1974), from East Twin on Finlayson (1977), from the River Ystwyth on Cryer (1978), from Yendacott on Foster (1977), and from Ebyr N. and Ebyr S. on Oxley (1974).

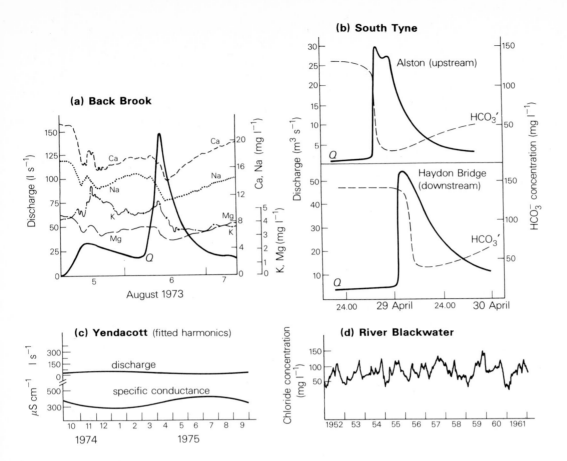

(b) South Tyne

(a) Back Brook

August 1973

(c) Yendacott (fitted harmonics)

(d) River Blackwater

year (Fig. 5.13e), and for some catchments and some instances seasonal contrasts in solute response (Fig. 5.13f) may be isolated statistically (e.g. Foster 1978a). Similar contrasts have been isolated in respect of hydrological conditions (e.g. Wilkinson 1971, Oxley 1974, Walling 1974) and separate rating relationships have been established for rising and falling stages (Fig. 5.13g) and for quickflow and delayed flow components of total runoff (Fig. 5.13h).

It is increasingly recognised that the storm-period solute behaviour of British rivers may be highly complex (e.g. Walling 1975, 1978, Burt 1979) and subject to multivariate control (Foster 1978b). Flushing of previously accumulated soluble material (e.g. Walling 1974, Spraggs 1976) especially during the first storms of autumn months (e.g. Edwards 1973b), may complicate stream solute behaviour (Fig. 5.14a), and this phenomenon may be greatly exaggerated when extreme meteorological events are juxtaposed as in the drought of 1976 (Slack 1977, Walling & Foster 1978, Walling 1980). In contrast, the occurrence of several closely spaced flood events may deplete solute supplies (Walling & Foster 1975). Solute behaviour in larger British catchments may be further complicated by the development of a kinematic differential between floodwave and flood water velocities (Glover & Johnson 1974), which causes the timing of the solute response to progressively lag behind the flood peak in a downstream direction (Fig. 5.14b), and by the aggregation and routing of solute responses from contrasting tributary areas, which may produce a wide range of solute behaviour at the catchment outlet (Walling & Webb 1980).

Figure 5.14 Storm-period flushing of solutes in the Back Brook, Devon (a), and a progressive lag effect recorded for bicarbonate concentrations during a storm event in the River South Tyne (b). Annual harmonic curves fitted to fluctuations in discharge and specific conductance levels in the Yendacott catchment, Devon (c), and seasonal changes in chloride concentrations of the River Blackwater resulting from varying dilution of sewage inputs (d). Results from the River South Tyne are based on Glover and Johnson (1974), from Yendacott on Foster (1977), and from the River Blackwater on Davis and Slack (1964).

151

Annual patterns of solute behaviour may also be isolated in British rivers. A distinctive annual cycle of solute accumulation and leaching, which is inversely related to annual discharge fluctuations, is discernible in some British catchments (Fig. 5.14c), whereas at other sites the annual march of total and individual solute levels have been found to strongly reflect autumn flushing and vegetation die-back (Edwards 1973b, Foster & Walling 1978), the contribution of dissolved material from precipitation (Sutcliffe & Carrick 1973), seasonal uptake by plants and animals (Edwards 1974, Casey 1975) and the varying dilution of sewage inputs (Davis & Slack 1964, Fig. 5.14d). In the longer term, it has been suggested that the solute concentrations of streams draining agricultural areas may have increased over the last 25 to 30 years in response to changes in cultivation, improvements in drainage and increases in fertiliser use and waste discharges. This trend has been particularly evident in Eastern England where, for example, Davis and Slack (1964) have noted a doubling of sulphate concentrations in the Rivers Chelmer and Blackwater between 1931 and 1963, and Edwards and Thornes (1973) have demonstrated that levels of conductivity, chloride, nitrate–nitrogen, ammoniacal nitrogen and non-carbonate hardness significantly increased in the River Stour between 1951 and 1970.

Consideration of temporal variations reveals that background solute levels in British rivers are far from being static, and that temporal behaviour of many solute species is complex. Storm-period fluctuations and annual cycles are super-imposed on longer-term trends in solute levels, and contrasting temporal solute responses in different areas of Britain will further diversify national, regional and local patterns of background water quality.

River water temperatures

The systematic recording of river water temperatures in British rivers can be traced back about 40 years to the measurements made on the River Nene in 1937 (Herschy 1965). Since that time, measuring stations have been established at a number of sites in order to provide information for fishery management, assessment of thermal pollution, and more broad-based water quality monitoring as well as specialised research investigations. However, activity has varied considerably from region to region and there is no nationally co-ordinated network of water temperature monitoring stations. The publication *Surface water: United Kingdom 1971–73* lists 68 locations where detailed records are maintained, and the instrumentation employed at these sites includes daily-read maximum and minimum thermometers, mercury-in-steel thermographs and the temperature measuring facilities of automatic water quality monitoring stations. The detail and quality of the data are variable, intermittent records are frequently encountered and data availability varies considerably from station to station. This general paucity of water temperature data has been paralleled by a lack of attempts to produce a countrywide analysis of this facet of water quality, but the work of Smith (1979) must stand as a notable exception. Furthermore, most of the studies that have been undertaken have been at the local scale and have been slanted towards biological considerations (e.g. Crisp & Le Cren 1970, Macan 1958, Gameson *et al.* 1959, Langford 1972) rather than the hydrological viewpoint.

Discussion of the temperature characteristics of British rivers must therefore be somewhat constrained by limited data availability, but can usefully commence with a brief consideration of a typical thermal regime. Figure 5.15 presents

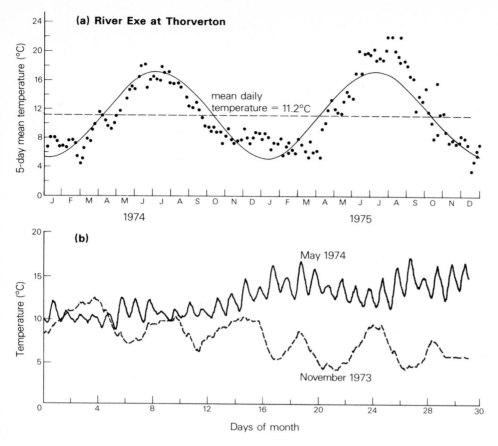

Figure 5.15 Variations in water temperature in the River Exe at Thorverton, illustrating (a) the annual variation of 5-day mean water temperatures and (b) the continuous traces of river water temperature for May 1974 and November 1973.

information on the annual (a) and diurnal (b) patterns of temperature variation recorded in the River Exe at Thorverton, Devon, with a catchment of 601 km². The annual pattern exhibits a well defined seasonal cycle with minimum temperatures in the period December to February and maximum values during June, July and August. A number of authors (e.g. Johnson 1971) have noted how this seasonal cycle can be approximated by a simple harmonic curve as has been superimposed on Figure 5.15a. At the diurnal level, water temperatures respond to day to day and diurnal variations in the energy budget, which are in turn reflected by variations in air temperature. Marked diurnal fluctuations may occur during the summer months (e.g. Fig. 5.15b) but, during the winter months, day to day variations associated with different weather conditions commonly provide the major source of variation (e.g. Fig. 5.15b). Where diurnal fluctuations are clearly developed, a phase lag between maximum air and water temperatures is generally evident, with maximum water temperatures occurring during the mid- or late afternoon.

In considering these general characteristics of the thermal regime of British rivers, it may be noted that temperatures rarely exceed 25°C or fall below 0°C, and that the upper limit is normally 16–22°C. Smith (1979) has found it useful to distinguish between streams and rivers in this context, since the smaller flows of streams are more responsive to heat exchange and their temperatures exhibit greater variation than larger rivers. Typical temperature characteristics of rivers and streams, as proposed by Smith (1979), are listed in Table 5.9.

Figure 5.16 provides an attempt to highlight countrywide variations in water

153

Table 5.9 Typical characteristics of the thermal regimes of British rivers.

Characteristic	Streams	Rivers
annual maximum	25°C	20°C
annual minimum	0°C	1°C
diurnal range (winter)	2°C	<1°C
diurnal range (summer)	10–12°C	3°C
maximum rate of change	3°C hr^{-1}	0.5–1.0°C hr^{-1}

Based on Smith (1979).

temperature regimes by plotting the maximum and minimum temperatures recorded at a number of recording stations on major rivers during the calendar year 1978. No clear pattern is immediately apparent but the considerable variation evident may be related to a number of controls including climate and human activity. Both maximum and minimum temperatures are influenced by general climatic conditions, since temperatures commonly decrease with increasing latitude and altitude. Thus the maximum temperature of 18.8°C recorded on the River Almond in Scotland may be contrasted with that of 22.3°C from the River Culm in South-West England. This general climatic control is further evidenced in Figure 5.17a which plots monthly mean temperatures for two upland rivers in Scotland and northern England and for two lowland rivers in southern England. At certain times of the year, there is as much as 5°C difference between the monthly mean temperature recorded in the River Wear (202 m OD) and that reported for the Bristol Avon (17 m OD). The precise character of the runoff

Figure 5.16 Countrywide variation in the maximum and minimum water temperatures recorded at a number of measuring sites during 1978.

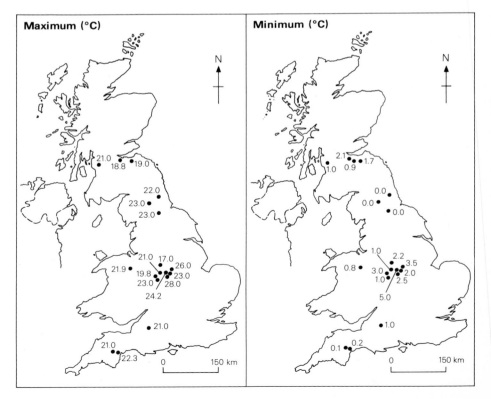

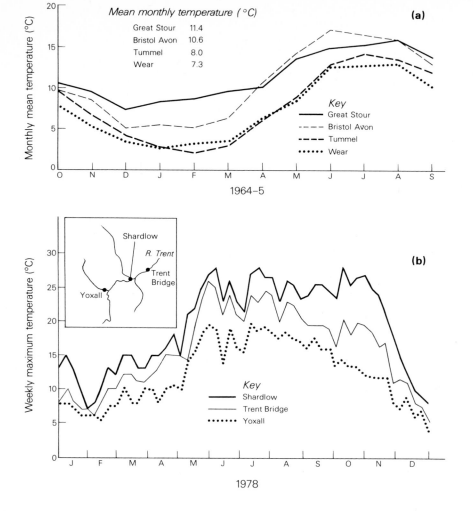

Figure 5.17 Annual variation of monthly mean water temperatures, 1964–5, for 4 British rivers (a) and a comparison of weekly maximum temperatures during 1978 at three stations on the River Trent (b). The data presented in (b) were kindly made available by the Severn–Trent Water Authority.

regime is also important, since it is frequently observed that rivers exhibiting a large groundwater flow component exhibit less annual variation in temperature due to the relatively constant temperature of groundwater outflow. The elevated monthly mean temperatures evidenced during the winter by the Great Stour in Figure 5.17a may, for example, be related to this influence.

The countrywide pattern of maximum and minimum temperatures depicted in Figure 5.16 also reflects the influence of thermal pollution. The values plotted for a number of stations in the Trent basin are considerably higher than those in neighbouring areas and may be related to the effects of thermal discharges from electricity generating stations sited along this river. Thermal pollution from industrial effluent and particularly from power stations is also important in several other British rivers including the Severn (Langford 1970), the Lea (Gameson *et al.* 1959) and the Ouse (Alabaster 1969). Over 50% of Britain's electricity is now produced at power stations sited on rivers, and surface water abstraction by the Central Electricity Generating Board for cooling purposes accounts for about half of the licensed water abstraction in England and Wales (Smith 1979). Modern British power stations require about 3.5 $m^3 s^{-1}$ of cooling water per 100 MW generated (Hawes 1970), and cooling is frequently indirect in the larger stations

155

because of the large volumes required. This involves the circulation of water through cooling towers and the abstraction of only about 3% of the water requirement from the river, in order to replenish a 1% evaporative loss and a 2% return necessary to avoid excessive build-up of dissolved solids in the cooling water (Ross 1970).

An example of the impact of thermal pollution on the temperature regime of the River Trent is provided in Figure 5.17b. This presents weekly maximum temperatures recorded for an upstream station at Yoxall, for a measuring point at Shardlow, about 5 km below Castle Donington Power Station, and for Trent Bridge a further 15 km downstream. The temperatures recorded at Yoxall may be viewed as essentially natural, whereas those found at Shardlow, which are up to 8°C higher, reflect thermal pollution from a series of upstream power stations as well as from the station in the immediate vicinity. The partial recovery apparent for the temperatures recorded at Trent Bridge may be ascribed both to heat loss from the river and to the influence of tributary inflows. Maximum temperatures in excess of 30°C have been reported for the Trent but the maximum temperature recorded for a river influenced by thermal pollution is probably the value of 32°C cited by Langford and Aston (1972) for the Great Ouse.

It must be recognised that the general countrywide trends apparent in Figure 5.16 and discussed above will be further complicated by the influence of local catchment characteristics and channel conditions on river water temperatures. The presence or absence of trees lining a river channel and providing shade can exert an important control on the temperature regime of a stream causing lower maximum temperatures and higher minima. For example, Roberts and James (1972) have compared the forested headwaters of the River Severn in Central Wales with the adjacent headwaters of the River Wye draining an area of open sheep pasture and have reported that monthly mean temperatures in the Severn are generally 2°C cooler in summer and up to 1°C warmer in winter. Similarly Gray and Edington (1969) describe how felling of woodland bordering a small tributary of the River Coquet in Northumberland produced an increase in summer maxima of up to 6.5°C.

The influence of vegetation cover and other local factors including channel character and flow volume on river water temperatures is also demonstrated in Figure 5.18a, which depicts the monthly maximum, mean and minimum temperatures recorded at 18 sites within the Exe basin during July 1976 and 1977. During both years there was considerable local variation in the maximum, mean and minimum temperatures recorded at the individual sites and a clear tendency for temperatures to increase along the course of the trunk stream so that, for example, the maximum temperature of 18.4°C recorded in the headwaters of the River Exe during July 1976 contrasted with values of 25.2°C and 27.0°C in the lower reaches of the Rivers Exe and Culm. This trend is different from that reported by Smith (1975) in a study of the downstream temperature profile of the River Tees, for in that case the highest absolute maxima were recorded in the upper basin.

The summer of 1976 was a period of drought conditions and extremely low river flows and a comparison of the temperature values depicted for the individual years therefore provides some indication of the influence of flow volumes on water temperature. Maximum temperatures recorded during July 1976 were in all cases higher than those recorded in July 1977, with increases of 3.6°C evident at certain stations. These increases partly reflect increased air temperatures but the reduced thermal inertia of the dwindling river flows was clearly also significant since minimum temperatures were in some cases lower during 1976. Further evidence of the influence of drought conditions on temperature regimes within the Exe basin is provided in Figure 5.18b which compares the complete record for August 1976 from the River Exe at Thorverton and the River Barle at Brushford with that for 1974. Both rivers clearly demonstrate increased temperatures during 1976 but certain contrasts in behaviour are evident. The pronounced diurnal variation of up to 4°C recorded at Brushford may be related to the extremely low flow volumes and the shallow rock-floored channel. At Thorverton, the diurnal variation is probably less than that recorded during the more normal conditions of 1974 and

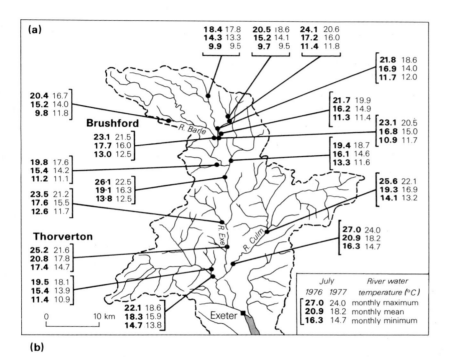

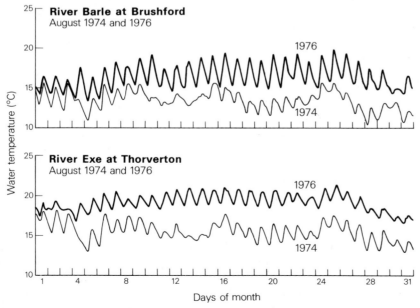

Figure 5.18 A comparison of July monthly maximum, mean and minimum water temperatures recorded within the Exe basin during the drought conditions of 1976 and during the summer of 1977 (a). The continuous traces of water temperature for August 1974 and August 1976 from the River Barle at Brushford and the River Exe at Thorverton are compared in (b).

157

both this feature and the greater overall increase in temperatures may be related to the extended residence times and slow downstream transfer of channel flow which produced a temperature response in the main channel more akin to that of a static water body.

Suspended sediment transport

Measurements of suspended sediment transport are not explicitly included in any of the current monitoring programmes operated by national and regional authorities in Britain. In the past, the former Trent River Authority instituted a number of sediment load investigations (Potter 1973), but these were discontinued after reorganisation of the river authorities and they probably represent the only exception to the general lack of coverage of this aspect of river water quality. The absence of a national programme of sediment measurement contrasts with the situation in many other European countries, including Sweden (WMO 1977), West Germany (Bundesanstalt für Gewasserkunde 1977), and Poland (Branski 1968) where such activity is firmly established, and may be largely accounted for by an apparent lack of need for data of this type in Britain. Reservoir sedimentation problems are considered to be minimal in most areas, sediment concentrations rarely rise to levels presenting serious difficulties to water treatment works and problems associated with soil erosion and channel sedimentation are similarly viewed as being of insufficient significance to merit such a programme. Recent awareness of the role of suspended sediment in the transport of nutrients and contaminants in sediment-associated form (e.g. Shear & Watson 1977) may, however, provide a new perspective on this question and the inclusion of the assessment of particulate matter transport within the scope of the Harmonised Monitoring Programme may awaken interest in measurement of sediment transport.

Fortunately, this lack of activity at the national level has been partly offset by the efforts of workers in academic institutions and other research establishments who have responded to the lack of data by initiating sediment measuring programmes in local rivers. The stimulus for such work has frequently been a geomorphological interest in rates of erosion and landscape development as well as concern for practical problems of estuary and harbour sedimentation. Early work by Marshall (1957) at the University of Leeds was followed by that of Hall (1967) on the River Tyne, Fleming (1969a) on rivers draining to the Clyde estuary, Walling (1971) on Devon rivers, Collins (1973) on Sussex rivers and a number of more recent studies (cf. Table 5.11). These studies have involved a variety of approaches, and the techniques employed have included traditional manual sampling procedures (e.g. Hall 1967), the use of automatic sampling equipment (e.g. Walling & Teed 1971) as well as the application of photo-electric turbidity sensing equipment to the continuous recording of suspended sediment concentrations (e.g. Fleming 1969b, Walling 1977b).

The nature of these investigations is, however, such that any attempt to provide a countrywide evaluation of the results obtained faces several problems. Many of the measurement programmes only continued for a few years and their short duration means that it is difficult, if not impossible, to estimate properties of the long-term record such as mean annual sediment yield for the sites concerned. Similarly, the resultant lack of contemporaneity of the measurement programmes introduces certain problems into any attempt to compare results from one area to another. The longest detailed record of suspended sediment transport in a British river is probably that available for the River Creedy in Devon (cf. Walling 1977b) which commenced in 1972 and at present extends to nearly 8 years. Considerable uncertainty also surrounds the reliability and comparability of the data produced. For example, Walling (1977b) has shown that different methods of calculating sediment yields may produce considerable variation in the resultant estimates and this variability must inevitably be further compounded by the use of different measurement and sampling strategies. These problems and uncertainties may be highlighted by reference to two instances in which the estimates of sediment yield from a catchment produced by different workers show little agreement. Thus values of annual suspended sediment yield of 56.9 t km^{-2} yr^{-1} and 6.9 t km^{-2} yr^{-1} have been cited for the River Esk in Yorkshire by Marshall (1957) and Arnett (1979) respectively, and values as different as 488 t km^{-2} yr^{-1} and 2.1 t km^{-2} yr^{-1} have been reported by Imeson (1970a) and Arnett (1979) for the Hodge Beck in Yorkshire. Caution is also required in any attempt to use information on sediment transport provided by a water quality sampling programme not specifically designed for that purpose. A large proportion of the suspended sediment yield from a drainage basin will be transported during a small number of major floods and these are unlikely to be sampled by a programme involving regular weekly or fortnightly sampling.

In addition to the information provided by measurements undertaken at river gauging stations, estimates of sediment yield may also be obtained from surveys of reservoir deposition. In Britain, data from this source is very limited but, nevertheless, provides a valuable perspective on long-term sediment yields, since the measured accumulation usually relates to a period in excess of 50 years. Again, measurements of this type have been undertaken as isolated case studies rather than as part of a national programme and involve a number of uncertainties as to the trap efficiency of the reservoir, and the methods used to estimate the volume and bulk density of the deposits.

Notwithstanding the problems of data availability and reliability outlined above, it is possible to make a number of meaningful generalisations concerning suspended sediment transport in British rivers. This review can usefully consider first, the magnitude and pattern of variation of suspended sediment concentrations; secondly, the composition of the sediment involved; and finally the magnitude of suspended sediment yields and their regional variation.

Maximum levels of suspended sediment concentration encountered in British rivers rarely exceed 5000 mg l^{-1} and in many rivers concentrations do not rise above 1000 mg l^{-1}. Values in excess of 5000 mg l^{-1} are probably restricted to small streams draining areas disturbed by human activity. Robinson (1979) documents concentrations in excess of 7500 mg l^{-1} in a stream draining an area disturbed by forest ditching operations and Walling (1974) has reported a concentration of 9000 mg l^{-1} in a small stream draining an area of residential development on the margin of Exeter, Devon. Even higher values of over 50000 mg l^{-1} have been encountered in some Cornish streams receiving drainage from china clay workings (Richards 1979). Figure 5.19 provides information on the sediment concentrations measured in four rivers representative of contrasting areas of Britain by depicting the suspended sediment rating plots or concentration–discharge relationships for these rivers. In all four cases, concentrations exhibit the universally documented positive relationship with discharge and range from about 1.0 mg l^{-1} during low flows to approximately 1000 mg l^{-1} during extreme flood discharges. In this respect, therefore, there is little difference between the River Rother which drains

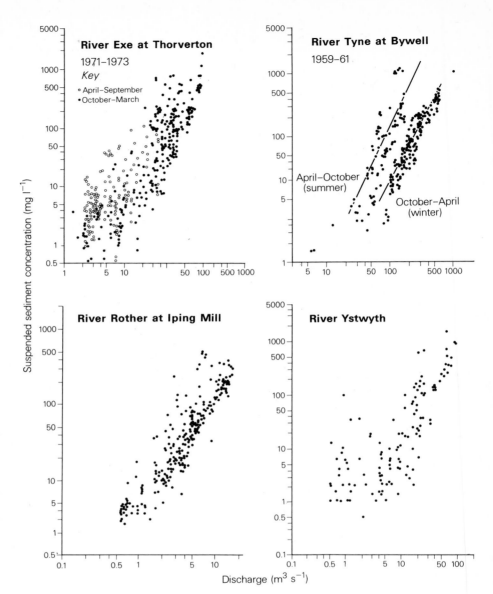

Figure 5.19 Suspended sediment concentration–discharge rating relationships for four British rivers. Results from the River Tyne are based on Hall (1967), from the River Rother on Wood (1977), and from the River Ystwyth on University of Wales (1977).

an area of Cretaceous rocks in South-East England and the River Ystwyth draining an upland catchment in Central Wales, the River Tyne in North-East England and the River Exe in South-West England.

The scatter associated with the rating plots depicted in Figure 5.19 is typical of sediment transport systems which are supply limited and may be related to seasonal effects, to hysteresis in the concentration–discharge relationship during individual events and to progressive exhaustion of sediment supply during a sequence of storm hydrographs (e.g. Walling 1974, 1978, Wood 1977). The seasonal effect is marked by the tendency for concentrations for a particular discharge to be higher in summer than in winter. This is clearly evident in the plot for the River Exe where summer and winter samples have been distinguished, and that for the Tyne where the best-fit lines for the two periods are shown. The effects of exhaustion are exemplified in Figure 5.20a which shows the variation of

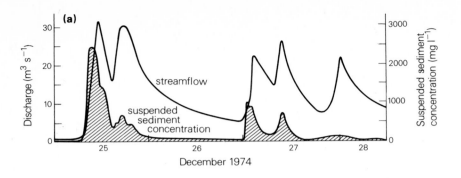

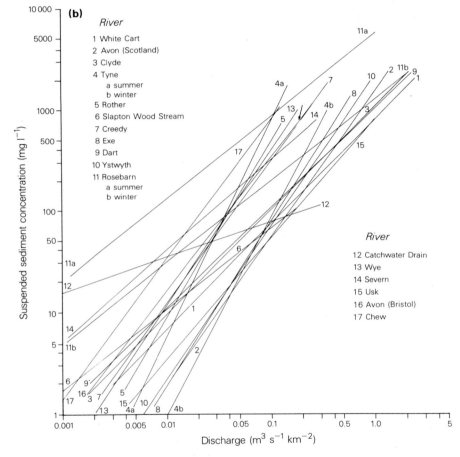

Figure 5.20 Variations in suspended sediment concentration during a series of storm hydrographs on the River Dart, Devon (a) and a compilation of the straight line sediment concentration/discharge relationships for a selection of British rivers (b). Further details of the rivers represented on (b) are listed in Table 5.11.

suspended sediment concentration during a multiple peaked storm runoff event in the River Dart, a tributary of the River Exe in Devon.

A number of workers (e.g. Bogardi 1961, Bauer & Tille 1967, Rannie 1978) have suggested that the exponent (*b*) and constant (*a*) in the suspended sediment concentration (*C*)/discharge (*Q*) relationship of the form:

$$C = aQ^b$$

may be related to the sediment generating characteristics of the contributing drainage basin. Thus while Wolman (1977) and Gregory and Walling (1973) have

161

noted that values of the exponent (b) commonly range between 1.0 and 2.0, it should prove possible to characterise British rivers in terms of a typical value. The straight line logarithmic rating relationship for a selection of British rivers have been plotted on Figure 5.20b, with discharge (Q) values expressed in terms of discharge per unit area ($m^3 \ s^{-1} \ km^{-2}$) in order to facilitate comparison. On the basis of this information it may be suggested that an exponent value of approximately 1.2 is typical of British rivers and that values range between about 0.3 and 2.0. This range may be compared with one of approximately 0.1 to 3.2 reported by Rannie (1978) from a global analysis. Figure 5.20b also indicates that there is a tendency for the exponent (b) and constant (a) values of these rating relationships to be inversely related and it can be tentatively proposed that low values of b and high values of a are associated with rivers draining lowland clay catchments and that high values of b and therefore low values of a are indicative of rivers draining upland catchments developed on resistant rocks.

The general lack of detailed data concerning suspended sediment transport by British rivers is paralleled by an absence of information on the properties of that sediment. Nevertheless, some limited evidence concerning particle size characteristics, organic matter content and mineralogy may be presented. Attempts to undertake particle size analysis on suspended sediment samples from British rivers have frequently been hampered by the difficulties of obtaining sufficient quantities of particulate material and the results produced by individual studies must be evaluated critically in the light of both the method of sample collection and the procedure employed for particle-size analysis. For example, the data presented by Brookes (1974) refer to particulate material trapped in mesh collectors and are doubtless biased towards the coarser fractions, and Collins (1973) indicates that the predominance of silt-sized material and the lack of a significant clay fraction in samples analysed from a number of Sussex streams was probably a function of the instrument (Coulter Counter) used.

Figure 5.21 presents information on the average particle-size distribution of suspended sediment from the River Dart, a tributary of the River Exe in Devon. The samples were not treated to remove organic material and were analysed dispersed in both natural river water and a chemical dispersing agent (sodium hexametaphosphate) using a Sedigraph apparatus. The results are viewed as

Figure 5.21 The average particle-size distribution of suspended sediment from the River Dart, Devon. A distinction has been made between chemically dispersed sediment and sediment dispersed in natural river water.

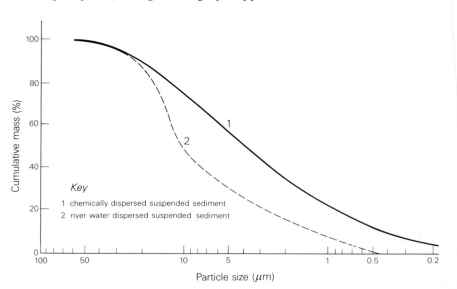

Key
1 chemically dispersed suspended sediment
2 river water dispersed suspended sediment

Table 5.10 Values of organic matter content of suspended sediment reported for British rivers.

	Organic matter content %	Method of determination	Source
Ystwyth	1.9–18.5	hydrogen peroxide oxidation	University of Wales (1977)
Sussex rivers	10–30	ashing	Collins (1973)
East Twin	15–37	dichromate oxidation	Finlayson (1977)
Dorset Frome	5–60	loss on ignition, POC × 2	Far (pers. comm., 1978)
N. York Moor rivers	24–71 (low flows) average 20 (storms)	dichromate oxidation	Arnett (1978)
Clyde	average 18		
Kelvin	average 15	loss on ignition	Fleming (1969a)
White Cart	average 27		
Rother	average 20	loss on ignition	Wood (1976)
Exe Basin streams	average 7–14	organic carbon × 2	Walling and Peart (1980)

providing a meaningful characterisation of the suspended sediment transported by this river. The difference between the two curves has been related to the tendency for sediment to be transported as aggregates which are broken down when the material is chemically dispersed. This contrast has important implications for any attempt to study the mechanics of suspended sediment transport in terms of the particle-size distribution of chemically dispersed material. Nevertheless, reference will be made to the size distribution of chemically dispersed sediment since results presented by other workers are generally of this nature. In this river, which has a cobble-lined channel, there is an absence of sand-sized material and a considerable fraction (*c.* 50%) of the sediment comprises particles in the clay size-range. Clearly, a greater proportion of sand-sized material could be expected in streams draining catchments with a significant source of such material either within the channel or in the soils, but the distribution shown in Figure 5.21 closely resembles those presented for suspended sediment samples from the River Ystwyth (University of Wales 1977). In that river, the sand-sized fraction of the samples analysed was less than 10% and the clay fraction varied between 60% and about 20%.

Similar problems of reliability surround any attempt to compile information on the organic matter content typical of suspended sediment from British rivers. Methods used for organic matter determinations have included loss on ignition, organic carbon determinations and a variety of wet-oxidation procedures. Table 5.10 presents results from a number of British rivers along with information on the method used to determine organic matter content. These values range between 1.9 and 71%, but values of 10–30% can probably be viewed as representative of British rivers. Furthermore, it must be recognised that the percentage of organic

Table 5.11 Suspended sediment yields of British catchments.

Catchment	Area (km²)	Period of record	Load t km⁻² yr⁻¹	Source
Almond	176	1972–4	59	Al-Ansari *et al.* (1977)
Earn	—	1972–4	97	
Clyde at Blairston	1700	1967–8	62	
Clyde at Daldowie	1900	1964–7	60	
White Cart	235	1964–7	122	
Kelvin	335	1967–8	33	Fleming (1970)
Leven	784	1966–7	36	
Avon	266	1964–7	174	
Tyne	2159	1959–61	61	Hall (1967)
Gullet Syke	1.0	long term estimate	194	
West Grain	1.51	long term estimate	256	Wilkinson (1971)
Langden Brook	15.3	long term estimate	232	
Swale at Grinton	220	1955–7	111	
Swale at Leckby	1383	1956	25	Marshall (1957)
Esk	310	1956–7	57	
Hodge Beck	18.9	1966–8	488	Imeson (1970a)
Catchwater Drain	15.0	1966–8	8.9	
Ystwyth	170	1973–5	164	University of Wales (1977)
Ebyr N.	0.07	1971	1.1	Oxley (1974)
Ebyr S.	0.09	1971	0.8	
Nene	1530	1968–70	11	Collins (1973)
Welland	531	1968–70	14	

Catchment	Area (km²)	Period of record	Load t km⁻² yr⁻¹	Source
Severn	6850	1937–72	65	
Usk	912	1957–72	46	
Wye	4040	1949–72	51	
Chew Stoke Stream	6.47	1971–2	70	
Chew	133	1971–2	26	
Wellow Brook	70	1971–2	48	Brookes (1974)
Midford Brook	147	1971–2	37	
Frome	256	1971–2	35	
Semington Brook	152	1971–2	15	
Marden	96	1971–2	52	
Gauze Brook	24	1971–2	28	
Avon	666	1971–2	27	
East Twin	0.18	1972–3	2.0	Finlayson (1977)
Creedy	262	1972–4	53	
Dart	46	1975	91	Walling (1978)
Exe	601	1974–5	24	
East Devon catchments				
1	0.11	1967–8	9.5	
2	0.47	1967–8	37	
3	0.78	1967–8	50	Walling (1971)
4	4.97	1967–8	46	
5	6.4	1967–8	56	
Sid	39.3	1967–8	47	
Slapton Wood	0.94	1971–2	8.4	Troake and Walling (1973)
Rother	154	1972	14	Wood (1976)
Balcombe	3.1	1968–70	44	
Billingshurst	7.6	1968–70	148	
Clayhill I	8.6	1968–70	13	
Clayhill II	5.18	1968–70	14	
Fulking	0.18	1968–70	12	
Nutley	0.86	1968–70	5.8	Collins (1973)
Winterbourne	17.6	1968–70	1.8	
W. Adur	108	1968–70	41	
Cuckmere	133	1968–70	9.2	
Ouse	179	1967–8	33	

In some instances, the period of record relates to the study period. In others, a sediment rating relationship derived from a relatively short period of measurement has been applied to flow records from a longer period to estimate sediment yield for that period.

matter will frequently increase during the summer months and that an inverse relationship between organic matter content and suspended sediment concentration may exist.

Little work has been undertaken to date on the mineralogy of suspended sediment from British rivers but the work of Wood (1978) on the Sussex Rother can usefully be cited. In this case, the mineralogy of suspended sediment was found to be closely related to that of the soils in the catchment, although more detailed analysis indicated that such factors as the incidence of bedrock erosion within the river channel, the precipitation of minerals from solution, the preferential deposition of certain minerals and the relative importance of groundwater and surface runoff contributions exercised an important control on the precise composition of the sediment. In many rivers, ion exchange reaction between clay

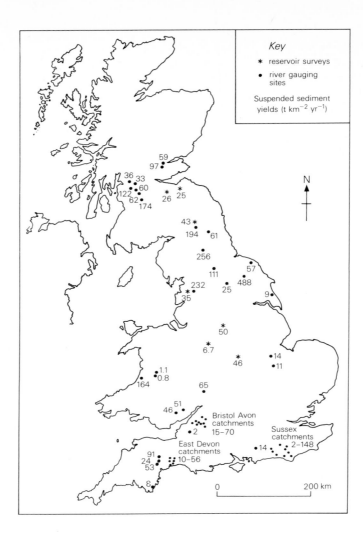

Figure 5.22 Countrywide variation in suspended sediment yields reported from river gauging stations (Table 5.11) and reservoir surveys (Table 5.12).

minerals and the solute phase could also be expected to exercise an influence.

Recognising the problem of reliability outlined above, measurements of annual suspended sediment yield from 56 British catchments are listed in Table 5.11. These values have also been plotted according to location in Figure 5.22. On the basis of this data compilation, sediment yields of British rivers may be seen to range from <1.0 t km^{-2} yr^{-1} to nearly 500 t km^{-2} yr^{-1}. Higher values could be encountered in small streams draining highly disturbed areas such as construction sites or clay workings. However, a value of 50 t km^{-2} yr^{-1} could be proposed as typical of British rivers and this must be viewed as low when compared with the global data presented by Walling and Kleo (1979) which exhibited a range between approximately 1 t km^{-2} yr^{-1} and 10000 t km^{-2} yr^{-1}. Available estimates of long-term sediment yield based on reservoir surveys are presented in Table 5.12. In this case the number of catchments involved is small but the estimates of sediment supply are entirely consistent with the data based on shorter term measurements of sediment yield at river gauging stations (Fig. 5.22). The average rate of sediment supply to these reservoirs is about 30 t km^{-2} yr^{-1}.

The number of rivers for which sediment yield data are available is inadequate to permit the construction of a meaningful map of sediment yield for Britain, but a number of tentative generalisations can be made on the basis of Figure 5.22. Loads in excess of 100 t km^{-2} yr^{-1} would seem to be associated primarily with upland areas receiving annual precipitation greater than 1000 mm and, within these areas, with small- and intermediate-sized catchments where sediment delivery ratios will be relatively high. Conversely low suspended sediment yields (<25 t km^{-2} yr^{-1}) would appear to reflect low annual precipitation (e.g. River Welland and River Nene), large basins where sediment delivery ratios will be relatively low (River Swale at Leckby Grange), and low relief (Catchwater Drain). Very low suspended sediment yields (<5 t km^{-2} yr^{-1}), represented by the East Twin catchment on the Mendip Hills and the Ebyr N. and Ebyr S. catchments in central Wales, may be accounted for in terms of the small headwater areas involved, the resistant bedrock and the essentially undisturbed conditions found in these upland areas. Local factors including land use and catchment lithology will clearly introduce further complexity and the relatively high sediment yield of the Billingshurst catchment in Sussex (148 t km^{-2} yr^{-1}) is, for example, undoubtedly influenced by the Weald Clay underlying this area. The availability of more reliable data and of a denser network of measuring stations must, however, be awaited before these local effects can be fully documented.

Table 5.12 Estimates of long-term sediment yield obtained from surveys of reservoir sedimentation.

River	Reservoir	Catchment area km^2	Sediment yield t km^{-2} yr^{-1}	Source
Rede	Catcleugh	40.0	43.1	Hall (1967)
Bradgate	Cropston	17.8	45.6	Cummins and Potter (1972)
Loxley	Strines	7.4	49.7	Young (1958b)
N. Esk	N. Esk	7.0	26.0	Ledger *et al.* (1974)
N. Tyne	Hopes	5.0	25.0	Ledger *et al.* (1974)
Churnet	Deep Hayes	9.8	6.7	Rodda *et al.* (1976)
Wyre	Abbeystead	47.3	34.8	Rodda *et al.* (1976)

To assist in comparison, volumes of reservoir sediment have been converted to estimates of sediment yield using uniform conversion factors. These assume that deposited sediments contain 82% water and have a specific gravity of 2.1 (cf. Ledger *et al.* 1974).

Geomorphologists have frequently used a comparison of the magnitude of the suspended sediment and the dissolved solids yield from a drainage basin as a means of assessing the relative efficacy of mechanical and chemical denudation processes. This approach necessarily involves numerous problems such as the need to account for the non-denudational component of the solute load and contrasts in the delivery mechanisms influencing sediment and solute yields. Nevertheless, it is appropriate to conclude this brief consideration of suspended sediment transport by British rivers by referring to Table 5.13 which compares the annual suspended and gross dissolved loads for a number of rivers. Solute loads generally exceed suspended sediment loads and in many instances solute yields account for more than 90% of the combined load. Values of the sediment:solute ratio in excess of 1.0 are largely associated with upland areas where the underlying rocks are chemically resistant and where stream solute concentrations are therefore relatively low (cf. Fig. 5.3). More detailed comparative analysis involving such considerations as the transport of cations or nutrients in solution and in

167

Table 5.13 The relative magnitude of suspended sediment and total dissolved solids loads reported for British rivers.[a]

River	Suspended sediment load $t\,km^{-2}\,yr^{-1}$	Solute load $t\,km^{-2}\,yr^{-1}$	Sediment:solute ratio
Tyne	61	38	1.6
Gullet Syke	194	66	2.96
West Grain	256	102	2.51
Langden Brook	232	110	2.11
Swale at Grinton	111	143	0.77
Swale at Leckby	25	123	0.20
Esk	57	51	1.12
Hodge Beck	488	53	9.1
Catchwater Drain	8.9	129	0.07
Ebyr N.	1.1	5.4	0.21
Ebyr S.	0.8	4.1	0.19
Severn	65	109	0.60
Usk	46	129	0.36
Wye	51	92	0.55
Avon	27	148	0.18
East Twin	2.0	21	0.10
Creedy	53	61	0.87
Dart	91	61	1.50
Exe	24	85	0.28
East Devon catchments			
1	9.5	35	0.26
2	37	57	0.65
3	50	42	1.18
4	46	84	0.53
5	56	69	0.81
Slapton Wood	8.4	57	0.15
Balcombe	44	95	0.46
Billingshurst	148	124	1.2
Clayhill I	13	61	0.22
Clayhill II	14	67	0.21
Fulking	12	539	0.02
Nutley	5.8	63	0.09
Winterbourne	1.8	44	0.04
W. Adur	41	95	0.43
Cuckmere	9.2	74	0.12
Ouse	33	86	0.39

[a] Further information concerning the areas of the catchments cited and the source of data is provided in Table 5.11.

sediment-associated form would provide an additional facet on this theme but suitable data are again lacking.

Figure 5.23 which presents a plot of suspended load versus dissolved load for the stations listed in Table 5.13 also provides a British perspective on the general controversy surrounding the interrelationship of these two load components. Thus while Meybeck (1976) and Strahkov (1967) argue for a positive relationship, Judson and Ritter (1964) propose that the relationship is inverse. The data presented in Figure 5.23 are not conclusive in this context, since considerable

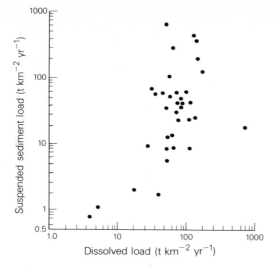

Figure 5.23 The relationship between suspended sediment and dissolved loads provided by available British data.

scatter exists. Nevertheless they suggest that a positive relationship between the two load components is characteristic of British rivers and that increased solute loads are generally paralleled by increased suspended sediment loads. Figure 5.23 also evidences a contrast in the range of values associated with the two load components. Thus whereas the majority of the dissolved loads fall within the relatively narrow band of 30–150 t km^{-2} yr^{-1}, the associated suspended sediment loads range over nearly two orders of magnitude between 5 and 300 t km^{-2} yr^{-1}.

Conclusions

In comparison with many other areas of equivalent size, Britain exhibits a remarkable diversity of natural and cultural environments, and the considerable variation in water quality conditions, encountered in British rivers and outlined in the present chapter, inevitably reflects differences in the physical and human landscape. A strong contrast between gross pollution in a small proportion of rivers and the absence of contamination from the majority of watercourses in Britain is obvious from national surveys and is readily attributable to the activities of man. Less immediately apparent, but no less significant, is the variation of background water quality in unpolluted streams. Solute levels in Britain are characterised by rapid fluctuations in space and time, and concentrations and loads are highly sensitive to geological, climatic, land use and topographic conditions. Furthermore, spatial patterns of solute variation become increasingly complex as the scale of resolution is changed from the national to the local level. Suspended sediment transport and temperature characteristics of British rivers are also strongly influenced by physiographic contrasts and are by no means uniform across the country. However, these physical aspects of background water quality perhaps exhibit somewhat less variation than might be encountered in areas of comparable size elsewhere in the world.

The present chapter has primarily sought to define the nature and extent of variations in water quality conditions in Britain. However, it should also be recognised that the presence of watercourses varying greatly in quality characteristics has important implications for the utilisation of British rivers, and attention is given to this aspect of water management in the next chapter.

169

6 River management

T. R. Wood

River management is the art of resolving conflicting demands upon a natural resource and at the same time attempting to define and conserve the essential features of that resource. In Britain, the high population density and high level of water consumption mean that substantial demands are made of rivers both to support abstractions and to accept industrial and domestic effluent. The uneven spread of population and the east–west rainfall gradient combine to make some English rural rivers and many British urban rivers very badly over-subscribed. However, even in remote rural areas conflicting demands are evident, for example, in the form of leisure activities such as angling, with its need to conserve a variety of physical river characteristics, and the demands of the agricultural community to improve land drainage by lowering the water table. There are few British rivers and almost no English rivers where the regime is unaltered by such demands. As a consequence there are now several common ground rules employed in the Water Industry to aid the definition of a river's essential characteristics and to test the acceptability of the demands that are made. These essential characteristics range from the hydraulic capacity of the channel to the frequency and magnitude of low flows and the quality of the river water itself. These ground rules are not immutable and often are not expressed within one document easily available to the public, but they have been developed through a long history of river engineering and water supply practice. Much of this chapter is devoted to their discussion.

Democratic land drainage institutions in Britain date back at least to the 13th century (Dangerfield 1979). However, it was the Industrial Revolution with the consequent growth in demand for water supply and for water-borne sewage disposal which necessitated legislation to deal with river water quality and resource management. In the 19th century epidemics of water-borne disease prompted the newly emergent towns and cities to secure remote and therefore wholesome water supplies via a series of private Acts of Parliament and to provide more adequate means of sewage disposal, for by that time many rivers were in an appalling condition. The Thames, for example, was in a particularly bad state, the stench being so bad that sheets drenched in disinfectant had to be hung over the windows of Parliament. In 1865 a Rivers Commission was appointed to look into means for preventing the pollution of rivers. This resulted in the Rivers Pollution Prevention Acts of 1876 and 1893. However, these Acts disregarded one of the Commission's conclusions which was that effective river management could only be conducted over entire river basins, unhampered by the artificial boundaries of local government. Again, the 1902 Royal Commission on Salmon Fisheries and the Royal Commission on Sewage both urged the formation of local river boards, but that was only achieved in England and Wales in 1930 with the establishment of Catchment Boards to exercise pollution control and drainage functions. In 1948 the River Boards Act created river basin bodies responsible for land drainage, pollution prevention and fisheries. In 1963 the Water Resources Act added the function of groundwater and surface water resource management to the other functions and achieved a measure of amalgamation of the River Boards, renaming them River Authorities. Although this was a major step forward, and still today is the cornerstone of resource management legislation, the River Authorities themselves have been replaced by multi-purpose river basin bodies in England and Wales. These Regional Water Authorities, created by the 1973 Water Act, are responsible for providing water and treating sewage, as well as exercising the other functions of the predecessor River Authorities.

Figure 6.1 shows the boundaries of the Regional Water Authorities and Figure 6.2 the boundaries of the Scottish Regions and the Scottish River Purification Boards, who share between them most of the functions of the English and Welsh Regional Water Authorities. The Scottish Regional Councils are responsible, *inter alia,* for water supply, sewerage and sewage disposal, and the seven Scottish River Boards look after the cleanliness of Scottish rivers, consenting effluent discharges and conserving water resources. In the Scottish island communities, the Island Councils have the responsibility for water supply, sewage disposal, sewerage and pollution prevention. In Northern Ireland a third form of organisation occurs with the Department of the Environment for Northern Ireland providing water supply and sewerage and sewage disposal. The Department also has powers to control effluent discharges and to regulate abstraction control.

Regional Water Authorities spend relatively small sums on river functions compared to the monies they spend on their water supply, sewerage and sewage disposal responsibilities. About 4% of Severn–Trent Water Authority's capital expenditure, some £3.1 m, was spent in 1976–7 on land drainage works, and less than £1.8 m was spent, in the same year, on the water resources revenue account, out of a total revenue expenditure of £152.8 m. Many examples of the British river management philosophy can be seen within the catchment of the Severn and the Trent and the proportion of the Authority's income spent on each of the three services of water supply, sewage disposal and river management is typical of other

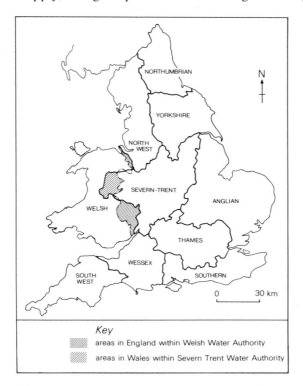

Figure 6.1 The Regional Water Authorities of England and Wales.

171

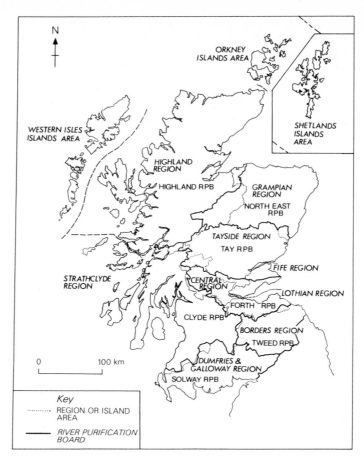

Figure 6.2 The Scottish Regions and the Scottish River Purification Boards.

Water Authorities. Although the river functions are subordinate in terms of expenditure, they are important particularly in the relationship to the consumer, who might be largely ignorant of the needs of new sewers and takes a wholesome supply of drinking water for granted, but may be vociferous where, for example, flood damage is concerned.

The management organisations that have been created have evolved policies to resolve the conflicting demands made on rivers by people living in or near their catchments. River management is, therefore, a pragmatic science, with few predetermined rules for any given situation, each problem being decided by the interplay of natural and man-made influences.

In Britain as elsewhere most lessons have been learnt at times of high or low flow, because for much of the time a river can manage itself and man's demands upon it are, in many cases, of little consequence. However, at times of high or low flow, the consequences of man's actions can be important. Indeed, man can influence the frequency of such extremes, and can modify their impact both on the river and on his own society.

172

The dry summers of 1975 and 1976 taught British hydrologists a number of lessons, only some of which have yet appeared in print. However, publication of some rather unfortunate statistics at the end of 1976 left many people with the impression that similar conditions might only re-occur once every two or three centuries, or even once a millennium. This sort of return period refers to rainfall statistics; indeed for some periods certain areas of southern England suffered quite rare rainfall events in 1975 and 1976. Rainfall data has, however, only limited relevance to drought as it affects Water Authorities. Of more direct interest are river flow and reservoir level and the state of the water table in water bearing strata. These are the parameters which influence water supply, and in each drought, the condition of each parameter can be assigned a probability. This varies according to the duration of the period considered, the location and characteristic of the source itself and in certain cases the intensity of the conditions. Much of this is self evident. Obviously the probability varies according to duration; a drought with a mean monthly runoff of x mm of say 9 months duration might be much rarer than a 5-month drought having a similar mean monthly runoff. This variation is very important (Hamlin & Wright 1978) for different types of source works are designed to withstand droughts of differing duration. For example an impounding direct supply reservoir is often designed to provide its minimum safe supply (yield) during droughts of up to 9 months, and in some cases 18 months. However, droughts of much shorter duration are critical to the operation of river regulation schemes. Major aquifers respond only to several seasons of dry weather, and in particular only to dry winter weather since little replenishment occurs during any summer. Hence, we must be careful to define the duration of the dry period in discussing the return period of a drought just as we must specify which source or which stream we are considering.

These points may be made more clearly by comparing the performance of three sources of public water supply in the severe summers of 1975 and 1976. Figure 6.3a shows the Nottingham Bunter Sandstone, an aquifer from which abstraction for public water supply has occurred for over a 100 years. Nottinghamshire is an area where very careful resource evaluation has to be made since natural recharge is small due to the low effective rainfall (130–300 mm per annum are the mean values of measured rainfall less actual evapotranspiration in Nottinghamshire). Observed water levels are available at a number of sites, and Figure 6.3a shows the decline during the 1970s consequent upon a series of dry winters, but with little variation relative to the total quantity of saturated rock and little change during the dry summers of 1975 and 1976. 40% of Severn–Trent Water Authority's supplies are derived from underground sources, largely from Triassic sandstones such as this, and a similar pattern can be seen at nearly all public supply boreholes. The only exceptions are boreholes in shallow aquifers such as fluvioglacial sands and gravels often supplying isolated communities. The total number of these shallow boreholes is small but they can produce localised supply problems where there are no alternative sources. An additional hazard is that such shallow sources can suffer bacteriological and chemical pollution subsequent to drought when heavy rainfall, carrying its post-drought extreme levels of dissolved and suspended loads, finds easy ingress to the aquifer.

Figure 6.3b shows the frequency of the inflow to the Derwent Valley Reservoirs for the six months of May to October for 1975 and 1976. These are direct supply reservoirs designed to produce about 200 Ml d^{-1}. Neither 1975 nor 1976 are the

(a)

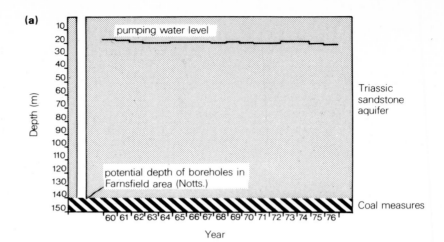

(b)

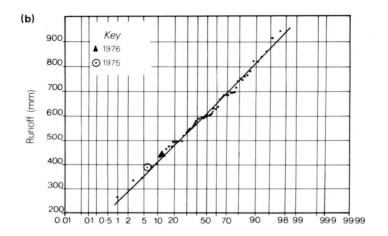

(c)

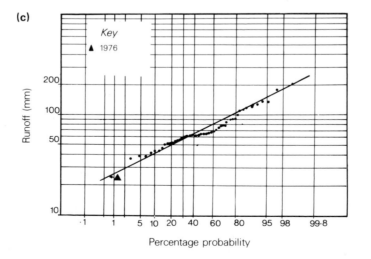

Figure 6.3 How different measures of a dry summer give differing results. (a) Groundwater levels in the Nottinghamshire Triassic sandstones; (b) the probability of the six months runoff May to October for the Derwent Valley Reservoirs of South Yorkshire, showing 1975 and 1976 conditions which might be expected to occur, on average, at least every 20 years; (c) the probability of the August mean discharges for the River Severn at Bewdley, the regulation control point for the River Severn; 1976 shown separately.

174

Figure 6.4 The exposed banks of Llyn Clywedog in 1976 (photograph by P. Cliff).

most severe design sequence. The dry intervening winter of 1975–6 would with a two season reservoir (one having poorer winter refill characteristics) have made the period from May 1975 to September 1976 a very severe test. Nevertheless, the fact that the Derwent Valley Reservoirs did refill in the intervening winter makes neither the summer of 1975 nor 1976 a particularly severe test of that supply system.

In contrast to those examples Figures 6.3c and 6.4 show the severe conditions met with in 1976 on the River Severn, which since 1968 has seen the large scale use of river abstraction supported by a head water regulating reservoir at Clywedog. This system was designed to meet a 90- to 100-day critical period with maximum daily releases of the order of 500 Ml d^{-1} being anticipated in a dry year under full demand. The three months of June to August 1976 were extremely dry and seem to be likely to occur perhaps less frequently than once every 100 years. Managing the reservoir and the river in that 90 days brought home its own lessons and a number of operational and legislative changes are being, or have already been, introduced. These include improved hydrometry and revised prescribed flow rules which allow a 5-day average instead of an instantaneous flow at the point of regulation. This will still give identical protection to the river, but will make for easier and more efficient management of the source.

These examples do no more than demonstrate the self-evident, that 1975 and 1976 vary in significance according to the period examined and the characteristics of the supply source. In water supply terms, only small direct supply reservoirs and regulated sources have short critical periods, and only these are affected by the type of drought familiar to the public. Short-term rainfall deficiency is not a serious problem unless, like some Water Authorities, there are few large reservoirs and limited groundwater in the supply system. What, however, may not be realised is the possibility of further amendments to frequency by interlinking sources and by varying operational policies. With the advent of Regional Water Authorities, considerably more flexibility was available both by physically inter-linking supply areas to two or more sources, each of which had differing characteristics, but also by developing control rules to take advantage of natural or artificially created interdependence of sources. If security against drought were the only objective in developing control rules, a simple line such as Figure 6.5 for a single site would suffice. When two or more sources are involved (say a direct supply reservoir and an aquifer) one could develop secure rules which would pay little attention to costs, or to other objectives such as preservation of reservoir level for amenity or preservation of flood storage. The skill is to design rules which meet carefully agreed objectives, generally minimising cost of operations in average years (usually achieved by reducing winter pumping of groundwater or run of river abstractions) and in dry years, preserving security of supply by recognising a developing drought situation early enough to have brought in the background sources (higher unit cost sources, normally the aquifer) so delaying reservoir storage falling to critical levels.

The management of sources in this manner is a developing science, with its few practitioners learning rapidly. For example, one of the several uncertainties still to be understood is the tolerance of the public to drought or rather to restrictions. Design rules vary with their objectives, and at the moment many of the drought objectives are hazy in that little is known about the public acceptability of restrictions. For example, how often should drought orders (to reduce reservoir compensation water) be introduced on rivers? How often should the public be banned from watering their gardens, and, more seriously, how often should industry be asked to reduce production because of water shortage? Some research has been carried out into the acceptability of restriction but the results are inconclusive (Hamlin, pers. comm.) and appear to depend heavily upon the recent experience of the subject, i.e. the tolerance to drought restrictions depends on whether or not such restrictions have recently been imposed.

The frequency of these restrictions can be altered, since each is dependent largely upon the willingness of the public to invest in capital works or to subsidise increased operating costs. At the present time drought orders and hosepipe bans (1976 Drought Act, Section 1) are sought perhaps more frequently than in the past in order to reduce the frequency of more severe restrictions, because a small

Figure 6.5 An operating curve for Tittesworth Reservoir designed to ensure a secure minimum yield of 20 Ml d^{-1}.

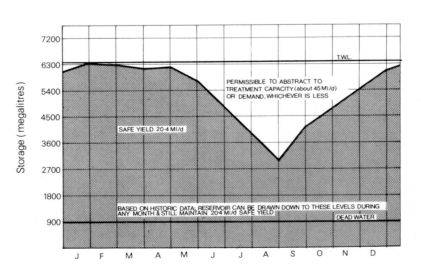

176

measure, say a cut in compensation water, introduced early enough in a drought can have a significant effect on reservoir levels. Such a policy avoids the need for frequent drastic action (cuts to industry) but does mean an increase in the occurrence of minor restrictions such as compensation water reductions. Many environmentalists would initially oppose such a policy, but experience in 1975 and 1976 showed that few ecological problems arose in rivers normally supported by reservoir compensation water, if such supplies were reduced, at least to a level allowing the survival of biological communities. This resulted in part from improved self-cleansing in the rivers due to the low travel times and higher water temperatures experienced in those hot dry summers, but also because no one knew (and still no one knows) the tolerance of biological communities to low flows. Compensation water was often fairly generously assessed when reservoirs were constructed in the past, especially where there was a strong angling lobby or a need for water power and today many streams supported by compensation water would otherwise be nearly dry in times of drought. Nevertheless, one should ask whether it is right to introduce compensation water reductions at the possible expense of amenity interest or even of the survival of biological communities. Clearly there is a need to establish how frequently restrictions should be imposed. At present there is a tendency to adopt somewhat more severe restrictions than are justified by the existing conditions, although this cautious approach to water supply in part reflects the public's wish to see their Water Authority 'doing something positive' in a drought.

During a drought hydrologists can offer very little to the practising water engineer provided that earlier hydrological advice has been taken. There can be no certainty about the end of the drought and projections based upon unreliable rainfall predictions are useless. To overcome the uncertainty element, Severn-Trent Water Authority has adopted the practice of designing control rules based on one of the conventional approaches (see for example McMahon & Mein 1978 for a recent comprehensive review of the subject) but having a measure of reserve storage to safeguard against the worse than design situation. This reserve, together with progressive restrictions on supply from individual sources, is a reflection of the growing acknowledgement that no water authority can countenance extensive failure of supply. It is a statement of the non-acceptability of high risks to a public utility.

Much of the foregoing has been concerned with frequency, and yet the techniques of frequency analysis are themselves often misunderstood. A hydrologist often finds himself being asked to define the frequency of an event from a short data record when he suspects that the event is fairly rare. Further, the record may have missing data and almost certainly will have some spurious entries. It may have bias or be incorrectly computed.

Data generation techniques, much in favour in the late 1960s and early 1970s, have more recently lost ground since they appear still to depend upon the same judgement as other techniques in deciding the distribution of low flows, having only the limited sample of the site record available. Instead hydrological simulation techniques are used widely today, taking advantage of the 80–100 years of rainfall data normally available in Britain, and tuning the models on 3–5 years of flow data (Manley 1978). These techniques have their advocates and their detractors, but in the absence of a high quality flow record, appear to offer the next best choice. They do not, however, overcome the problem of deciding the value of a 1–2% drought or the return period of a particular season, and for that one is thrown back to the mathematical fitting of extreme value distributions.

In summary, drought management is concerned with the correct interpretation of the wishes of the general public, via the manipulation of control rules on resource systems to achieve a balance between secure supply, economy and the interest of the rivers themselves. The key to this is an appreciation of frequency and the establishment of operational rules long before a drought starts.

Low-flow management

Apart from periods when public water supply is in danger, river management is concerned to define more frequently occurring low flows and to ensure an adequate balance of interest at such times. At extreme flows, those seen for example in 1976, river managers, fishery interests and others would acknowledge the overriding need to maintain public water supplies albeit on a restricted basis. However, they are concerned to ensure a balance in more normal conditions. This balance is one where at more frequently encountered flows, but still low flows, there should be no derogation of water rights, no fish stress, no prejudice to amenity and no adverse effects on water quality.

The 1963 Water Resources Act sought to achieve this balance of interest by giving to the then River Authorities the powers to license all abstractors of water. Existing abstractors in 1965 obtained a 'licence of right' but new abstractors were to have their applications vetted by the River Authorities to ensure that other existing interests including fisheries and water quality were not jeopardised by the applicants' requirements. Under the same legislation, River Authorities were asked to establish 'minimum acceptable flows' by which a river's environmental needs were to be recognised and below which no new abstraction would be permitted.

In practice, although the licensing system has worked very well, a number of problems may still be encountered both with licensing and with the establishment of minimum acceptable flows. These have been solved in a variety of ways. One of these problems is that the Act embodies the principle of 'first come, first served' where water abstraction is concerned, which means that no matter how deserving the later applicant may be, it is the date of his application which decides the merit of his case. In turn this has led to some over-sizing of applications, thus ensuring a measure of insurance against a growth in demand (particularly true of some early public water supply applications). However, licences were reduced voluntarily when more effective charging schemes were introduced. Nevertheless, the principle of first come first served does frustrate, in some measure, the ability of the Water Authorities to plan an equitable distribution of water. However, it would be impossible to overturn this principle since it is one of the cornerstones of English Common Law. Instead, the licensing system seeks to protect existing rights and this it achieves by approving new licensing applications only where water is available, establishing periods of the year or flow thresholds when water is unavailable. Such thresholds, frequently termed prescribed flow conditions, have become widely used in two different ways. The first is by the establishment of some river basin thresholds at one key point controlling several abstractions, often where good flow data is available. Alternatively, there is the use of a local site where a gauge board can be readily erected close to the point of abstraction and where the applicant is asked only to abstract above an agreed level. Obviously the former has advantages where policing is concerned, and will ensure greater accuracy in determination of flows and their frequency. However, local arrangements are often preferred especially for small seasonal abstractors, despite difficulties of policing the licence and doubts about the stability or accuracy of the flows ascribed to a given river reach. One problem that often arises with prescribed flows is the question of how frequently such flows should be tolerated, and not just what the value of the flow should be. A system of secondary and even tertiary thresholds has recently been introduced in Severn–Trent Water Authority whereby new applicants can be restricted at higher prescribed flows so ensuring earlier abstractors their continued access to medium flows. Other Water Authorities have employed seasonally variable thresholds and some licences are time dependent, either in the sense of being restricted to some period of the year, or reviewable after some period of years.

Clearly much depends for the success of such a system on the value of the prescribed flows chosen. In 1979, Severn–Trent undertook a review of prescribed flows, examining each river basin, and within each basin, each major river reach. Water quality, fishery, hydrological, licensing and water supply interests jointly decided upon revised prescribed flows which would protect existing interests and the environment but which might in some cases make previously unavailable river water licensable in the future. Particular care had to be exercised where river flows were supported by flow from permeable strata, in that groundwater licences also derogate surface water assets. Difficulties in the calculation of base flow from aquifers where groundwater abstraction may have been progressively increasing add a further tier of complication to the already difficult problem of deciding environmentally necessary prescribed flows. Other difficulties include those of attempting to define, in flow or level terms, the minimum acceptable conditions for fish life. Fish stress appears to be related to several factors, including BOD and ammonia levels, and only some of these parameters are related to flow. By attempting to use only flow as a measure of minimum acceptable conditions we are in danger of over-simplifying a complex situation. It is for similar reasons that the concept of minimum acceptable flows has been largely side-stepped both by the River Authorities and subsequently the Water Authorities since no single flow can effectively define the environmental protection needed for any river.

Nevertheless, despite such problems, a considerable number of surface water and groundwater abstraction licences (7700 in Severn–Trent Water Authority alone) successfully co-exist, and each year squabbles over water rights between competing interests are few. Equally a considerable income is derived from the use of water by abstractors whether it be for potable supplies, for agricultural purposes (e.g. spray irrigation), for industrial cooling, or for power generation. In 1976 Severn–Trent Water Authority obtained an income of some £2.4 m from these charges of which nearly half was a paper transaction being the income rechargeable to public water supply abstractions.

Although Water Authorities have side-stepped the use of minimum acceptable flows, they are careful to safeguard the interests of the river as well as the requirements of existing river users. Because fisheries, water quality, amenity and existing users all require different measures of low flow, methods of estimating low flows and their frequency have recently been developed. Measured flows are not available on all rivers, and because of the extensive use of British rivers, natural river flows are rarely directly measured. Care therefore has to be exercised in inferring flow at one site from measured flow at another. The Institute of Hydrology (1980a) have published methods of deriving low flows of various frequencies and durations based on a collection of British national data. This is an extremely useful source of information where local data is poor. However, the

179

study largely employed non-naturalised data because of the difficulties of accounting for abstractions and discharges. In an attempt to provide better information for low flows on the heavily utilised rivers of the English Midlands, Severn–Trent Water Authority have produced residual flow diagrams for all their major rivers, each of which shows the composition of the flow in both its natural element and its abstractions and discharges. Derived from these are two techniques, firstly a method of assessing natural flow per unit area, which allows the construction of a flow-duration curve relating flow and frequency according to soil type, lithology and annual average rainfall, and secondly a method of mapping areas of similar low-flow regime. These techniques, which are essentially similar to those published nationally by the Institute of Hydrology, are important regionally because of the use of naturalised data, and the incorporation of the very large numbers of occasional measurements made at points other than gauging stations during low-flow periods. These basin-wide co-ordinated surveys of low flows gave a series of snapshots showing the interrelationship of flows at many points. It is this wealth of information which these surveys produced, together with the details of abstractions and discharges, which has allowed the production of high quality residual flow diagrams.

Until the introduction of the Institute of Hydrology's low-flow study and these regional studies, low-flow information was sparse, except at gauging stations. For the latter, flow duration curves were produced and most users tended to select the flow exceeded 95% of the time as being a suitable measure of low flow. However, Hindley (1973) showed that for short records this was a somewhat dangerous practice and suggested the use of the seven-day minimum flow, defined as the average of each year's lowest consecutive seven days flow. This tends to reduce the effect of very low flows seen in any one year, for example the bias is removed of the extreme low flows of 1975 and 1976. In Britain there is still a tendency to use the 95% exceedance flow as a measure of low flows but a number of Authorities are moving towards Hindley's seven-day minimum.

Whatever low-flow measure is used, choice of acceptable low flows is somewhat subjective and the relationships between flow and several factors including fish and quality are not fully known. However, the success of the British licensing control system and of quality management (see the following section) suggests that while improvements are being made in low-flow estimation techniques, by and large river management in Britain over the past decade has been successful in resolving conflicting demands at times of low flow as well as preserving the essential characteristics of the rivers themselves. The Water Act (1973) has offered the opportunity to manage resources on a catchment wide scale for the benefit of amenity, of private abstractors, of water quality and fisheries and of public water supply. For example, river regulation schemes are no longer operated solely for the benefit of public water supply. Llyn Clywedog, the major river regulating reservoir on the Severn, was used solely to support a limited number of downstream public water supply abstractions in the days of single function Authorities (the so-called Clywedog 'Club'). However, today such schemes are used to support many forms of abstraction, including farmers' summer spray irrigation requirements. It is the wide responsibilities of the Regional Water Authorities which should ensure good low-flow management in England and Wales in the future, and the experience since 1973, when the RWAs were created, supports this view.

Management of water quality

In Britain, one of the principal uses of rivers is for the disposal of domestic and industrial waste, a feature dating back only to the closing years of the 19th century when the water closet was generally introduced as a means of safely and conveniently removing human sewage from industrial communities. The growth of large urban areas was not in itself the cause of river pollution, nor of the impoundment of remote upland streams to produce cheap supplies of water, but it was the widespread introduction of water-borne sewage disposal together with the growth in industrial effluent which produced both these phenomena some generations after the Industrial Revolution was underway.

Table 6.1 shows the march in demand for public water supplies in Birmingham since 1859 which is reflected in the quantities of sewage discharged to the River Tame. The decrease in demand for Central Birmingham water supply since 1965 reflects the decline of the inner city seen elsewhere in British conurbations and is not reflected in an overall decreased discharge of sewage to the river system.

Therefore the extensive use of British rivers for effluent disposal is less than 120 years old, and post-dates the Industrial Revolution and the development of major urban areas by several generations. Indeed, both the River Trent at Nottingham and the River Tame in Birmingham were separately used in the middle years of the 19th century as local sources of water supply. Figure 6.6 shows the River Tame at Salford Bridge in 1980, better known as the bottom layer of the motorway intersection of the M6 termed 'Spaghetti Junction'. This was the site of a reservoir abstracting River Tame water constructed as late as 1826 and which provided water to the City of Birmingham until 1871 despite occasional pollution incidents with gas liquors and other discharges. Today, the River Tame downstream of Birmingham contains about 90% effluent in its low flows ($6.6\ \mathrm{m^3\ s^{-1}}$ in $7.4\ \mathrm{m^3\ s^{-1}}$). In the summer of 1976 even the River Severn near Gloucester with a catchment area of 10 000 square kilometres was almost entirely dependent for its flow upon a

Table 6.1 Public water supply to Birmingham.

	Ml d^{-1}
1859	15
1880	45
1895	73
1912	104
1965	356
1977	298

Figure 6.6 The River Tame at Salford Bridge, adjacent to a former public water supply reservoir used until 1871.

181

combination of releases from reservoir storage and effluent discharges. The natural discharge of the River Severn was virtually nil at Gloucester because of the effects of abstraction. The management of river water quality is thus extremely important, both at times of normal low flow in urban rivers and rivers used for public water supply, and in rural rivers in times of drought.

In Britain, the first significant pollution prevention legislation was passed in 1876. This prohibited four forms of pollution; from mine water, from sewage, from trade effluent and from solids disposal. The 1876 Act was not successful, and attempts at controlling rather than prohibiting polluting discharges followed. In 1912, the Eighth Report of the Royal Commission on Sewage Disposal recommended, amongst many other standards now forgotten (Roberts 1974), two criteria for an acceptable standard of a sewage effluent, provided that there was an adequate dilution available from the receiving watercourse. That dilution was taken to be a minimum of eight times the quantity of the effluent under low-flow conditions. The criteria for the effluent discharge itself put forward by the Royal Commission were a maximum demand of 20 parts per million of dissolved oxygen (BOD) and a maximum of 30 parts per million of suspended solids. This would result in a river water downstream of the discharge which would have a BOD of less than $4 \, \text{mg} \, \text{l}^{-1}$. Since 1912, these Royal Commission limits of '20/30' have been widely applied and almost to the present day have been used as a standard for sewage effluents.

In 1951, the Rivers (Prevention of Pollution) Act replaced the earlier 1876 legislation. Prohibition was replaced by a system of discharge consents with new discharges being required to comply with minimum standards. In 1961 this system was extended to cover existing discharges. The establishment of these consent conditions lay in the hands of the River Boards and then was given to their successors, the River Authorities, and in turn is now exercised by the Water Authorities.

While Water Authorities are public bodies and therefore open in their government, they are both responsible for setting river quality standards and for managing the sewage plants themselves. Is it, to use a frequently quoted metaphor, possible to be gamekeeper and poacher? Would it have been better in the 1973 Water Act to have established an independent body responsible for the inspection of quality standards, similar perhaps to the Health and Safety Executive? Alternatively does the corporate management approach, with both sides met around the table, make for more efficient management? Several Water Authorities, conscious of the need to monitor their own performance in an open and responsible manner, independently report upon the quality of river water, of sewage effluent and of water treated for public supply. In Severn–Trent Water Authority, a five-man Water Quality Advisory Panel has been established to undertake this monitoring function, each year examining a series of detailed reports on water quality performance. Together with the annual publication of water quality statistics, which since 1974 show a 25% increase in the quality of sewage effluent, this type of approach has considerably softened criticism of the 1973 Act.

In 1974, the Control of Pollution Act (COPA) received the Royal Assent, but Part II of the Act, which refers to river pollution has not yet been implemented. Amongst other powers, COPA will allow any person or group to take proceedings against a polluter, including of course the Water Authorities, themselves responsible for the operation of the sewage works which are the chief source of pollution load. Furthermore, when Part II is implemented, the consent standards and the degree of compliance with those standards will become public knowledge, whereas earlier legislation kept confidential both of these items of information. The previous consents, established under the 1951 and 1961 Rivers (Prevention of Pollution) Acts were long-term goals, operated by agreement, prosecution only occurring where there was wilful disregard of standards, or gross negligence and rarely where standards were marginally exceeded. In order to avoid prosecution when COPA Part II is implemented and in recognition of the need to monitor existing plant rather than imply any future objective, the Water Authorities have introduced 'interim consents'. These are consents with which existing works, if well managed, can just comply and which in some cases are less stringent than the existing standards. In some cases, however, they are more stringent. These will be reviewed periodically and considerable effort has gone into allaying the fear of environmentalists that lower standards are being adopted. In practice, the quality of river water and of effluents will change little (Lester 1979). In Scotland the Procurator Fiscal still has to sanction any prosecution by the general public and the Scottish River Purification Boards (the Scottish Pollution Prevention Authorities) have decided against an interim review of consents. In other words, the interim review largely results from the right of the public in England and Wales to prosecute the industrial discharger and the Water Authorities.

The twin suspicions aroused by the gamekeeper/poacher role of the Water Authorities and the interim consents are not easily allayed, and in the relatively short period since the 1974 reorganisation, the financial restraint imposed on public bodies and the changing objectives of both the EEC and of national government probably make definitive statements about the success of current legislation meaningless at such a time. Nevertheless, while the impetus to improve rivers, one of the crusades of the environmental lobby of the 1960s, has had to be moderated in the light of financial restraint, the record of the British Water Industry in improving water quality over the past 30 years has been very good indeed. For example, between 1958 and 1975 in England and Wales there was a rise from 86.1% to 91.4% of total river length which could be classed as of good quality (DOE 1978b). This apparent slight rise of only 5% represents a very significant national investment in pollution control and some dramatic changes in particular areas. For example, the tidal Thames, which in the middle of the 18th century had a good run of salmon, had become seriously polluted by 1800. Even in 1950, the lower Thames was so heavily polluted that for several months of the year no dissolved oxygen could be detected. To all extent and purpose the tidal Thames was a dead river with no fish life, an unpleasant and characteristic smell and a poor appearance. However, by the improvement and diversion of sewage effluent and by stricter trade effluent control, in 1967 some 50 species of fish had been caught in the tidal Thames and in 1977 over 100 species. The offensive odour had disappeared and amenity and appearance were vastly improved.

Similar dramatic improvement has been seen in other major rivers, for example the Clyde, the Tees, the Trent and the Pennine Rivers of Yorkshire and Lancashire. Some of the changes in river water quality in the Severn and the Trent between 1962 and 1978 can be seen in Figure 6.7. The more than halving of BOD levels and the general improvement of river water from one class to the next highest class, seen, for example, for much of the Trent is testimony both to the investments made in effluent treatment and to the hard work of the pollution control authorities.

The reorganisation of the Water Industry appeared to promise not only a continuation of the battle against pollution, but an increase in the rate at which improvements were to be made. In 1973 the DOE expressly said (DOE 1973) that

183

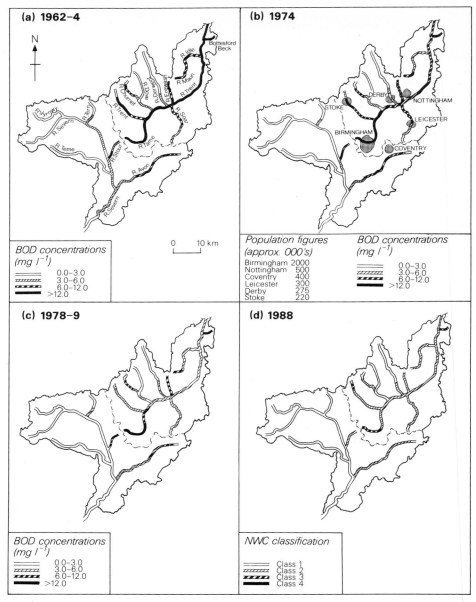

Figure 6.7 River water quality in Severn–Trent Water Authority – past, present and future. (a) River water quality in 1962–4; (b) river water quality in 1974; (c) river water quality in 1978–9; (d) proposed water quality objectives for 1988.

'there would be a massive clean-up of the country's rivers and estuaries by the early 1980s'. However, since considerable improvements had already been made prior to 1973 and since then a series of financial recessions have occurred, the immediate objectives of water quality management in 1980 are much more limited. The NWC publication, *The next stage,* in 1978 pointed the way to methods of maintaining water quality despite the financial situation. Water Authorities were required to ensure sufficient quantity and quality of river water for public supply and for industry and agriculture. They were also reminded of their duties to prevent nuisance and safeguard public health, to maintain and restore inland and tidal water quality, to have regard for the fauna and flora and to maintain and improve fisheries. Water Authorities were equally asked to achieve these objectives at the least possible cost. This is a notable toning down of the

184

enthusiasm of the 1973 DOE statement. However, it may well represent a more pragmatic approach to the problems of quality management and in particular to the willingness of the general public to pay for improvements. Although many would applaud the intention to improve river water quality still further, unless there is a specific objective such as the use of a river for public water supply, it is extremely difficult to estimate the benefits attributable to the improvements of a particular river reach. Indeed if one attempts to estimate the increased amenity deriving from such improvements, by counting the numbers of anglers or dinghy sailors or casual visitors to the river bank, then a very low return on the investment is seen. Clearly, management of water quality is vitally important but identifying the point on the curve of diminishing returns of effluent improvement is difficult unless clearly recognisable objectives are available. Severn–Trent Water Authority has recently identified the river water quality objectives which should lead in the next decade to river quality as shown in Figure 6.7d. Essentially the established principles are that existing river quality should not deteriorate, that grossly polluted rivers be eliminated, and fishless rivers be improved to levels where they can support a reasonable fishery or have moderate amenity value.

In 1979, central government imposed a limit on the capital expenditure of Water Authorities and this has prejudiced the likelihood of achieving all of these objectives within ten years. At the time of writing is is unlikely that the objectives themselves will change, although capital expenditure of public bodies is frequently the subject of control by central government. In other words, the intentions will probably remain as they are, but the timetable may well alter.

Lying behind the discussion on objectives, standards and consent conditions, is a vast data-base, in particular a data base of chemical quality parameters but also of biological and to a lesser extent of bacteriological information. Simply to gather, analyse, process and to publish this body of information is an enormous undertaking, Toms (1975) recognises that before there can be comprehensive management of river quality there has to be knowledge of the background quality of the river and its variability under a variety of natural conditions. Indeed, that information has to be married to flow data since on its own quality determinations are less meaningful because both variability and total loads are both dependent on the quantity of available water. When COPA is introduced, flow will become an important factor in quality assessment of effluents since the quality of the receiving watercourse rather than the quality of the effluent becomes important.

The question of how and where water quality sampling should occur has been investigated by Montgomery and Hart (1974). However, pollution incidents may not be detected by routine sampling since there is a need to recognise quickly changes in water quality. Water quality monitors with either alarm facilities or telemetry output facilities are being introduced in Britain, but several difficulties have been experienced with the sensors (Briggs 1971). Reducing storage at public water supply river intakes is not yet practised and is still the subject of discussion, but this seems a possibility with good pollution monitors and where pollution incidents are short-lived. At present water quality monitors are restricted to monitoring pH, dissolved oxygen, temperature, ammonia, conductivity and turbidity and are mainly used as continuous recorders of present conditions. Such monitors are already extensively used in Britain, for example on the River Lea, and the River Dove. Improved performance due to a reduced delay between sample observation and human inspection of the monitor's results as well as improved utilisation can be expected when these monitors are coupled to telemetry systems.

185

The use of fish as indicators of river quality is a good example of real time biological sampling (Hellawell 1978) and there is fairly comprehensive routine biological sampling of rivers. However, biological and bacteriological parameters, let alone radiological or virological parameters, are not as frequently used in the water industry as chemical measures of quality. In the 1950s, the importance of thermal pollution was recognised with the growth in generating capacity on many British rivers. Similarly, one may well see in the 1980s other methods of assessing pollution being adopted more widely than at present (Wilhm 1975).

Thermal pollution is itself a particularly interesting example of a heavy demand for a quantity of water and as a consequence a marked effect taking place on the quality of the river downstream. Approximately one third of the British national generating capacity (some 15 000 MW) is installed along the Trent and the net effect of the direct cooled stations is to increase the temperature of the middle Trent by about 5°C while the evaporative power stations could reduce flow by up to 390 Ml d^{-1}. Power station operation is highly dependent on the terms of the abstraction licences and upon the consent conditions and equally the Water Authority depends for a substantial part of its surface water abstraction charges on the revenue raised by the CEGB licences.

As Porter (1978) points out there is no attempt to charge for direct discharges made to the river systems, a method which would allow both an increased income to finance further water quality improvements and an opportunity to control pollution by the price mechanism. If charges were correctly set, this would allow the price to reduce the level of pollution to the point where costs of further treatment would be greater than the damage caused by the pollution itself. Although this ideal may sound attractive it is likely to be difficult to introduce since all would depend on the nature of the charging scheme and a careful judgement of the effects of any discharge. Furthermore, the Water Authority would be the main contributor. However, it is nevertheless true that substantial use is made of rivers as effluent carriers without adequate charge being levied on the discharges made directly to that system.

Although much of river quality management depends on control of discharges to the river system, in recent years an attempt has been made to improve river habitat and in-river quality by more direct means. The introduction of shallow weirs, leading to the maintenance of minimum depths, is an example whereby fish habitat has been protected. This is often carried out as part of a land drainage or river regulation scheme, or in certain cases of extreme low flow when river conditions prevent the normal use of minimum prescribed flows usually employed to protect the biological and chemical characteristics of river waters. The deliberate introduction of spillways and weirs in raw water reservoirs is common practice, but is not often employed in river systems to improve river water quality, since weirs or other impoundments are both expensive to build and lead inevitably to local drainage problems not welcomed by riparian owners. Furthermore, the effects on river water quality can be mixed and are not all advantageous.

On the River Tame a river purification lake is being constructed (Lester, Woodward & Raven 1972, Binnie & Partners 1973). Although the River Tame has relatively good river quality at times of low flow, fish kill occurs after heavy rainfall due to urban storm runoff, untreated sewage and trade effluent being swept into the river. The chosen solution is a 25-ha lake downstream of the Birmingham conurbation designed primarily for purification purposes: this lake is due for completion in 1981. Figure 6.8 shows the long-term plans for a series of lakes at Kingsbury. The first lake will act as a large-scale settlement tank, retaining

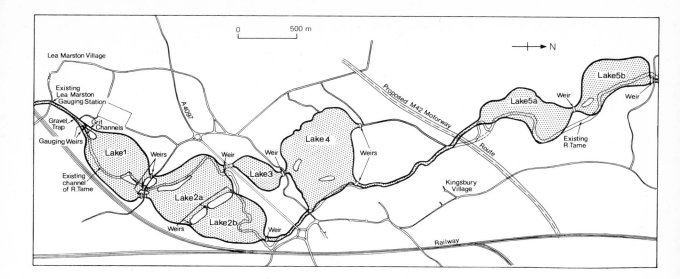

and allowing the settlement of suspended solids, while the other lakes will have amenity and water quality functions. This exciting project will be a positive way of improving water quality in an area formerly notorious for the quantity and quality of its polluting discharges.

Stormwater balancing tanks within the sewerage system or at sewage treatment plants have been used elsewhere in Britain to reduce the effects of heavy rainfall on river quality. For example, the River Avon near Coventry is extensively protected by large storm tanks but apart from the River Tame there are no other British examples of large-scale, on-line purification lakes.

In summary, water quality management, so necessary over the past 100 years, has achieved a great deal in the last 30 years, but its future objectives and the availability of capital to achieve those objectives are prescribed by the will of the general public and the mood of central government.

Figure 6.8 The Kingsbury Purification Lakes – showing the long-term plans for purification and amenity lakes in the River Tame. Diagram based on Binnie and Partners (1973) report to Trent River Authority on the Kingsbury Purification Lakes.

Flood-flow management

Nationally, Britain spends some £30 m per year on capital works to drain land and to protect against the effects of floods. This includes £4 m spent on coastal defences, but excludes a further £13 m spent annually on maintenance of existing works. Over many years these capital works have effectively changed the landscape of many British river basins. In particular, the Eastern counties of England between Essex and Yorkshire and the low-lying lands of Somerset and the riparian washlands of Cheshire and Lancashire have been radically altered by traditional drainage techniques of channel deepening and widening, by field drainage and by artificial control of the water table. In Eastern England, frequent resort is made to pump drainage, introduced as long ago as 1727 near Ely. The extent to which these Eastern counties have been changed is perhaps little realised by the modern traveller, but brief examination of the pre-drainage maps of the Lower Trent (Fig. 6.9), compared to today's landscape, shows how effectively both the physiography and man's activities have been altered. Today the landscape, with straight and level roads crossing the multi-cropped fields of Lincolnshire or the East Anglian grain fields, is a long way removed from the

187

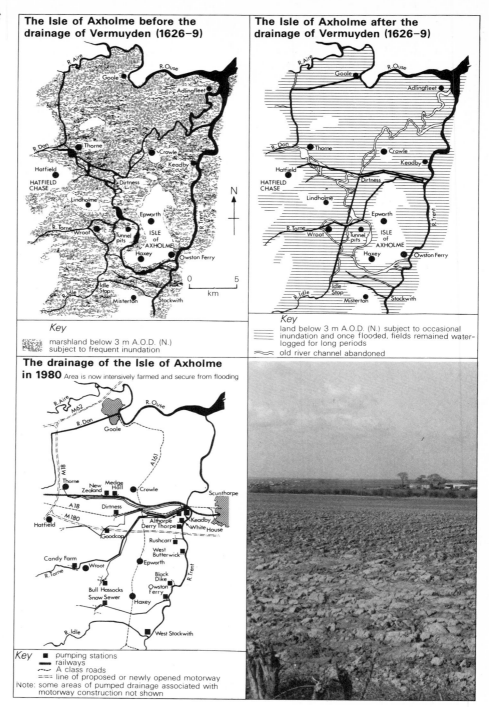

The Isle of Axholme before the drainage of Vermuyden (1626–9)

R. Aire
R. Ouse
Goole
Adlingfleet
R. Don
Thorne
Crowle
Keadby
Hatfield
Dirtness
HATFIELD CHASE
Lindholme
Epworth
R. Torne
Wroot
Tunnel pits
ISLE of AXHOLME
R. Trent
Haxey
Owston Ferry
N
0   5 km
Idle Stop
R. Idle
Misterton
Stockwith

Key

▨ marshland below 3 m A.O.D. (N.) subject to frequent inundation

The Isle of Axholme after the drainage of Vermuyden (1626–9)

R. Aire
R. Ouse
Goole
Adlingfleet
R. Don
Thorne
Crowle
Keadby
Hatfield
Dirtness
HATFIELD CHASE
Lindholme
Epworth
R. Torne
Wroot
Tunnel pits
ISLE of AXHOLME
R. Trent
Haxey
Owston Ferry
Idle Stop
R. Idle
Misterton
Stockwith

Key

═══ land below 3 m A.O.D. (N.) subject to occasional inundation and once flooded, fields remained water-logged for long periods

〰 old river channel abandoned

The drainage of the Isle of Axholme in 1980 Area is now intensively farmed and secure from flooding

R. Aire
M62
R. Don
R. Ouse
Goole
A161
M18
Thorne
New Zealand
Medge Hall
Crowle
Scunthorpe
A18
Dirtness
M180
Althorpe
Derry Thorpe
Keadby
White House
Hatfield
Goodcop
Rushcarr
West Butterwick
Candy Farm
Wroot
Epworth
R. Torne
Black Dike
R. Trent
Bull Hassocks
Snow Sewer
Owston Ferry
Haxey
R. Idle
West Stockwith

Key
■ pumping stations
▬▬ railways
〜 A class roads
═══ line of proposed or newly opened motorway
Note: some areas of pumped drainage associated with motorway construction not shown

Figure 6.9 The Isle of Axholme (a) before 1600, (b) after the drainage of Vermuyden in 1626–9 and (c) in 1980. (d) Photograph of the well-drained and intensively-farmed River Idle basin of the 1980s.

188

difficult communications of the poverty- and disease-ridden lands of the 16th century.

Conventional arterial drainage (the improvement of river channel conveyance capacity) is now moving increasingly towards a care and maintenance role since much of Britain is now drained to standards suitable for arable farming. However, field drainage still progresses apace (Green 1976). Environmental protection of wetlands is a phenomenon of recent origin but is another factor now causing the slowing pace of arterial drainage (Water Space Amenity Commission 1978). In contrast, the other element of the drainage engineer's work, flood protection, is very active in Britain, with many towns and villages and considerable coastal areas still requiring the construction of flood defences. Some of this expenditure is undertaken by Local Authorities, especially in urban areas. In fact, the most expensive flood protection works ever undertaken in Britain, the Thames Barrier, is the product of the Greater London Council. The main feature is a rising sector gate barrier constructed at Woolwich which can be closed in the event of surge conditions. Including major protection works to the estuary downstream of the barrier, the scheme at 1978 prices was costed at some £478 m. The finished scheme will offer flood protection to over 130 km² of Greater London's low-lying land.

The Ministry of Agriculture and the Welsh and the Scottish Office give grant aid which, in England and Wales, averages some 55% of the capital cost of such schemes, although in the case of the Thames Barrier grant aid was 75%. Grant aid effectively relieves Water or Local Authorities of the total financial cost of schemes, but also ensures a degree of control and uniformity of standard between different schemes.

Despite the sums of money involved in land drainage, data allowing the design of such schemes is rarely adequate. Figures 1.1–1.4 presented the existing national network of gauging stations which gives Britain one of the highest densities anywhere in the world. Nevertheless, although the information necessary to design land drainage schemes is much more available than without such a network, rarely is record length adequate, nor is data quality as high as one would wish. Frequently, records are of the order of five to ten years in length and scheme design may be far greater than this.

Figure 6.10 shows the upper end of a distribution of level records for the River Severn, the lower part of the record having been omitted since this lay below a distinct break occurring at or about bankfull. The importance of accurately estimating the design levels or design flows is emphasised at a site such as Tewkesbury shown in Figure 6.11 with its wide floodplain and quite enormous storage and consequent small change in level for substantial change in flow. In the Lower Severn, exceptionally long daily level records were available, of the order of 150 years, recorded at locks constructed in the 19th century. Apart from the River Thames, few other such long records are available from major British rivers for analysis and estimation of the 1 in 50- or 1 in 100-year return period flow becomes an even more hazardous venture than was the case for the River Severn.

Birmingham and the River Tame are good examples of the difficulties encountered in urban design flow estimation. Local flooding problems are often caused in urban areas from inadequate culvert capacities. The peculiar development history of the Black Country meant that flood runoff was delayed due to the countless 18th and 19th century channel restrictions formed in the headwaters of the Tame which in turn allowed the later development of the washlands (floodplain) of the middle Tame in the early 20th century. Recent 'improvement' schemes in the headwaters have now endangered the housing in these washlands and remedial

189

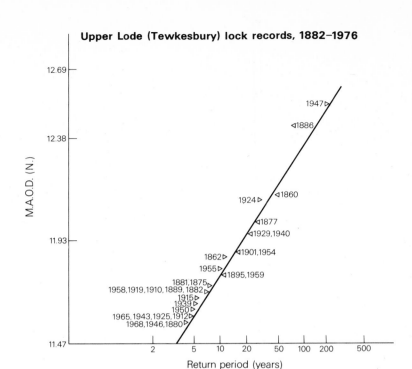

Upper Lode (Tewkesbury) lock records, 1882–1976

Figure 6.10 Frequencies of flood levels for Tewkesbury, on the River Severn.

measures will have to be provided. Within the urban area, off-line lakes are being provided to give flood protection to the upper river (Fitzsimons 1979). The particular advantages of these lakes are their cheapness relative to other solutions and the improvement of water quality not given by other schemes. Nevertheless, their cheapness is only relative, for at 1979 prices, the six urban lakes of the upper and middle Tame, excluding the Kingsbury Purification Lakes are to cost nearly £9 m. Clearly, it is vitally important to use the best available techniques to design such a scheme, for it is the volume of the design hydrograph which dictates the size of the balancing lakes and in turn the cost of the project. In urban areas, there are substantial difficulties in choosing the correct design flows for little data exists and the Flood Studies Report has only recently been extended to areas which have greater than 25% of their catchments which are urbanised (Institute of Hydrology 1980b). The further complications of estimating the geomorphological effects of river improvements is of considerable academic interest and conflicting opinion exists (see for example Gregory 1977, Hollis 1979). In the case of Birmingham, extensive improvements in carrying capacity have occurred already in the head-waters without any perceptible change in the flood-flow characteristics of the lower river, let alone the morphology. Studies are now in hand to establish whether further extensive improvements in the conveyance capacity of headwater streams will appreciably affect downstream hydrology.

In areas of urban development as opposed to urban channel improvement where the amount of urban land is increasing in a catchment, several authors (Hollis 1974) have identified considerable change in flood flows. Undoubtedly, such changes will occur as the impermeability of a catchment is increased. These changes also appear to affect snow melt runoff (Taylor & Roth 1979) and Packman (1977) has shown the changing magnitude of low return period urban floods. At higher return periods, of the order of 50–100 years, little data is available and yet it is these standards which are normally used to provide flood protection in an urban

Figure 6.11 The extensive floodplain of the River Severn at Tewkesbury photographed during floods having a return period of once in five years.

environment. Current practice is to use the same design flood at the 50- and 100-year levels as would be used in a rural catchment, since it is argued (Packman 1977) that under such extreme conditions a rural catchment and an urban catchment would have similar characteristics.

Although the River Tame provides a good example of the difficulties associated with producing design flows, it is not typical of land drainage work, either in terms of the chosen civil engineering or hydrological solutions. More usual are channel improvement schemes or conventional flood protection schemes involving either widening and deepening of channels or the construction of earth banks and masonry walls. Figure 6.12 shows a flood protection scheme under construction in the Derbyshire Derwent area at Matlock where environmental and amenity interests had to be balanced against the need to protect the local community against a severe flood risk. The chosen solution was a combination of channel deepening and flood wall construction. Such schemes require estimates of instantaneous peak flows rather than the whole flood hydrograph, making the hydrologist's job easier. However, in the case of extensive schemes, the common practice is to produce either a physical or mathematical model of the existing river conditions, fitting it to some known event, and then altering its physical characteristics to show the effects on the design flood of a variety of alternative solutions. Frequently this involves both considerable expense and the need to provide the full hydrograph. The Hydraulics Research Station provides an excellent service in this field and has produced numerous models, both physical and mathematical, to aid land drainage design.

Another aspect of land drainage work which is rapidly developing and becoming more important in today's cost conscious climate, is the assessment of benefit. Clearly, any public expenditure should be able to demonstrate the effects of a chosen course of action, and in the field of water services, benefit assessment is a technique now common to many new schemes. For example, where agricultural land might in the past have been given a general level of protection of say 5–10

Figure 6.12 Channel deepening operation in the River Derwent at Matlock where a sympathetic approach was necessary to protect the river's visual amenity (photograph by P. Cliff).

Figure 6.13 Example of the relationships (a) between return period and design flows for a flood protection scheme, (b) between return period and benefits of a flood protection scheme and (c) between costs of constructing a flood protection scheme and design flow.

years, recently developed techniques (Penning-Rowsell & Chatterton 1977) allow a standard of protection to be given commensurate with the benefits, so that if little benefit could be given over say the 5-year level and considerable additional cost were involved, that protection would not now normally be offered. These techniques have been applied by the same authors to urban areas as well and are again highly dependent on the accuracy of the hydrological data, in particular the return period allocated to a flood event. Considerable room for error exists here, in that the general relationship between flood flows and return periods has the form shown in Figure 6.13a. This means that one needs little change in flow to produce a substantial change in return period. Hence, whilst one may produce error of little consequence to the chosen design, the economic justification is highly dependent on return period, for a doubling of the return period will halve the benefit of the scheme. Where one is protecting against say the highest flood in

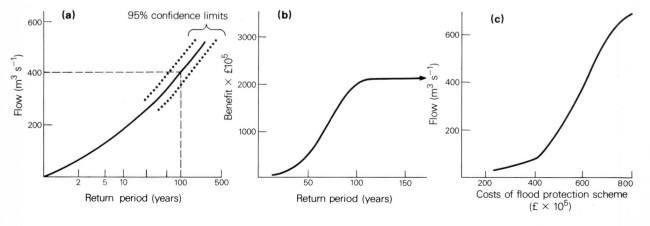

a 10-year record, there is obviously considerable doubt about the actual return period of that flood. The example in Figure 6.13 may help to clarify this point. Take a design flow of $400 \, m^3 \, s^{-1}$ having a 100-year return period. The benefits of a scheme to protect against such a flow might be £2000 $\times$ 10^5 and the cost might be £600 $\times$ 10^5. However, if the flow of $400 \, m^3 \, s^{-1}$ was really, say, a 50-year flood then the effects on the cost of the scheme might be very little, but the benefits would fall to £500 $\times$ 10^5, i.e. to less than the cost of the scheme. Figure 6.13a shows that such poor estimates are not unlikely given the data we possess.

In realisation of the consequences of overtopping conventional flood protection schemes and of inundation in unprotected areas, many Water Authorities provide a flood warning service. Indeed, benefit assessment techniques have been extended to flood warning (Chatterton, Pirt & Wood 1979) so that there is firm evidence to show the need for the further development of flood forecasting and warning services. Already in Britain a high level of service exists, providing many large centres of population with several hours warning. Most of these services are currently based on level-to-level correlation techniques. Such techniques are known to suffer from a number of drawbacks, and attempts are currently being made to develop both rainfall–runoff models to forecast floods in the headwaters and flood routing models to deal with the lower reaches. A number of alternative rainfall–runoff models are available (Lambert 1972, Rockwood 1961) and it is not yet evident that any one is better than another. What is clear is that the quality of the data and the density of the sampling network of data points tends to influence strongly the characteristics of the end product (Simpson, Wood & Hamlin 1980). As far as flood routing is concerned, Price (1977) has developed a variable parameter Muskingem–Cunge technique which gives extremely useful results both in the design mode and when applied to flood forecasting. What is important is the need to develop an integrated flood forecasting system, capable of rapid data collection, assimilation and forecasting. In the late 1960s and early 1970s, radio telemetry was a popular method of swift data assembly but as telephone connections have become more reliable in extreme events with the advent of pressurised lines, and as shorter signalling times have been realised, conventional telephone systems have become competitive both in cost and performance. Jones (1980) describes a forecasting system of telephone 'scanners' which can frequently interrogate some 200 out-stations (rainfall and river level recorders) and which cascade data to mini-computers carrying the main rainfall to runoff and flood routing models. It would seem likely that the considerable additional benefits of flood forecasting by flow modelling will be realised in the 1980s in Britain and at the moment we have both the technology and the hydrological modelling capacity to undertake this work. What is needed is simply the public wish to realise these benefits.

Many members of the public ask why they should pay for forecasts provided to others foolish enough to live in areas where flooding occurs. In view of the public concern over water charges, this is a legitimate question, but seemingly most people are happy to accept the need for a common basis of charging for most other public services regardless of the localisation of benefit. Surprisingly perhaps, flood insurance is not calculated or provided in a similar manner (Smith & Tobin 1979) although in the United States where development control of washlands is much weaker than in Britain, some compulsory flood insurance is accepted in certain areas (Gillett 1974). In England and Wales all planning applications in the washlands are subject to planning control by the Water Authorities, and normally no property is now constructed which either is subject to flooding or which would

193

make flooding worse elsewhere. Floodplain maps are produced showing the extent of floods of fairly severe return periods and these form the basis of planning control. A recent development is the use of photogrammetry to produce such maps (Collin & Chisholm 1979).

Despite substantial academic interest in the erosive power and sediment movement potential of floods, the British river engineer sees relatively few practical problems posed by sediments. For example, in Britain, siltation in major reservoirs is a very slow process and the cost of land lost to bank erosion is small relative to other costs of major floods. Some sedimentological problems do exist, but many are localised in nature and therefore demand individual study. For example, the question of the origin of the extensive silt deposits in the Lower Severn is of interest since there are proposals to erect a tidal barrier across the Severn estuary. Clearly, if a significant proportion of the silt were of recent fluvial origin, the consequences of erecting such a barrier would be very significant. Similarly, studies have been undertaken of the effects of sediment movement in rivers subject to artificially high flows produced by regulation releases. Nevertheless, of the engineering problems posed by high flows, sedimentological problems are secondary considerations to be dealt with after designing for the river flows themselves.

Apart from flood protection schemes, flood warning and development control, the management of high river flows now extends to the operation of reservoirs to provide some measure of flood protection. Even conventional direct supply reservoirs, originally constructed to supply water and little else, can today, by judicious management, provide some measure of flood relief. This may often be in summer time when the reservoir is naturally drawn down, but by deliberately drawing down the reservoir to a level where it can still safely provide its nominal yield, a measure of flood protection can be given to areas downstream. In the winter similar draw-down can be arranged, but except in the advent of lying snow, draw-down is modest. The 1974 reorganisation of the Water Industry offered the possibility of multi-purpose reservoir management and it has been eagerly seized. However, there are relatively few opportunities where all-year-round flood protection can be given and the costs of constructing purpose-built flood protection reservoirs are prohibitive except in the case of balancing lakes in urban areas. Hence in the United Kingdom, flood protection is likely to continue to be dominated by conventional river channel works, albeit that flood forecasting may in the future be seen to provide protection beyond the range of conventional flood defences, and only in urban areas or below existing reservoirs will there be alternative solutions sought.

Conclusions

Whether it is a drought, flood, low flow or quality objective, river management is largely founded on the selection and effective application of appropriate information, and one common theme running through much of this chapter is that such data is usually limited. Despite a dense network of gauging stations, both high and low flows are not well measured, although this applies quite as much elsewhere as in Britain. Although developments have occurred in both ultrasonic and electromagnetic gauging (Herschy 1978), few rivers are gauged anywhere in the world such that there is confidence in the measurement of either the high or the low flows. Hence estimation and extrapolation techniques still tend to play an

important role in hydrology and therefore river management, for it is the magni-1
tude and frequency and often the duration of flow that form some of the key variables determining management decisions. Water quality management is also founded on a large data-base and similar considerations and reservations can be made in this field. Good data is expensive to collect, even where the current state of technology allows its collection, but because of its scarcity, it is often beyond price when it comes to the making of important decisions.

A second theme which is also common to all river management decisions is the need for the scientific community to be able to measure what people want from their rivers. For example, how often will pollution incidents or cuts in compensation water be tolerated? How often will people accept flooding of homes and are they prepared to pay the economic cost of flood protection or of flood warning? Even more difficult to define is the acceptable level of expenditure on pollution prevention and the intangible quality standards to which rivers should be restored. River management has attained in Britain a great deal of improvement in water quality, in drainage, in conservation and in flood protection in the past, but as it edges closer to the point where diminishing returns begin, it must establish the needs of its consumers and their willingness to foot the bill.

When one looks at the record of British river management, although there are areas for improvement, the overall impression is of a balance of interest between the many demands made on the rivers and a care for the essential features of the rivers themselves. The last decade has seen an emerging care for the environment; perhaps the next decade will be marked by caring, at a price, for both demands and for environment.

References

Abrahams, A. D. and R. F. Cull 1979. The formation of alluvial landforms along New South Wales coastal streams. *Search* **10,** 187–8.

Ackers, P. and F. G. Charlton 1970. The geometry of small meandering streams. *Proc. Inst. Civ. Engrs* suppl. **12,** 289–317.

Adams, W. A. 1974. Pedogenesis of soils derived from Lower Palaeozoic mudstones in mid-Wales. *Welsh Soils Discussion Group* **15,** 61–9.

Alabaster, J. S. 1969. Effects of heated discharges on freshwater fish in Britain. In *Biological aspects of thermal pollution,* P. A. Krenkel and R. L. Parker (eds), 354–70. Vanderbilt: Vanderbilt University Press.

Al-Ansari, N. A., M. Al-Jabbari and J. McManus 1977. The effect of farming upon solid transport in the River Almond, Scotland. In *Int. Assoc. Hydrol. Sci. Publ. 122,* 118–125.

Amey, G. 1974. *The collapse of the Dale Dyke Dam 1864.* London: Cassell.

Anderson, M. G. and T. P. Burt 1978. The role of topography in controlling throughflow generation. *Earth Surface Processes* **3,** 331–44.

Anderson, M. G. and A. Calver 1977. On the persistence of landscape features formed by a large flood. *Trans Inst. Br. Geogs* **2,** 234–54.

Anderson, M. G. and A. Calver 1980. Channel plan changes following large floods. In *Timescales in geomorphology,* R. A. Cullingford, D. A. Davidson and J. Lewin (eds), 43–52. Chichester: Wiley.

Arnett, R. R. 1978. Regional disparities in the denudation rate of organic sediments. *Z. Geomorph.* supp. Bd. **29,** 169–79.

Arnett, R. R. 1979. The use of differing scales to identify factors controlling denudation rates. In *Geographical approaches to fluvial processes,* A. F. Pitty (ed.), 127–47. Norwich: Geobooks.

Ashby, M. 1979. *Water power survey of the Dovey Valley.* Machynlleth, Powys: Centre for Alternative Technology.

Ashmore, P. 1977. Unpublished B.Sc. dissertation. Department of Geography, University of Hull.

Atkinson, B. W. 1980. Climatic regions within the drought area. In *Atlas of drought in Britain 1975–6,* J. C. Doornkamp and K. J. Gregory (eds), 31–2. London: Institute of British Geographers.

Atkinson, T. C. 1971. The danger of pollution of limestone aquifers with special reference to the Mendip Hills, Somerset. *Proc. Univ. Bristol Spelaeol. Soc.* **12,** 281–90.

Atkinson, T. C. 1977. Diffuse flow and conduit flow in limestone terrain in the Mendip Hills, Somerset (Great Britain). *J. Hydrol.* **35,** 93–110.

Atkinson, T. C. and D. P. Drew 1974. Underground drainage of limestone catchments in the Mendip Hills. In *Inst. Br. Geogs Sp. Publ. 6,* 87–106.

Atkinson, T. C., D. I. Smith, J. J. Lavis and R. J. Whitaker 1973. Experiments in tracing underground waters in limestones. *J. Hydrol.* **19,** 323–46.

Bagnold, R. A. 1960. *Some aspects of the shape of river meanders.* USGS Prof. Paper 282-E.

Bagnold, R. A. 1977. Bedload transport by natural rivers. *Water Resources Res.* **13,** 303–12.

Bathurst, J. C. 1978. Flow resistance of large-scale roughness. *Proc. Am. Soc. Civ. Engrs, J. Hydraul. Div.* **104**(HY6), 1587–1603.

Bathurst, J. C., R. M. Li and D. B. Simons 1979. *Hydraulics of mountain rivers.* Fort Collins, Colorado: Civil Engineering Department, Engineering Research Centre, Colorado State University.

Bauer, L. and W. Tillie 1967. Regional differentiation of the suspended sediment transport in Thuringia and their relation to soil erosion. In *Int. Assoc. Sci. Hydrol. Publ. 75,* 367–77.

Bayfield, N. G. 1974. Burial of vegetation by erosion debris near ski lifts on Cairngorm, Scotland. *Biol. Conserv.* **6,** 246–51.

Beckinsale, R. P. and L. Richardson 1964. Recent findings on the physical development of the Lower Severn Valley. *Geog. J.* **130,** 87–105.

Beven, K. 1979. On the generalised kinematic routing method. *Water Resources Res.* **15,** 1238–42.

Beven, K., K. Gilman and M. D. Newson 1979. *Towards a simple physically-based variable contributing area model of catchment hydrology.* Working Paper 154, Department of Geography, University of Leeds.

Biddle, P. and J. H. Miles 1972. The nature of contemporary silts in British estuaries. *Sediment. Geol.* **7,** 23–33.

Binnie & Partners 1973. *The Tame purification lakes.* Report to Trent Water Authority.

Bleasdale, A. 1963. The distribution of exceptionally heavy daily falls of rain in the United Kingdom, 1953–60. *J. Inst. Water Engrs* **17,** 45–55.

Bluck, B. J. 1971. Sedimentation in the meandering River Endrick. *Sc. J. Geol.* **7,** 93–138.

Bluck, B. J. 1976. Sedimentation in some Scottish rivers of low sinuosity. *Trans R. Soc. Edinb.* **69,** 425–56.

Bluck, B. J. 1979. Structure of coarse-grained braided stream alluvium. *Trans R. Soc. Edinb.* **70,** 181–221.

Board, P. A. 1973. The fate of rubbish in the Thames estuary. *Marine Pollut. Bull.* **4,** 165–66.

Bogardi, I. 1961. Some aspects of the application of the theory of sediment transportation to engineering problems. *J. Geophys. Res.* **66,** 3337–46.

Boulton, A. G. 1966. *Surface water survey and modernisation.* Informal discussion of the Hydrological Group, Institute of Civil Engineers, London.

Boulton, G. S., A. S. Jones, K. M. Clayton and M. J. Kenning 1977. A British ice sheet model and patterns of glacial erosion and deposition in Britain. In *British Quaternary studies,* F. W. Shotton (ed.), 231–46. Oxford: Oxford University Press.

Bowen, D. Q. 1978. *Quaternary geology.* Oxford: Pergamon Press.

Branski, J. 1968. Zmacenie wody i transport rumowiska unoszonego w rzekach Polskich. *Prace Panst. Inst. Hydrol.-Meteorol.* **95,** 49–67.

Bridge, J. S. 1976, Bed topography and grain size in open channel bends. *Sedimentology* **23,** 407–14.

Bridge, J. S. and J. Jarvis 1976. Flow and sedimentary processes in the meandering River South Esk, Glen Cova, Scotland. *Earth Surface Processes* **1,** 303–36.

Bridges, E. M. 1969. Eroded soils of the Lower Swansea Valley. *J. Soil Sci.* **20,** 236–45.

Briggs, D. J. and D. D. Gilbertson 1980. Quaternary processes and environments in the upper Thames Valley. *Trans Inst. Br. Geogs* n.s. **5,** 53–65.

Briggs, R. 1971. Assessment of water quality field instrumentation. *Measurement and Control* **4,** T54–T58.

Briggs, R. 1972. Water quality monitoring networks – practice in Great Britain. In *Casebook on hydrological network design practice.* Geneva: World Meteorological Office.

Brookes, R. E. 1974. Unpublished Ph.D. thesis. University of Bristol.

Browning, K. A., C. W. Pardoe and F. F. Hill 1975. The nature of orographic rain at winter time cold fronts. *Q. J. R. Met. Soc.* **101,** 333–52.

Bull, W. B. 1979. Threshold of critical power in streams. *Geol. Soc. Am. Bull.* **90,** 453–64.

Bundesanstalt für Gewasserkunde 1977. *Internationale Hydrologische Dekade Jahrbuch Bundesrepublik Deutschland 1974.* Koblenz.

Bunting, B. T. 1961. The role of seepage moisture in soil formation, slope development and stream initiation. *Am. J. Sci.* **259,** 503–18.

Burt, T. P. 1979. The relationship between throughflow generation and the solute concentration of soil and stream water. *Earth Surface Processes* **4,** 257–66.

Burton, J. D. and P. S. Liss 1976. *Estuarine chemistry.* London: Academic Press.

Calder, I. R. and M. D. Newson 1979. Land use and upland water resources in Britain – a strategic look. *Water Resources Bull.* **15,** 1628–39.

Calver, A., M. J. Kirkby and D. R. Weyman 1972. Modelling hillslope and channel flow. In *Spatial analysis in geomorphology,* R. J. Chorley (ed.), 197–218. London: Methuen.

Carling, P. A. 1979. *Survey of physical characteristics of salmon spawning riffles in the river North Tyne.* Freshwater Biological Association, Teesdale Unit.

Casey, H. 1969. The chemical composition of some southern English chalk streams and its relation to discharge. In *River Authorities Association Yearbook 1969,* 110–13.

Casey, H. 1975. Variation in chemical composition of the River Frome, England, 1965–72. *Freshwater Biol.* **5,** 507–14.

Catt, J. A. 1978. The contribution of loess to soils in lowland Britain. In *The effect of man on the landscape: the lowland zone,* S. Limbrey and J. G. Evans (eds), 12–19. CBA Research Report 21.

References Cawse, P. 1977. *Deposition of trace elements from the atmosphere in the UK.* Paper SS/OC/77/3, ADAS Conference on Inorganic Pollution and Agriculture, Imperial College, London.

Centre for Agricultural Strategy 1980. *Strategy for the UK forest industry.* University of Reading.

Chandler, R. J. 1970. The degradation of Lias Clay slopes in an area of the East Midlands. *Q. J. Engng Geol.* **2,** 161–81.

Chang, H. H. 1979. Minimum stream power and river channel patterns. *J. Hydrol.* **41,** 303–27.

Charlton, F. G., P. M. Brown and R. W. Benson 1978. *The hydraulic geometry of some gravel rivers in Britain.* Report INT-180, Wallingford: Hydraulics Research Station.

Chatterton, J., J. Pirt and T. R. Wood 1979. The benefits of flood forecasting. *J. Inst. Water Engrs and Scientists* **33,** 237–52.

Cheetham, G. H. 1976. Palaeohydrological investigations of river terrace gravels. In *Geoarchaeology: Earth science and the past,* D. A. Davidson and M. L. Shackley (eds), 335–44. London: Duckworth.

Church, M. and J. M. Ryder 1972. Paraglacial sedimentation: a consideration of fluvial processes conditioned by glaciation. *Geol. Soc. Am. Bull.* **83,** 3059–72.

Clayton, C. L. 1951. The problem of gravel in highland water courses. *J. Inst. Water Engrs* **5,** 400–6.

Clayton, K. M. 1977. River terraces. In *British Quaternary studies,* F. W. Shotton (ed.), 153–67. Oxford: Oxford University Press.

Cole, G. 1966. An application of regional analysis of flood flows. In *River flood hydrology,* 39–57. London: Institute of Civil Engineers.

Coleman, A. 1970. The conservation of wildscape: a quest for facts. *Geog. J.* **136,** 199–205.

Collin, R. L. and N. W. T. Chisholm 1979. *Washland mapping of the River Sence, South Leicestershire – a photogrammetric and computer-aided approach.* Report to the Severn-Trent Water Authority. Aberystwyth: University College of Wales.

Collins, M. B. 1973. Unpublished D.Phil. thesis. Brighton: University of Sussex.

Cooke, G. A. n.d. *Topographical and statistical description of the principality of Wales, Part II: South Wales.* London.

Countryside Commission 1978. *Upland land use in England and Wales.* Cheltenham: HMSO.

Costa, J. E. 1975. Effects of agriculture on erosion and sedimentation in the Piedmont zone, Maryland. *Geol. Soc. Am. Bull.* **86,** 1281–86.

Crisp, D. T. 1966. Input and output of minerals for an area of Pennine moorland: the importance of precipitation, drainage, peat erosion and animals. *J. Appl. Ecol.* **3,** 327–48.

Crisp, D. T., P. R. Cubby and S. Robson 1980. *A survey of fish populations in the streams of the Plynlimon experimental catchments.* Report 3, Freshwater Biological Association, Teesdale Unit Project 18.

Crisp, D. T. and E. D. Le Cren 1970. The temperature of three different small streams in North-West England *Hydrobiologia* **35,** 305–23.

Crisp, D. T., M. Rawes and D. Welch 1964. A Pennine peat slide. *Geol. J.* **130,** 519–24.

Crisp, D. T. and S. Robson 1979. Some effects of discharge upon the transport of animals and peat in a north Pennine headstream. *J. Appl. Ecol.* **16,** 721–36.

Cross, P. and J. M. Hodgson 1975. New evidence for the glacial diversion of the River Teme near Ludlow, Salop. *Proc. Geol. Assoc.* **86,** 313–31.

Cryer, R. 1976. The significance and variation of atmospheric nutrient inputs in a small catchment system. *J. Hydrol.* **29,** 121–37.

Cryer, R. 1978. Unpublished Ph.D. thesis. University College of Wales, Aberystwyth.

Cryer, R. 1980. The chemical quality of some pipeflow waters in upland mid-Wales and its implications. *Cambria* **6,** 28–46.

Cummins, W. A. and H. R. Potter 1972. Rate of erosion in the catchment area of Cropston Reservoir, Charnwood Forest, Leicestershire. *Mercian Geol.* **6,** 149–57.

Curran, J. C., G. E. Peckham, D. Smith, A. Thorn, J. S. G. McCulloch and T. C. Strangeways 1977. Cairngorm summit automatic weather station. *Weather* **32,** 61–4.

Dangerfield, B. J. (ed.) 1979. *The structure and management of the British water industry.* London: Institution of Water Engineers.

Davies, B. E. (ed.) 1980. *Applied soil trace elements.* Chichester: Wiley.

198

Davies, B. E. and J. Lewin 1974. Chronosequences in alluvial soils with special reference to historic lead pollution in Cardiganshire, Wales. *Environ. Pollut.* **6**, 49–57.

Davis, A. L. and J. G. Slack 1964. The rivers Blackwater and Chelmer – hardness, sulphate, chloride and nitrate content. *Proc. Soc. Water Treatment and Examination* **13**, 12–19.

Dendy, F. E. 1968. Sedimentation in the nation's reservoirs. *J. Soil Water Conserv.* **23**, 135–37.

Department of the Environment for Northern Ireland 1978. *Water statistics 1978.* Belfast: HMSO.

Dobbie, C. H. and P. O. Wolf 1953. The Lynmouth flood of August 1952. *Proc. Inst. Civ. Engrs* **2**, 522–88.

DOE (Department of the Environment) 1971. *Report of a river pollution survey of England and Wales, 1970.* London: HMSO.

DOE 1972. *River pollution survey of England and Wales, updated 1972.* London: HMSO.

DOE 1973. *A background to the water reorganisation in England and Wales.* London: HMSO.

DOE 1978a. *Water data 1977.* London: HMSO.

DOE 1978b. *River pollution survey of England and Wales, updated 1975.* London: HMSO.

DOE 1978c. *Surface water: United Kingdom 1971–3.* London: HMSO.

Doornkamp, J. C., K. J. Gregory and A. S. Burn (eds) 1980. *Atlas of drought in Britain 1975–6.* London: Institute of British Geographers.

Douglas, I. 1970. Sediment yields from forested and agricultural lands. In *The role of water in agriculture,* J. A. Taylor (ed.), 57–88. Oxford: Pergamon Press.

Douglas, I. and P. Crabb 1972. Conservation of water resources and management of catchment areas in upland Britain. *Biol. Conserv.* **4**, 109–16.

Dunne, T. 1978. Field studies of hillslope flow processes. In *Hillslope hydrology,* M. J. Kirkby (ed.), 227–93. Chichester: Wiley.

Dury, G. H. 1958. Tests of a general theory of misfit streams. *Trans Inst. Br. Geogs* **25**, 105–18.

Dury, G. H. 1964a. *Principles of underfit streams.* USGS Prof. Paper 452-A.

Dury, G. H. 1964b. *Subsurface exploration and chronology of underfit streams.* USGS Prof. Paper 452-B.

Dury, G. H. 1974. Magnitude and frequency analysis and channel morphometry. In *Fluvial geomorphology,* M. E. Morisawa (ed.) 91–121. Binghamton: State University of New York.

Dury, G. H. 1976. Discharge prediction, present and former, from channel dimensions. *J. Hydrol.* **30**, 219–45.

Dury, G. H., C. A. Sinker and D. J. Pannett 1972. Climatic change and arrested meander development on the River Severn. *Area* **4**, 81–5.

Edwards, A. M. C. 1973a. Dissolved load and the tentative solute budgets of some Norfolk catchments. *J. Hydrol.* **18**, 201–17.

Edwards, A. M. C. 1973b. The variation of dissolved constituents with discharge in some Norfolk rivers. *J. Hydrol.* **18**, 219–42.

Edwards, A. M. C. 1974. Silicon depletions in some Norfolk rivers. *Freshwater Biol.* **4**, 267–74.

Edwards, A. M. C. and J. B. Thornes 1973. Annual cycle in river water quality: a time series approach. *Water Resources Res.* **9**, 1286–95.

Ellis, J. B. 1979. The nature and sources of urban sediments and their relation to water quality: a case study from north-west London. In *Man's impact on the hydrological cycle in the United Kingdom,* G. E. Hollis (ed.), 199–216. Norwich: Geobooks.

Evans, J. G. 1966. Late-glacial and Postglacial subaerial deposits at Pitstone, Buckinghamshire. *Proc. Geol. Assoc.* **77**, 347–64.

Evans, R. and R. P. C. Morgan 1974. Water erosion of arable land. *Area* **6**, 221–25.

Fairbairn, W. A. 1967. Erosion in the River Findhorn valley. *Sc. Geog. Mag.* **83**, 46–52.

Farquarson, F. A. K., D. Mackney, M. D. Newson and A. J. Thomasson 1978. *Estimation of runoff potential of river catchments from soil surveys.* Harpenden: Soil Survey of England and Wales, Special Survey 11.

Fearnsides, W. G. and W. H. Wilcockson 1928. A topographical study of the flood-swept course of the Porth Llwyd above Dolgarrog. *Geog. J.* **72**, 401–19.

199

References   Ferguson, R. I. 1973a. Regular meander path models. *Water Resources Res.* **9,** 1079–86.

Ferguson, R. I. 1973b. Channel pattern and sediment type. *Area* **5,** 38–41.

Ferguson, R. I. 1975. Meander irregularity and wavelength estimation. *J. Hydrol.* **26,** 315–33.

Ferguson, R. I. 1976. Disturbed periodic model for river meanders. *Earth Surface Processes* **1,** 337–47.

Finlayson, B. L. 1977. *Runoff contributing areas and erosion.* Res. Paper 18, School of Geography, University of Oxford.

Finlayson, B. L. 1978. Suspended solid transport in a small experimental catchment. *Z. Geomorph.* NF **22,** 192–210.

Fitzsimons, J. 1979. *The use of balancing lakes and washlands for flood alleviation in the upper and middle Tame.* Paper read to the River Engineering Section, Institution of Water Engineers, unpublished.

Fleming, G. 1969a. Unpublished Ph.D. thesis. University of Strathclyde.

Fleming, G. 1969b. Suspended solids monitoring: a comparison between three instruments. *Water and Water Engng* **73,** 377–82.

Fleming, G. 1970. Sediment balance of the Clyde Estuary. *Proc. Am. Soc. Civ. Engrs, J. Hydraulics Div.* **96** (HY11), 2219–30.

Ford, J. D. (ed.) 1977. *Limestones and caves of the Peak District.* Norwich: Geobooks.

Foster, I. D. L. 1977. Unpublished Ph.D. thesis. University of Exeter.

Foster, I. D. L. 1978a. Seasonal solute behaviour of stormflow in a small agricultural catchment. *Catena* **5,** 151–63.

Foster, I. D. L. 1978b. A multivariate model of storm-period solute behaviour. *J. Hydrol.* **39,** 339–53.

Foster, I. D. L. and D. E. Walling 1978. The effects of the 1976 drought and autumn rainfall on stream solute levels. *Earth Surface Processes* **3,** 393–406.

Gameson, A. L. H., J. W. Gibbs and M. J. Barrett 1959. A preliminary temperature survey of a heated river. *Water and Water Engng* **63,** 13–17.

Gaunt, G. D., R. A. Jarvis and B. Matthews 1971. The Late Weichselian sequence in the Vale of York. *Proc. Yorks Geol. Soc.* **38,** 281–84.

Geyl, W. F. 1976. Tidal palaeomorphs in England. *Trans Inst. Br. Geogs* ns **1,** 203–224.

Gillet, P. 1974. National flood insurance program enlarged. *Water for Texas* **4,** 9–11.

Gilman, K. and M. D. Newson 1980. *Soil pipes and pipeflow – a hydrological study in upland Wales.* Norwich: Geobooks.

Glasspoole, J. 1924. Fluctuations of annual rainfall: three driest consecutive years. *Trans Inst. Water Engrs* **29,** 83–101.

Glover, B. J. and P. Johnson 1974. Variations in the natural chemical concentration of river water during flood flows and the lag effect. *J. Hydrol.* **22,** 303–16.

Godwin, H. 1938. The origin of roddons. *Geog. J.* **91,** 241–50.

Godwin, H. and M. E. Clifford 1939. Studies of the Postglacial history of British vegetation. *Phil. Trans R. Soc.* **229B,** 324–406.

Gorham, E. 1956a. The ionic composition of some bog and fen waters in the English Lake District. *J. Ecol.* **44,** 142–52.

Gorham, E. 1956b. On the chemical composition of some waters from the Moor House nature reserve. *J. Ecol.* **44,** 375–82.

Gorham, E. 1961. Factors influencing supply of major ions to inland waters with special reference to the atmosphere. *Geol. Soc. Am. Bull.* **72,** 795–840.

Gray, J. R. A. and J. M. Edington 1969. Effect of woodland clearance on stream temperature. *J. Fish. Res. Bd Can.* **26,** 299–403.

Green, F. H. W. 1964. A map of annual average potential water deficit in the British Isles. *J. Appl. Ecol.* **1,** 151–8.

Green, F. H. W. 1976. Recent changes in land use and treatment. *Geog. J.* **142,** 12–26.

Gregory, K. J. (ed.) 1977. *River channel changes.* Chichester: Wiley.

Gregory, K. J. 1979a. Changes of drainage network composition. *Acta Univ. Oulu* A **82 3,** 19–28.

Gregory, K. J. 1979b. Drainage network power. *Water Resources Res.* **15,** 775–7.

Gregory, K. J. and C. C. Park 1974. Adjustment of river channel capacity downstream from a reservoir. *Water Resources Res.* **10,** 870–3.

Gregory, K. J. and C. C. Park 1976a. Stream channel morphology in north-west Yorkshire. *Rev. Géomorph. Dynamique* **25,** 63–72.

Gregory, K. J. and C. C. Park 1976b. The development of a Devon gully and man. *Geography* **61**, 77–82.

Gregory, K. J. and D. E. Walling 1973. *Drainage basin form and process: a geomorphological approach.* London: Edward Arnold.

Gregory, K. J. and D. E. Walling 1979. *Man and environmental process.* Folkestone: Dawson.

Grimshaw, D. L. and J. Lewin 1980a. Source identification for suspended sediments. *J. Hydrol.* **47**, 151–62.

Grimshaw, D. L. and J. Lewin 1980b. Reservoir effects on sediment yield. *J. Hydrol.* **47**, 163–71.

Grimshaw, D. L., J. Lewin and R. Fuge 1976. Seasonal and short-term variations in the concentrations and supply of dissolved zinc to polluted aquatic environments. *Environ. Pollut.* **11**, 1–7.

Grove, A. T. 1953. Account of a mudflow on Bredon Hill, Worcestershire, April 1951. *Proc. Geol. Assoc.* **64**, 10–13.

Hack, J. T. 1957. *Studies of longitudinal stream profiles in Virginia and Maryland.* USGS Prof. Paper 294-B, 45–97.

Hadfield, C. 1966. *The canals of the West Midlands.* Newton Abbot: David & Charles.

Hadfield, C. 1969. *The canals of South and South-East England.* Newton Abbot: David & Charles.

Hall, D. G. 1967. The pattern of sediment movement in the river Tyne. In *Int. Assoc. Sci. Hydrol. Publ. 75*, 117–40.

Hall, D. G. 1968. The assessment of water resources in Devon, England, using limited hydrometric data. In *Int. Assoc. Sci. Hydrol. Publ. 76*, 110–20.

Hamlin, M. J. and C. E. Wright 1978. The effect on the river system. In *Scientific aspects of the 1975–6 drought in England and Wales.* London: The Royal Society.

Hamlin, R. and J. B. Thornes 1974. *Width variations in small perennial stream channels.* Discussion Paper 51, Department of Geography, London School of Economics.

Harding, D. M. and D. J. Parker 1972. *A study of the flood hazard at Shrewsbury, UK.* Calgary: 22nd International Geographical Congress.

Harriman, R. 1978. Nutrient leaching from fertilised forest watersheds in Scotland. *J. Appl. Ecol.* **15**, 933–42.

Harrison, A. J. M. 1965. Some problems concerning flow measurement in steep rivers. *J. Inst. Water Engrs* **19**, 469–77.

Harrison, S. 1864 (1974). *A complete history of the great flood at Sheffield.* Ilkley: Scholar Press.

Harvey, A. M. 1969. Channel capacity and the adjustment of streams to hydrologic regime. *J. Hydrol.* **8**, 82–98.

Harvey, A. M. 1974. Gully erosion and sediment yield in the Howgill Fells, Westmorland. In *Inst. Br. Geogs Sp. Publ.* **6**, 45–58.

Harvey, A. M. 1975. Some aspects of the relations between channel characteristics and riffle spacing in meandering streams. *Am. J. Sci.* **275**, 470–8.

Harvey, A. M. 1977. Event frequency in sediment production and channel change. In *River channel changes*, K. J. Gregory (ed.), 301–15. Chichester: Wiley.

Hawes, F. B. 1970. Thermal problems 'old hat' in Britain. *Elect. Wld* April, 40–2.

Hawkes, H. A. 1978. Biological surveillance of river water quality, conceptual basis and ecological validity. In *Pollution Report No. 3*. 82–91. First UK/USSR Seminar held at Valdai, USSR, 1976.

Hellawell, J. M. 1978. *Biological surveillance of rivers.* London: Natural Environment Research Council.

Herschy, R. W. 1965. *River water temperature.* Technical Note No. 5. Reading: Water Resources Board.

Herschy, R. W. 1978. *Hydrometry.* Chichester: Wiley.

Hey, R. D. 1975a. Design discharges for natural channels. In *Science, technology and environmental management*, R. D. Hey and T. D. Davies (eds), 73–88. Farnborough: Saxon House.

Hey, R. D. 1975b. Response of alluvial channels to river regulation. *Proc. 2nd Wld Congr. Int. Water Resources Assoc., New Delhi* V, 183–8.

Hey, R. D. 1976a. Geometry of river meanders. *Nature* **262**, 482–4.

References   Hey, R. D. 1976b. Impact prediction in the physical environment. In *Environmental impact assessment*, T. O'Riordan and R. D. Hey (eds), 71–81. Farnborough: Saxon House.

Hey, R. D. 1978. Determinate hydraulic geometry of river channels. *Proc. Am. Soc. Civ. Engrs, J. Hydraul. Div.* **104** (HY6), 869–85.

Hey, R. D., C. R. Thorne and J. C. Bathurst 1976. Drought. *New Scientist* **71**, 660–1.

Hickin, E. J. 1974. The development of meanders in natural river channels. *Am. J. Sci.* **274**, 414–42.

Higginbottom, I. E. and P. G. Fookes 1971. Engineering aspects of periglacial features in Britain. *Q. J. Engng Geol.* **3**, 85–117.

Hill, A. R. 1973. Erosion of river banks composed of glacial till near Belfast, Northern Ireland. *Z. Geomorph.* NF **17**, 428–42.

Hindley, D. R. 1973. The definition of dry weather flow in river measurement. *J. Inst. Water Engrs* **27**, 438–40.

Hitchcock, D. 1977. Channel pattern changes in divided reaches: an example in the coarse bed material of the Forest of Bowland. In *River channel changes*, K. J. Gregory (ed.), 206–20. Chichester: Wiley.

Hodgson, J. M., J. A. Catt and A. H. Weir 1967. The origin and development of clay-with-flints and associated soil horizons on the South Downs. *J. Soil Sci.* **18**, 85–102.

Holden, A. V. 1966. A chemical study of rain and stream waters in the Scottish Highlands. *Freshwater Salmon Fish. Res.* **37**, Edinburgh: HMSO.

Holeman, J. N. 1968. The sediment yield of major rivers of the world. *Water Resources Res.* **4**, 737–47.

Holgate, H. T. D. 1973. Rainfall forecasting for River Authorities. *Met. Mag.* **102**, 33–48.

Hollis, G. E. 1974. The effect of urbanisation on floods in the Canon's Brook, Harlow, Essex. In *Inst. Br. Geogs Sp. Publ. 6*, 123–39.

Hollis, G. E. (ed.) 1979. *Man's impact on the hydrological cycle in the United Kingdom*. Norwich: Geobooks.

Hollis, G. E. and J. K. Luckett 1976. The response of natural river channels to urbanisation: two case studies from South-East England. *J. Hydrol.* **30**, 351–63.

Hooke, J. M. 1977. The distribution and nature of changes in river channel patterns: the example of Devon. In *River channel changes*, K. J. Gregory (ed.), 265–79. Chichester: Wiley.

Hooke, J. M. 1979. An analysis of the processes of river bank erosion. *J. Hydrol.* **42**, 39–62.

Hooke, J. M. 1980. Magnitude and distribution of rates of river bank erosion. *Earth Surface Processes* **5**, 143–56.

Horton, A. 1970. *The drift sequence and subglacial topography in parts of the Ouse and Nene basin*. Report 70/9. Institute of Geological Sciences.

Horton, R. E. 1932. Drainage basin characteristics. *Trans Am. Geophys. Union* **13**, 350–61.

Howe, G. M., H. O. Slaymaker and D. M. Harding 1967. Some aspects of the flood hydrology of the upper catchments of the Wye and Severn. *Trans Inst. Br. Geogs* **41**, 33–58.

Hudson, J. A. 1977. *Meltwater gauge (snow gauge)*. Report 43, 28–32. Wallingford: Institute of Hydrology.

Huggett, R. J. 1976. Lateral translocation of soil plasma through a small valley basin in the Northaw Great Wood, Hertfordshire. *Earth Surface Processes* **1**, 99–109.

Hughes, B. D. and R. W. Edwards 1977. Flows of sodium, potassium, magnesium and calcium in the River Cynon, South Wales. *Water Res.* **11**, 563–6.

Hutchinson, J. N. 1980. The record of peat wastage in the East Anglian Fenland at Holme Post, AD. 1848–1978 *J. Ecol.* **68**, 229–49.

Imeson, A. C. 1970a. Unpublished Ph.D. thesis. University of Hull.

Imeson, A. C. 1970b. Variation in sediment production from three East Yorkshire catchments. In *The role of water in agriculture*, J. A. Taylor (ed.), 39–56. Oxford: Pergamon Press.

Imeson, A. C. 1974. The origin of sediment in a moorland catchment with particular reference to the role of vegetation. In *Inst. Br. Geogs Sp. Publ. 6*, 59–72.

Imeson, A. C. and R. C. Ward 1972. The output of a lowland catchment. *J. Hydrol.* **17**, 145–59.

Ingram, H. A. P. 1967. Problems of hydrology and plant distribution in mires. *J. Ecol.* **55**, 711–24.

Ingram, H. A. P. 1978. Soil layers in mires: function and terminology. *Soil Sci.* **29**, 224–7.

Institute of Geological Sciences 1977. *Quaternary map of the United Kingdom,* 2 sheets. Leeds: IGS.

Institute of Hydrology 1980a. *Low flow studies report.* Wallingford: the Institute.

Institute of Hydrology 1980b. *Flood studies supplementary report no. 5.* Wallingford: the Institute.

Jackson, M. C. 1971. Evaluating the probability of heavy rain. *Met. Mag.* **106,** 185–92.

Jackson, M. C. 1974. Largest two-hour falls of rain in the British Isles. *Weather* **29,** 71–3.

Jacobi, R. M. 1978. Population and landscape in Mesolithic lowland Britain. In *The effects of man on the landscape: the lowland zone,* S. Limbrey and J. G. Evans (eds), 75–85. CBA Research Report 21.

Johnson, F. A. 1971. Stream temperatures in an alpine area. *J. Hydrol.* **14,** 322–36.

Johnson, P. 1975. Snowmelt. In *Flood studies conference,* 5–10. London: Institution of Civil Engineers.

Jones, A. 1971. Soil piping and stream channel initiation. *Water Resources Res.* **7,** 602–10.

Jones, H. H. 1980. An overview of hydrological forecasting in a multi-functional Water Authority. In *Proc. Oxford Symp.,* 195–202. International Association of Scientific Hydrology Publ. 129.

Jones, J. A. A. 1978. Soil pipe networks: distribution and discharge. *Cambria* **5,** 1–21.

Jones, O. T. 1924. The longitudinal profiles of the Upper Towy drainage system. *Q. J. Geol. Soc.* **80,** 568–609.

Judson, S. and D. F. Ritter 1964. Rates of regional denudation in the United States. *J. Geophys. Res.* **69,** 3395–401.

Keller, E. A. 1972. Development of alluvial stream channels: a five-stage model. *Geol. Soc. Am. Bull.* **83,** 1531–6.

Keller, E. A. and W. N. Melhorn 1978. Rhythmic spacing and origin of pools and riffles. *Geol. Soc. Am. Bull.* **89,** 723–30.

Kellerhals, R., M. Church and D. I. Bray 1976. Classification and analysis of river processes. *Proc. Am. Soc. Civ. Engrs, J. Hydraul. Div.* **102,** 813–29.

Kellerhals, R., M. Church and L. B. Davies 1979. Morphological effects of interbasin river diversions. *Can. J. Civ. Engng* **6,** 18–31.

King, L. C. 1953. Canons of landscape evolution. *Geol. Soc. Am. Bull.* **64,** 721–52.

Kirkby, M. J. 1963. Unpublished Ph.D. thesis. University of Cambridge.

Kirkby, M. J. 1967. Measurement and theory of soil creep. *J. Geol.* **75,** 359–78.

Kirkby, M. J. (ed.) 1978. *Hillslope hydrology.* Chichester: Wiley.

Klein, L. 1962. *River pollution 2: causes and effects.* London: Butterworths.

Knapp, B. J. 1974. Hillslope throughflows and the problem of modelling. In *Inst. Br. Geogs Sp. Publ.* **6,** 23–31.

Knight, A. H., R. Boggie and H. Shepherd 1972. The effect of ground water level on water movement in peat: a study using tritiated water. *J. Appl. Ecol.* **9,** 633–41.

Knight, C. 1979. Urbanisation and natural stream channel morphology: the case of two English new towns. In *Man's impact on the hydrological cycle in the United Kingdom,* G. E. Hollis (ed.), 181–98. Norwich: Geobooks.

Knighton, A. D. 1972. Changes in a braided reach. *Geol. Soc. Am. Bull.* **83,** 3813–22.

Knighton, A. D. 1973. River bank erosion in relation to streamflow conditions, River Bollin-Dean, Cheshire. *East Midland Geog.* **5,** 416–26.

Knighton, A. D. 1974. Variation in width-discharge relation and some implications for hydraulic geometry. *Geol. Soc. Am. Bull.* **85,** 1059–76.

Knighton, A. D. 1977. Short-term changes in hydraulic geometry. In *River channel changes,* K. J. Gregory (ed.), 101–19. Chichester: Wiley.

Kopaliani, Z. D. and V. V. Romashin 1970. Channel dynamics of mountain rivers. *Soviet Hydrol.: Selected Papers* **5,** 441–52.

Krutilla, J. V. and O. Eckstein 1958. *Multiple purpose river development.* Baltimore: Johns Hopkins University Press.

Lambert, A. O. 1972. Catchment models based on Iso functions. *J. Inst. Water Engrs* **26,** 413–22.

Lambert, J. M., J. N. Jennings, C. T. Smith, C. Green and J. N. Hutchinson 1960. *The making of the Broads.* London: Royal Geographical Society.

References   Langford, T. E. 1970. The temperature of a British river upstream and downstream of a heated discharge from a power station. *Hydrobiologia* **35**, 355–75.

Langford, T. E. 1972. A comparative assessment of thermal effects in some British and North American rivers. In *River ecology and man*, R. T. Oglesby *et al.* (eds), 319–51. New York: Academic Press.

Langford, T. E. and R. J. Aston 1972. The ecology of some British rivers in relation to warm water discharges from power stations. *Proc. R. Soc., Lond.* **1808**, 407–19.

Law, F. 1956. The effect of afforestation upon the yield of water catchment areas. *J. Br. Waterworks Assoc.* **38**, 484–94.

Ledger, D. C., J. P. B. Lovell and A. T. McDonald 1974. Sediment yield studies in upland catchment areas in South-East Scotland. *J. Appl. Ecol.* **11**, 201–6.

Leopold, L. B. and T. Maddock 1953. *The hydraulic geometry of stream channels and some physiographic implications.* USGS Prof. Paper 252.

Leopold, L. B. and M. G. Wolman 1957. *River channel patterns – braided, meandering and straight.* USGS Prof. Paper 282-B.

Leopold, L. B., M. G. Wolman and J. P. Miller 1964. *Fluvial processes in geomorphology.* San Francisco: W. H. Freeman.

Lester, W. F. 1967. Pollution in the River Trent and its tributaries. *J. Inst. Water Engrs* **21**, 261–74.

Lester, W. F. 1979. River quality objectives. *J. Inst. Water Engrs and Scientists* **33**, 429–50.

Lester, W. F., G. M. Woodward and T. W. Raven 1972. *River purification lakes.* Reading: Water Resources Board, Trent Research Programme.

Lewin, J. 1972. Late-stage meander growth. *Nature Phys. Sci.* **240**, 116.

Lewin, J. 1976. Initiation of bedforms and meanders in coarse-grained sediment. *Geol. Soc. Am. Bull.* **87**, 281–5.

Lewin, J. 1977. Palaeohydrology. *Cambria* **4**, 112–23.

Lewin, J. 1978a. Meander development and floodplain sedimentation: a case study from mid-Wales. *Geol J.* **13**, 25–36.

Lewin, J. 1978b. Floodplain geomorphology. *Prog. Phys. Geog.* **2**, 408–37.

Lewin, J. and B. J. Brindle 1977. Confined meanders. In *River channel changes*, K. J. Gregory (ed.), 221–33. Chichester: Wiley.

Lewin, J., R. Cryer and D. I. Harrison 1974. Sources for sediments and solutes in mid-Wales. In *Inst. Br. Geogs Sp. Publ. 6*, 73–85.

Lewin, J., B. E. Davies and P. Wolfenden 1977. Interactions between channel change and historic mining sediments. In *River channel changes*, K. J. Gregory (ed.), 353–67. Chichester: Wiley.

Lewin, J. and D. Hughes 1976. Assessing channel change on Welsh rivers. *Cambria* **3**, 1–10.

Lewin, J., D. Hughes and C. Blacknell 1977. Incidence of river erosion. *Area* **9**, 177–80.

Lewin, J. and M. J. C. Weir 1977. Morphology and recent history of the lower Spey. *Sc. Geog. Mag.* **93**, 45–51.

Lewin, J. and P. J. Wolfenden 1978. The assessment of sediment sources: a field experiment. *Earth Surface Processes* **3**, 171–8.

Lewis, W. K. 1957. Investigation of rainfall, runoff and yield on the Alwen and Brenig catchments. *Proc. Instn Civ. Engrs* **8**, 17–51.

Limbrey, S. 1978. Changes in quality and distribution of the soils in lowland Britain. In *The effects of man on the landscape: the lowland zone*, S. Limbrey and J. G. Evans (eds), 21–7. London: CBA Research Report 21.

Loveday, J. 1962. Plateau deposits of the southern Chiltern Hills. *Proc. Geol. Assoc.* **73**, 83–102.

Lowing, M. J., R. K. Price and R. A. Harvey 1975. *Real time conversion of rainfall to runoff for flow forecasting in the River Dee.* Malvern: Water Research Centre/Royal Radar Establishment.

Macan, T. T. 1958. The temperature of a small stony stream. *Hydrobiologia* **12**, 89–106.

Mackereth, F. J. H. 1966. Some chemical observations on Postglacial lake sediment. *Phil. Trans R. Soc.* **250B**, 165–213.

Maclean, W. N. 1927. Rainfall and flow-off in the River Garry, Invernesshire. *Trans Inst. Water Engrs* **32**, 110–46.

MAFF (Ministry of Agriculture, Fisheries and Food) 1967. *Potential transpiration.* Tech. Bull. 16, London: HMSO.

MAFF 1976. *Agriculture and water quality.* Tech. Bull. 32, London: HMSO.

Manley, G. 1975. Fluctuations of snowfall and persistence of snow cover in marginal oceanic climates. In *Proc. WMO/IAMAP Symp. on long-term climatic fluctuations*, 183–8.

Manley, R. E. 1978. Simulation of flows in ungauged basins. *Hydrol. Sci. Bull.* **23**, 85–101.

Marsh, T. J. and I. G. Littlewood 1978. An estimate of annual runoff from England and Wales, 1728–1976. *Hydrol. Sci. Bull.* **23**, 131–42.

Marshall, C. T. 1957. Unpublished Ph.D. thesis. University of Leeds.

McDonald, A. T. 1973. *Some views on the effect of peat drainage.* Working Paper 40, Department of Geography, University of Leeds.

McGill, J. D., R. S. Wilson and A. M. Brake 1979. The use of chironomid pupal exuviae in the surveillance of sewage pollution within a drainage system. *Water Res.* **13**, 887–94.

McMahon, T. A. and R. G. Meins 1978. *Reservoir capacity and yield.* Amsterdam: Elsevier.

McManus, J. 1979. The evolution of fluviatile sediments as demonstrated by QDa-Md analysis. *Earth Surface Processes* **4**, 141–46.

McManus, J. and N. A. Al-Ansari 1975. Calculation of sediment discharge in the River Earn, Scotland. In *Proc. 9th Int. Congr. Sediment., Nice,* 113–8.

Mellanby, K. 1974. A water pollution survey, mainly by British schoolchildren. *Environ. Pollut.* **6**, 161–73.

Meyback, M. 1976. Total mineral dissolved transport by world major rivers. *Hydrol. Sci. Bull.* **21**, 265–84.

Milne, J. A. 1979. The morphological relationships of bends in confined stream channels in upland Britain. In *Geographical approaches to fluvial processes,* A. F. Pitty (ed.), 215–39. Norwich: Geobooks.

Milne, J. A. 1980. Unpublished Ph.D. thesis. University of Hull.

Montgomery, H. A. C. and I. C. Hart 1974. The design of sampling programmes for rivers and effluents. *J. Inst. Water Pollut. Control* **73**, 3–27.

Morgan, R. P. C. 1979. *Soil erosion.* London: Longman.

Morgan, R. P. C. 1980. Soil erosion and conservation in Britain. *Prog. Phys. Geog.* **4**, 24–47.

Mosley, M. P. 1975. Channel changes on the River Bollin, Cheshire, 1872–1973. *East Midland Geog.* **6**, 185–99.

Munro, J. M. M., D. A. Davies and T. A. Thomas 1973. Potential pasture production on the uplands of Wales 3. Soil nutrient resources and limitations. *J. Br. Grassld Soc.* **28**, 247–55.

National Water Council 1978. *River water quality, the next stage: review of discharge consent conditions.* London: National Water Council.

NERC (Natural Environment Research Council) 1970. *Hydrological research in the United Kingdom, 1965–70.* London: NERC.

NERC 1975a. *Flood studies report.* London: NERC.

NERC 1975b. *Estuaries research.* London: NERC.

NERC 1979a. *Hydrological research in the United Kingdom, 1975–80.* London: NERC.

NERC 1979b. *The Humber Estuary.* London: NERC.

Newson, A. J. 1979. Heavy thunderstorms on Plynlimon, mid-Wales, 15 August 1977. *J. Met.* **2**, 292–4.

Newson, M. D. 1973. The Carboniferous limestone of the United Kingdom as an aquifer rock. *Geog. J.* **139**, 294–305.

Newson, M. D. 1975a. *Flooding and flood hazard in the United Kingdom.* Oxford: Oxford University Press.

Newson, M. D. 1975b. *The Plynlimon floods of 5–6 August 1973.* Wallingford: Institute of Hydrology.

Newson, M. D. 1976a. Soil piping in upland Wales: a call for more information. *Cambria* **3**, 33–9.

Newson, M. D. 1976b. Soil maps to predict catchment behaviour. *Welsh Soils Discussion Group* **17**, 174–93.

Newson, M. D. 1978. Drainage basin characteristics, their selection, derivation and analysis for a flood study of the British Isles. *Earth Surface Processes* **3**, 277–93.

Newson, M. D. 1979a. Framework for field experiments in mountain areas of Great Britain. *Stud. Geomorph. Carpatho-Baltanica* **XIII**, 163–74.

Newson, M. D. 1979b. The results of ten years' experimental study on Plynlimon, mid-

Wales, and their importance for the water industry. *J. Inst. Water Engrs and Scientists* **33**, 321–33.

Newson, M. D. 1980a. The geomorphological effectiveness of floods, a contribution stimulated by two recent events in mid-Wales. *Earth Surface Processes* **5**, 1–16.

Newson, M. D. 1980b. The erosion of drainage ditches and its effect on bedload yields in mid-Wales. *Earth Surface Processes* **5**, 275–90.

Newson, M. D. 1980c. Water balance at selected sites. In *Atlas of drought in Britain 1975–6*, J. C. Doornkamp, K. J. Gregory and A. S. Burn (eds), 38. London: Institute of British Geographers.

Newson, M. D. and J. G. Harrison 1978. *Channel studies in the Plynlimon experimental catchment*. Report 47, Wallingford: Institute of Hydrology.

Nixon, M. 1959. A study of bankfull discharges of the rivers of England and Wales. *Proc. Inst. Civ. Engrs* **12**, 157–74.

Nuttall, P. M. and E. H. Bielby 1973. The effect of china clay wastes on stream invertebrates. *Environ. Pollut.* **5**, 77–86.

Oborne, A. C., M. P. Brooker and R. W. Edwards 1980. The chemistry of the River Wye. *J. Hydrol.* **45**, 233–52.

Oldfield, F. 1977. Lakes and their drainage basins as units of sediment-based ecological study. *Prog. Phys. Geog.* **1**, 460–504.

Ovenden, J. C. and K. J. Gregory 1980. The permanence of stream networks in Britain. *Earth Surface Processes* **5**, 47–60.

Oxley, N. C. 1974. Suspended sediment delivery rates and solute concentration of stream discharge in two Welsh catchments. In *Inst. Br. Geogs Sp. Publ. 6*, 141–53.

Packman, J. C. 1977. *The effect of urbanisation on flood discharges – discussion and recommended procedures*. Cranfield Conference, MAFF.

Painter, R. B. 1971. A hydrological classification of the soils of England and Wales. *Proc. Inst. Civ. Engrs* **29**, 93–5.

Painter, R. B., K. Blyth, J. C. Mosedale and M. Kelly 1974. The effect of afforestation on erosion processes and sediment yield. In *Int. Assoc. Sci. Hydrol. Publ. 113*, 62–7.

Pardé, M. 1955. *Fleuves et rivières*, 3rd edn. Paris: Colin.

Park, C. C. 1975. Stream channel morphology in mid-Devon. *Trans Devon. Assoc.* **107**, 25–41.

Park, C. C. 1976. The relationship of slope and stream channel form in the River Dart, Devon. *J. Hydrol.* **29**, 139–47.

Park, C. C. 1977. Man-induced changes in stream channel capacity. In *River channel changes*, K. J. Gregory (ed.), 121–44. Chichester: Wiley.

Park, C. C. 1978. Allometric analysis and stream channel morphology. *Geog. Anal.* **10**, 211–28.

Park, C. C. 1979. Tin streaming and channel changes: some preliminary observations from Dartmoor, England. *Catena* **6**, 235–44.

Parry, M. L. 1978. *Climatic change, agriculture and settlement*. Folkestone: Dawson.

Penman, H. L. 1950. Evaporation in the British Isles. *Q. J. R. Met. Soc.* **76**, 372–83.

Penning-Rowsell, E. C. and J. Chatterton 1977. *Benefits of flood alleviation, a manual of assessment techniques*. Farnborough: Teakfield.

Penning-Rowsell, E. C. and J. R. G. Townshend 1978. The influence of scale on the factors affecting stream channel slope. *Trans Inst. Br. Geogs* ns **3**, 395–415.

Pennington, W. 1978. Responses of some British lakes to past changes in land use on their catchments. *Verhand. Int. Vereins Limnol.* **20**, 636–41.

Pennington, W. (Mrs T. G. Tutin), E. Y. Haworth, A. D. Bonny and J. P. Lishman 1972. Lake sediments in northern Scotland. *Phil. Trans R. Soc.* **264B**, 191–294.

Pennington, W. (Mrs T. G. Tutin), and J. P. Lishman 1971. Iodine in lake sediments in northern England and Scotland. *Biol. Rev.* **46**, 279–313.

Petts, G. E. 1977. Channel response to flow regulation: the case of the River Derwent, Derbyshire. In *River channel changes*, K. J. Gregory (ed.), 145–61. Chichester: Wiley.

Petts, G. E. 1979. Complex response of river channel morphology to reservoir construction. *Prog. Phys. Geog.* **3**, 329–62.

Petts, G. E. and J. Lewin 1979. Physical effects of reservoirs on river systems. In *Man's impact on the hydrological cycle in the United Kingdom*, G. E. Hollis (ed.), 79–91. Norwich: Geobooks.

Popov, I. V. 1964. Hydromorphological principles of the theory of channel processes and their use in hydrotechnical planning. *Soviet Hydrol.* 188–95.

Porter, E. 1973. *Pollution in four industrialised estuaries.* London: HMSO.

Porter, E. 1978. *Water management in England and Wales.* Cambridge: Cambridge University Press.

Potter, H. R. 1973. Sediment studies in the Trent Basin. *Assoc. River Auth. Yrbk,* 166–71.

Potts, A. S. 1971. Fossil cryonival features in central Wales. *Geograf. Ann.* **53A,** 39–51.

Price, D. H. E. 1975. The development of a Harmonised Monitoring Programme for rivers in the United Kingdom. *Prog. Water Technol.* **7,** 99–110.

Price, R. K. 1977. *FLOUT – a river catchment flood model.* Report IT 168, Wallingford: Institute of Hydrology.

Rabeni, C. F. and K. E. Gibbs 1978. Comparison of two methods used by divers for sampling benthic invertebrates in deep rivers. *J. Fish. Res. Bd Can.* **35,** 332–6.

Radley, J., and C. Simms 1967. Wind erosion in East Yorkshire. *Nature* **216,** 20–2.

Rannie, W. F. 1978. An approach to the prediction of sediment rating curves. In *Research in fluvial systems,* R. Davidson-Arnott and W. Nickling (eds), 149–67. Norwich: Geobooks.

Reynolds, G. 1959. Rainfall, runoff and evaporation on a catchment in west Scotland. *Weather* **24,** 90–8.

Richards, K. S. 1972. Meanders and valley slopes. *Area* **4,** 288–90.

Richards, K. S. 1976a. Channel width and the riffle-pool sequence. *Geol. Soc. Am. Bull.* **87,** 883–90.

Richards, K. S. 1976b. The morphology of riffle-pool sequences. *Earth Surface Processes* **1,** 71–88.

Richards, K. S. 1977. Channel and flow geometry: a geomorphological perspective. *Prog. Phys. Geog.* **1,** 65–102.

Richards, K. S. 1979. Channel adjustment to sediment pollution by the china clay industry in Cornwall, England. In *Adjustments of the fluvial system,* D. D. Rhodes and G. P. Williams (eds), 309–31. Dubuque, Iowa: Kendall-Hunt.

Richards, K. S. and R. Wood 1977. Urbanisation, water redistribution and their effect on channel processes. In *River channel changes,* K. J. Gregory (ed.), 369–88. Chichester: Wiley.

Risbridger, C. A. and W. H. Godfrey 1954. Rainfall, runoff and storage: Elan and Claerwen gathering grounds. *Proc. Inst. Civ. Engrs* **3,** 345–88.

Roberts, M. E. and D. B. James 1972. Some effects of forest cover on nutrient cycling and river temperature. In *Research papers in forest meteorology,* J. A. Taylor (ed.), 100–8. Aberystwyth: University of Wales.

Roberts, F. W. 1974. The Jubilee of the Royal Commission Standard. *J. Inst. Water Pollut. Control,* 129–37.

Robinson, A. R. 1973. Sediment – our greatest pollutant? In *Focus on environmental ecology,* R. W. Tank (ed.), 186–92. New York: Oxford University Press.

Robinson, D. N. 1968. Soil erosion by wind in Lincolnshire, March 1978. *East Midland Geog.* **4,** 351–62.

Robinson, M. 1979. *The effects of pre-afforestation ditching upon the water and sediment yields of a small upland catchment.* Working Paper 252, School of Geography, University of Leeds.

Robinson, M. 1981. *The effects of pre-afforestation drainage upon the streamflow and water quality of a small upland catchment.* Report, Wallingford: Institute of Hydrology.

Rockwood, P. M. 1961. Columbia Basin streamflows routing by computer. *Trans. Am. Soc. Civ. Engrs* **126,** 32–56.

Rodda, J. C. 1967. A countrywide study of intense rainfall for the United Kingdom. *J. Hydrol.* **5,** 58–69.

Rodda, J. C., R. A. Downing and F. M. Law 1976. *Systematic hydrology.* London: Newnes-Butterworth.

Rodda, J. C., A. V. Sheckley and P. Tan 1978. Water resources and climatic change. *J. Inst. Water Engrs and Scientists* **31,** 76–83.

Rose, J., C. Turner, G. R. Coope and M. D. Bryan 1980. Channel change in a lowland river catchment over the last 13000 years. In *Timescales in geomorphology,* R. A. Cullingford, D. A. Davidson and J. Lewin (eds), 159–75. Chichester: Wiley.

References   Ross, F. F. 1970. Warm water discharges into rivers and the sea. In *Proc. Ann. Conf. Inst. Water Pollut. Control,* Blackpool, UK.

Royal Commission on Environmental Pollution 1972. *Third report: pollution in some British estuaries and coastal waters.* London: HMSO.

Rudeforth, C. C. and A. J. Thomasson 1970. *Hydrological properties of soils in the River Dee catchment.* Special Survey 4, Harpenden: Soil Survey of England and Wales.

Rycroft, D. W., D. J. A. Williams and H. A. P. Ingram 1975. The transmission of water through peat. *J. Ecol.* **63,** 535–68.

Schumm, S. A. 1960. *The shape of alluvial channels in relation to sediment type.* USGS Prof. Paper 352-B.

Schumm, S. A. 1963a. Sinuosity of alluvial rivers on the Great Plains. *Geol. Soc. Am. Bull.* **74,** 1089–110.

Schumm, S. A. 1963b. *A tentative classification of alluvial river channels.* USGS Circular 477.

Schumm, S. A. 1971. Fluvial geomorphology – the historical perspective. In *River mechanics,* vol. 1, H. W. Shen (ed.), 4.1–4.30. Fort Collins: Water Resources Publications.

Schumm, S. A. and H. R. Khan 1972. Experimental study of channel patterns. *Geol. Soc. Am. Bull.* **83,** 1755–70.

Scottish Development Department 1972. *Report of a rivers pollution survey of Scotland, towards cleaner water,* Edinburgh: HMSO.

Scottish Development Department 1973. *A measure of plenty.* Edinburgh: HMSO.

Scottish Development Department 1976. *Towards cleaner water: 1975 report of a second rivers pollution survey of Scotland.* Edinburgh: HMSO.

Searcy, J. K. 1959. *Flow-duration curves, manual of hydrology: part 2, low-flow techniques.* USGS Water Supply Paper 1542-A.

Shaw, J. 1972. Sedimentation in the ice-contact environment from Shropshire (England). *Sedimentology* **18,** 23–62.

Shear, H. and A. E. P. Watson (eds) 1977. *The fluvial transport of sediment associated nutrients and contaminants.* Windsor, Ontario: International Joint Commission on the Great Lakes.

Shen, H. W. (ed.) 1973. *Environmental impact on rivers.* Fort Collins: Water Resources Publications.

Shotton, F. W. 1978. Archaeological inferences from the study of alluvium in the lower Severn–Avon valleys. In *The effect of man on the landscape: the lowland zone,* S. Limbrey and I. G. Evans (eds), 27–32. CBA Research Report 21.

Shreve, R. L. 1974. Variation of mainstream length with basin area in river networks. *Water Resources Res.* **10,** 1167–77.

Simons, D. B., E. V. Richardson and C. F. Nordin 1965. Sedimentary structures generated by flow in alluvial channels. In *Soc. Econ. Mineral. Petrol. Sp. Publ. 12,* 34–52.

Simpson, E. A. 1978. The harmonisation of the monitoring of the quality of inland fresh water. *J. Inst. Water Engrs and Scientists* **32,** 45–53.

Simpson, R. J., T. R. Wood and M. J. Hamlin 1980. Simple self-correcting models for forecasting flows on small basins in real time. In *Proc. Oxford Symp.,* 433–44. Int. Assoc. Sci. Hydrol. Publ. 129.

Sissons, J. B. 1976. *Scotland.* London: Methuen.

Skeat, J. D. and B. J. Dangerfield (eds) 1969. *Manual of British water engineering.* London: Institution of Water Engineers.

Skempton, A. W. and J. N. Hutchinson (organisers) 1976. A discussion on valley slopes and cliffs in southern England: morphology, mechanics and Quaternary history. *Phil. Trans R. Soc.* **283A,** 421–631.

Slack, J. G. 1977. River water quality in Essex during and after the 1976 drought. *Effluent Water Treat. J.* **17,** 575–8.

Smith, D. I. and D. P. Drew (eds) 1975. *Limestones and caves of the Mendip Hills.* Newton Abbot: David & Charles.

Smith, I. and A. Lyle 1979. *Distribution of freshwaters in Great Britain.* Edinburgh: Institute of Terrestrial Ecology.

Smith, K. 1975. Water temperature variations within a major river system. *Nordic Hydrol.* **6,** 155–69.

Smith, K. 1979. Temperature characteristics of British rivers and the effects of thermal

208

pollution. In *Man's impact on the hydrological cycle in the United Kingdom*, G. E. Hollis (ed.), 229–42. Norwich: Geobooks.

Smith, K. and G. A. Tobin 1979. *Human adjustment to the flood hazard*. London: Longman.

Spraggs, G. 1976. Solute variations in a local catchment. *Sthrn Hants Geog.* **8**, 1–14.

Stamp, L. D. 1950. *The world: a general geography*. London: Longman.

Stevenson, C. M. 1968. An analysis of the chemical composition of rain water and air over the British Isles and Eire for the years 1959–64. *Q. J. R. Met. Soc.* **94**, 56–70.

Stout, H. P. 1979. Prediction of oxygen deficits associated with effluent inputs to the rivers of the Forth catchment. *Proc. Inst. Civ. Engrs* **67**, 51–64.

Strahler, A. N. 1950. Equilibrium theory of erosional slopes approached by frequency distribution analysis. *Am. J. Sci.* **248**, 673–96, 800–14.

Strakhov, N. M. 1967. *Principles of lithogenesis*, vol. 1. Edinburgh: Oliver and Boyd.

Strangeways, I. C. 1972. Automatic weather stations for network operation. *Weather* **27**, 403–8.

Sutcliffe, D. W. and T. R. Carrick 1973. Studies on mountain streams in the English Lake District: 2. Aspects of water chemistry in the River Duddon. *Freshwater Biol.* **3**, 543–60.

Tallis, J. H. 1965. Studies on southern Pennine peats, IV: Evidence of recent erosion. *J. Ecol.* **53**, 509–20.

Tallis, J. H. 1973. Studies of southern Pennine peats, V: Direct observations on peat erosion and peat hydrology at Featherbed Moss, Derbyshire. *J. Ecol.* **61**, 1–22.

Taylor, C. H. and D. M. Roth 1979. Effects of suburban construction on runoff contributing zones in a small Southern Ontario drainage basin. *Hydrol. Sci. Bull.* **24**, 289–301.

Taylor, J. A. 1976. Upland climates. In *The climate of the British Isles*, T. J. Chandler and S. Gregory (eds), 264–87. London: Longman.

Taylor, J. A. and R. B. Tucker 1970. The peat deposits of Wales: an inventory and interpretation. In *Proc. 3rd Int. Peat Conf.*, 163–73. Ottawa: Runge Press.

Ternan, J. L. and A. G. Williams 1979. Hydrological pathways and granite weathering on Dartmoor. In *Geographical approaches to fluvial processes*, A. F. Pitty (ed.), 5–30. Norwich: Geobooks.

Thomas, T. M. 1956. Gully erosion in the Brecon Beacons area, South Wales. *Geog.* **41**, 99–107.

Thomas, T. M. 1964. Sheet erosion induced by sheep in the (Plynlimon) area, mid-Wales. In *Br. Geomorph. Res. Group Occ. Publ. 2*, 11–14.

Thorne, C. R. and J. Lewin 1979. Bank processes, bed material movement and planform development in a meandering river. In *Adjustments of the fluvial system*, D. D. Rhodes and G. P. Williams (eds), 117–37. Dubuque, Iowa: Kendall-Hunt.

Thornthwaite, C. W. and J. R. Mather 1955. *The water balance*. Centerton, NJ: Laboratory of Climatology.

Tomlinson, R. W. 1979. Water levels in peatlands and some implications for runoff and erosional processes. In *Geographical approaches to fluvial processes*, A. F. Pitty (ed.), 149–62. Norwich: Geobooks.

Tomlinson, T. E. 1970. Trends in nitrate concentrations in English rivers in relation to fertiliser use. *Water Treat. Examin.* **19**, 277–93.

Toms, R. G. 1975. Management of river water quality. In *River ecology*, vol. 2, B. A. Whittorn (ed.). Oxford: Blackwell Scientific.

Tooley, M. J. 1974. Sea-level changes during the last 9000 years in North-West England. *Geog. J.* **140**, 18–42.

Trimble, S. W. 1977. The fallacy of stream equilibrium in contemporary denudation studies. *Am. J. Sci.* **277**, 876–87.

Troake, R. P. and D. E. Walling 1973. The hydrology of the Slapton Wood stream. *Field Studies* **3**, 719–40.

Tuckfield, C. G. 1964. Gully erosion in the New Forest, Hampshire. *Am. J. Sci.* **262**, 795–805.

Tuckfield, C. G. 1973. Seepage steps in the New Forest, Hampshire, England. *Water Resources Res.* **9**, 367–77.

University of Wales 1977. *The sedimentation of Aberystwyth Harbour: a report to*

References   *Ceredigion District Council.* Departments of Geography and Geology, University College of Wales, Aberystwyth.

Walling, D. E. 1971. Sediment dynamics of small instrumented catchments in south-east Devon. *Trans Devon. Assoc.* **103,** 147–65.

Walling, D. E. 1974. Suspended sediment and solute yields from a small catchment prior to urbanisation. In *Inst. Br. Geogs Sp. Publ. 6,* 169–90.

Walling, D. E. 1975. Solute variations in small catchment streams: some comments. *Trans Inst. Br. Geogs* **64,** 141–7.

Walling, D. E. 1977a. Assessing the accuracy of suspended sediment rating curves for a small basin. *Water Resources Res.* **13,** 531–8.

Walling, D. E. 1977b. Limitations of the rating curve technique for estimating suspended sediment loads, with particular reference to British rivers. In *Int. Assoc. Sci. Hydrol. Publ. 122,* 34–48.

Walling, D. E. 1977c. Physical hydrology. *Prog. Phys. Geog.* **1,** 143–57.

Walling, D. E. 1978. Suspended sediment and solute response characteristics of the River Exe, Devon, England. In *Research in fluvial systems,* R. Davidson-Arnott and W. Nickling (eds), 169–97. Norwich: Geobooks.

Walling, D. E. 1980. Solute levels in two Devon catchments. In *Atlas of drought in Britain 1975–6,* J. C. Doornkamp, K. J. Gregory and A. S. Burn (eds). London: Institute of British Geographers.

Walling, D. E. and I. D. L. Foster 1975. Variations in the natural chemical composition of river water during flood flows and the lag effect: some further comments. *J. Hydrol.* **26,** 237–44.

Walling, D. E. and I. D. L. Foster 1978. The 1976 drought and nitrate levels in the River Exe basin. *J. Inst. Water Engrs and Scientists* **42,** 341–53.

Walling, D. E. and K. J. Gregory 1970. The measurement of the effect of building construction upon drainage basin dynamics. *J. Hydrol.* **11,** 129–44.

Walling, D. E. and A. H. A. Kleo 1979. Sediment yields of rivers in areas of low precipitation: a global view. In *Int. Assoc. Hydrol. Sci. Publ. 128,* 479–93.

Walling, D. E. and M. R. Peart 1980. Some quality considerations in the study of human influence on sediment yields. In *Proc. Helsinki Symp.* Int. Assoc. Hydrol. Sci. Publ. 130.

Walling, D. E. and A. Teed 1971. A simple pumping sampler for research into suspended sediment transport from small catchments. *J. Hydrol.* **13,** 325–37.

Walling, D. E. and B. W. Webb 1980. The spatial dimension in the interpretation of stream solute behaviour. *J. Hydrol.* **47,** 129–49.

Walling, D. E., M. R. Peart, F. Oldfield and R. Thompson 1979. Suspended sediment sources identified by magnetic measurements. *Nature.* **281,** 110–13.

Waltham, A. C. and M. M. Sweeting (eds) 1974. *Limestones and caves of North-West England.* Newton Abbot: David & Charles.

Ward, R. C. 1968. Some runoff characteristics of British rivers. *J. Hydrol.* **6,** 358–72.

Ward, R. C. 1976. Evaporation, humidity and the water balance. In *The climate of the British Isles,* T. J. Chandler and S. Gregory (eds), 183–98. London: Longman.

Water Resources Board 1969. *Conference on data retrieval and processing.* Reading: WRB.

Water Resources Board 1971. *The surface water yearbook of Great Britain 1965–6.* London: HMSO.

Water Space Amenity Commission 1978. *Conservation and land drainage guidelines.* London: The Commission.

Waylen, M. J. 1976. Unpublished Ph.D. thesis. University of Bristol.

Waylen, M. J. 1979. Chemical weathering in a drainage basin underlain by Old Red Sandstone. *Earth Surface Processes* **4,** 167–78.

Werritty, A. and R. I. Ferguson 1980. Pattern changes in a Scottish braided river over 1, 30 and 200 years. In *Timescales in geomorphology,* R. A. Cullingford, D. A. Davidson and J. Lewin (eds), 53–68. Chichester: Wiley.

Weyman, D. R. 1970. Throughflow on hillslopes and its relation to the stream hydrograph. *Bull. Int. Assoc. Sci. Hydrol.* **15**(3), 25–33.

Weyman, D. R. 1973. Measurements of the downslope flow of water in a soil. *J. Hydrol.* **20,** 267–88.

Weyman, D. R. 1974. Runoff processes, contributing area and streamflow in a small upland catchment. In *Inst. Br. Geogs Sp. Publ. 6,* 33–43.

Wheeler, D. A. 1979a. Unpublished Ph.D. thesis, University of Hull.

Wheeler, D. A. 1979b. The overall shape of longitudinal profiles of streams. In *Geographical approaches to fluvial processes,* A. F. Pitty (ed.), 241–59. Norwich: Geobooks.

White, E., R. S. Starkey and M. J. Saunders 1971. An assessment of the relative importance of several chemical sources to waters of a small upland catchment. *J. Appl. Ecol.* **8,** 743–9.

Whittel, P. A. 1979. The analysis of pebbles on the bed of the Upper Wharfe, Yorkshire. In *Geographical approaches to fluvial processes,* A. F. Pitty (ed.), 203–13. Norwich: Geobooks.

Wilcock, D. N. 1967. Coarse bedload as a factor determining bed slope. In *Int. Assoc. Sci. Hydrol. Publ. 75,* 143–50.

Wilcock, D. N. 1971. Investigation into the relation between bedload transport and channel shape. *Geol. Soc. Am. Bull.* 82, 2159–75.

Wilhm, J. F. 1975. Biological indicators of pollution. In *River ecology,* vol. 2, B. A. Whitton (ed.). Oxford: Blackwell Scientific.

Wilkinson, T. P. 1971. Unpublished Ph.D. thesis. University of Newcastle upon Tyne.

Williams, G. P. 1978. Bankfall discharge of rivers. *Water Resources Res.* **14,** 1141–54.

Wills, L. J. 1938. The Pleistocene development of the Severn from Bridgnorth to the sea. *Q. J. Geol. Soc.* **94,** 61–242.

Wilson, R. S. 1980. Classifying rivers using chironomid pupal exuviae. In *Chironomidae: ecology, systematics, cytology and physiology,* D. A. Murray (ed.). Oxford: Pergamon Press.

Wolfenden, P. J. and J. Lewin 1977. Distribution of metal pollutants in floodplain sediments. *Catena* **4,** 309–17.

Wolman, M. G. 1977. Changing needs and opportunities in the sediment field. *Water Resources Res.* **13,** 50–4.

Wood, P. A. 1976. Unpublished Ph.D. thesis. University of London.

Wood, P. A. 1977. Controls of variation in suspended sediment concentration in the River Rother, West Sussex, England. *Sedimentology* **24,** 437–45.

Wood, P. A. 1978. Fine-sediment mineralogy of source rocks and suspended sediment, Rother Catchment, West Sussex. *Earth Surface Processes* **3,** 255–63.

Woodiwiss, F. S. 1964. The biological system of stream classification used by the Trent River Board. *Chemy Ind.,* 443–7.

World Meteorological Organisation 1977. *Casebook of examples of organisation and operation of hydrological services.* Operational Hydrology Report No. 9. Geneva: WMO.

Yang, C. T. 1971. On river meanders. *J. Hydrol.* **13,** 251–3.

Young, A. 1958a. Unpublished Ph.D. thesis. University of Sheffield.

Young, A. 1958b. A record of the rate of erosion on Millstone Grit. *Proc. Yorks Geol. Soc.* **31,** 149–56.

Young, A. 1960. Soil movement by denudational processes on slopes. *Nature* **188,** 120–2.

Young, A. 1972. *Slopes.* Edinburgh: Oliver and Boyd.

Young, A. 1978. A twelve-year record of soil movement on a slope. *Z. Geomorph.* NF suppl. **29,** 104–10.

Index

213